# CEOE Field 44 OSAT
# Principal Common Core
## Teacher Certification Exam

**By:** Sharon Wynne, M.S
Southern Connecticut State University

"And, while there's no reason yet to panic, I think it's only prudent that we make preparations to panic."

# XAMonline, INC.
Boston

**Copyright © 2007 XAMonline, Inc.**
All rights reserved. No part of the material protected by this copyright notice may be reproduced or utilized in any form or by any means, electronic or mechanical, including photocopying, recording or by any information storage and retrievable system, without written permission from the copyright holder.

To obtain permission(s) to use the material from this work for any purpose including workshops or seminars, please submit a written request to:

XAMonline, Inc.
21 Orient Ave.
Melrose, MA 02176
Toll Free 1-800-509-4128
Email: info@xamonline.com
Web www.xamonline.com
Fax: 1-781-662-9268

Library of Congress Cataloging-in-Publication Data

Wynne, Sharon A.
 OSAT Principal Common Core Field 44: Teacher Certification / Sharon A. Wynne. -2nd ed.
 ISBN 978-1-58197-793-6
 1. OSAT Principal Common Core Field 44.  2. Study Guides.  3.CEOE
 4. Teachers' Certification & Licensure.  5. Careers

**Disclaimer:**
The opinions expressed in this publication are the sole works of XAMonline and were created independently from the National Education Association, Educational Testing Service, or any State Department of Education, National Evaluation Systems or other testing affiliates.

Between the time of publication and printing, state specific standards as well as testing formats and website information may change that is not included in part or in whole within this product. Sample test questions are developed by XAMonline and reflect similar content as on real tests; however, they are not former tests. XAMonline assembles content that aligns with state standards but makes no claims nor guarantees teacher candidates a passing score. Numerical scores are determined by testing companies such as NES or ETS and then are compared with individual state standards. A passing score varies from state to state.

**Printed in the United States of America** œ-1

# CEOE: OSAT Principal Common Core Field 44
ISBN: 978-1-58197-793-6

TEACHER CERTIFICATION STUDY GUIDE

## Table of Contents

**SUBAREA I.**                                       **SCHOOL VISION AND LEADERSHIP**

**COMPETENCY 1.0**    **UNDERSTAND HOW TO FACILITATE THE DEVELOPMENT AND ARTICULATION OF A SCHOOL VISION THAT PROMOTES LEARNING FOR ALL STUDENTS.** ............................................................. 1

Skill 1.1    Demonstrate knowledge of techniques for collaborating with other administrators, teachers, students, parents/guardians, community members, and state and federal agencies to develop a school vision of learning that promotes the success of all students. ............ 1

Skill 1.2    Analyze the use of data-based research strategies to develop a school vision of learning. ................................................................. 9

Skill 1.3    Demonstrate knowledge of strategies for developing a school vision based on relevant educational theories, models, and practices, including an understanding of the goals for learning in a pluralistic society, the needs of diverse learners, the nature of schools as interactive social and cultural systems, and the dynamics of social and organizational change. ........................................................... 14

Skill 1.4    Recognize the value of reflecting on the current status of the school and using that knowledge to inform the process of defining educational goals. ........................................................................ 16

Skill 1.5    Demonstrate knowledge of strategies and procedures for ensuring that the school vision addresses the diversity of learners and ...... 17

Skill 1.6    Demonstrate knowledge of strategies for articulating the school vision throughout the development process. ................................ 19

Skill 1.7    Demonstrate knowledge of communication techniques, including the use of technology, symbols, ceremonies, stories, and other activities, for conveying the school vision to staff, parents, students, and community members. .......................................................... 20

**PRINCIPAL COMMON CORE**

| | | |
|---|---|---|
| **COMPETENCY 2.0** | | **UNDERSTAND HOW TO FACILITATE IMPLEMENTATION AND STEWARDSHIP OF A SCHOOL VISION THAT PROMOTES LEARNING FOR ALL STUDENTS. ...................................................... 27** |
| Skill 2.1 | | Demonstrate knowledge of leadership processes necessary to implement and support the school vision, including effective communication strategies and strategies for motivating staff, students, and families. ............................................................... 27 |
| Skill 2.2 | | Identify procedures for implementing the school vision, including procedures for initiating change and for overcoming obstacles to change. ............................................................................................... 31 |
| Skill 2.3 | | Demonstrate knowledge of procedures for defining educational goals related to the school vision. ............................................... 32 |
| Skill 2.4 | | Analyze the use of data-based research strategies to monitor school improvement efforts, evaluate the school's progress toward achieving its goals and vision, ensure accountability, and make needed adjustments. ................................................................. 33 |
| Skill 2.5 | | Analyze the use of management techniques and group processes to define roles, assign functions, delegate effectively, facilitate teamwork and collegiality, encourage innovation and autonomy, and determine accountability for attaining goals related to the school vision. ............................................................................ 33 |

| COMPETENCY 3.0 | UNDERSTAND HOW TO PROMOTE COMMUNITY COLLABORATION AND INVOLVEMENT IN SUPPORTING THE SCHOOL VISION OF LEARNING ................................................................ 38 |
|---|---|
| Skill 3.1 | Analyze varied strategies for encouraging the involvement of staff, students, parents/guardians, and community members in supporting the school vision. ........................................................ 38 |
| Skill 3.2 | Identify strategies for drawing on the diversity of the community to improve educational programs, meet diverse student needs, and support the school vision. ............................................................ 43 |
| Skill 3.3 | Identify strategies for collaborating with community agencies to integrate health, social, cultural, and other services in the schools to address student needs. ............................................................ 45 |
| Skill 3.4 | Demonstrate knowledge of community relations techniques that make effective use of varied media to help support the school vision. ................................................................................................ 46 |
| Skill 3.5 | Identify outreach strategies for involving business, religious, political, and service organizations in supporting the school vision. ................................................................................................ 46 |
| Skill 3.6 | Analyze the use of community relations models, marketing strategies, and data-driven decision making to develop educational partnerships among schools, businesses, community organizations, government agencies, and higher education institutions. .............. 48 |
| Skill 3.7 | Describe ways to support the involvement of families in the education of their children ............................................................ 49 |
| Skill 3.8 | Describe ways to acknowledge that families have the best interests of their children in mind. ............................................................ 51 |

# TEACHER CERTIFICATION STUDY GUIDE

**COMPETENCY 4.0 UNDERSTAND THE SIGNIFICANCE OF DIVERSITY FOR THE SCHOOL'S VISION OF LEARNING AND WAYS TO EXERCISE LEADERSHIP IN SUPPORTING AND VALUING DIVERSITY ..................................................52**

Skill 4.1   Examine ways to use the experiences and perspectives of members of the school community with diverse backgrounds to help achieve the school vision and meet the learning needs of all students. ...............................................................................................52

Skill 4.2   Demonstrate knowledge of strategies for creating an atmosphere in the school that encourages respect, sensitivity, and appreciation for all people. ...........................................................................................54

Skill 4.3   Analyze factors involved in working effectively with diverse groups within the school and community. .......................................................55

Skill 4.4   Examine cultural, social, and economic factors affecting students and society. ...................................................................................57

Skill 4.5   Analyze the implications of diversity for education. ......................57

Skill 4.6   Demonstrate knowledge of ways to work with others in the school community to address prejudice and ensure that all students have an equal opportunity for educational success. ...............................58

Skill 4.7   Demonstrate knowledge of strategies for infusing diversity awareness into the curriculum. .....................................................60

Skill 4.8   Identify policies and strategies to help students and staff learn how to function effectively in a multilingual, multicultural, and economically diverse society. .........................................................61

**PRINCIPAL COMMON CORE**

**COMPETENCY 5.0　UNDERSTAND HOW TO SUPPORT THE SCHOOL VISION BY USING HUMAN RELATIONS SKILLS AND COMMUNICATION SKILLS TO SOLVE PROBLEMS AND FACILITATE DECISION MAKING. ...................... 63**

Skill 5.1　Analyze the use of communication skills and public relations techniques in disseminating information to the public and engaging the community in dialogue to support the school vision ................. 63

Skill 5.2　Demonstrate knowledge of techniques for facilitating communication with and among members of the school community. ............................................................................................... 63

Skill 5.3　Apply knowledge of skills for listening and speaking effectively in small- and large-group contexts. ................................................... 63

Skill 5.4　Identify procedures to promote collaborative decision making and creative problem solving in various school situations. .................... 63

Skill 5.5　Demonstrate knowledge of various theories of conflict resolution and appropriate application of these models to specific communities. ............................................................................... 63

Skill 5.6　Demonstrate knowledge of strategies for applying group process skills and for using research-based data to build consensus and resolve conflicts. ....................................................................... 66

## TEACHER CERTIFICATION STUDY GUIDE

**COMPETENCY 6.0 UNDERSTAND HOW SCHOOL LEADERSHIP AND THE SCHOOL VISION RELATE TO THE LARGER POLITICAL, SOCIAL, ECONOMIC, CULTURAL, LEGAL, AND ETHICAL CONTEXT OF EDUCATION. ............................................................... 67**

Skill 6.1 Examine how an understanding of the larger political, social, economic, and cultural context of education informs the development of effective policies and practices to benefit the school and its students. ................................................................. 67

Skill 6.2 Recognize how economic and political factors shape a community and affect the opportunities available to children in particular schools. ................................................................. 70

Skill 6.3 Recognize the importance of communicating regularly with all members of the school community, including representatives of diverse community groups, concerning trends, issues, and policies affecting the school................................................................. 71

Skill 6.4 Identify ways to advocate for policies and programs at the local, state, and federal levels that promote equitable learning opportunities and success for all students, regardless of socioeconomic background, ethnicity, gender, disability, or other individual characteristics................................................................. 79

Skill 6.5 Analyze community norms and values and explain how they relate to the role of the school in promoting social justice. ..................... 80

Skill 6.6 Recognize how the Oklahoma and U.S. Constitutions; district policies; and statutory, common, and case law regulate the behavior of students, staff, and administration in the schools. ...... 81

Skill 6.7 Demonstrate knowledge of the system of public school governance and strategies for working effectively with local governing boards. ................................................................. 82

Skill 6.8 Recognize how to demonstrate honesty, integrity, impartiality, fairness, sensitivity to student diversity, respect for confidentiality, and ethical behavior in interactions with members of the school community. ................................................................. 84

# TEACHER CERTIFICATION STUDY GUIDE

**SUBAREA II.**                                      **INSTRUCTIONAL LEADERSHIP**

**COMPETENCY 7.0**    **UNDERSTAND HOW TO USE KNOWLEDGE OF HUMAN DEVELOPMENT, LEARNING AND TEACHING THEORIES, EDUCATIONAL RESEARCH, AND BEST PRACTICE TO PROMOTE THE SUCCESS OF ALL STUDENTS.** .............. 89

Skill 7.1    Recognize the characteristics and stages of physical, cognitive, and social/emotional development and their educational significance............... 89

Skill 7.2    Analyze how sociological, linguistic, cultural, and other factors may affect students' development and needs and the implications of these factors for instruction. .......... 90

Skill 7.3    Examine ways to apply research-based knowledge of human development, learning, motivation, and best practice instruction to optimize learning for all students. ............... 91

Skill 7.4    Identify strategies for collaborating with counseling staff, teaching staff, and community agencies to address student needs and ensure student access to adequate counseling, guidance, and other services. ............... 92

Skill 7.5    Evaluate the implications of various behavior management practices. ............... 94

Skill 7.6    Examine strategies for promoting successful learning experiences for students with disabilities and ensuring that these students have access to appropriate resources. ............... 94

Skill 7.7    Recognize the role of various types of activity programs in meeting all students' developmental, social, cultural, athletic, leadership, and academic needs. ............... 96

| COMPETENCY 8.0 | UNDERSTAND HOW TO APPLY PRINCIPLES OF CURRICULUM PLANNING, DEVELOPMENT, AND EVALUATION TO PROMOTE THE SUCCESS OF ALL STUDENTS. ............100 |
|---|---|
| Skill 8.1 | Identify basic principles of curriculum design and recognize relationships between child/adolescent/adult development and the curriculum. ............100 |
| Skill 8.2 | Demonstrate knowledge of strategies for designing and implementing curricula that fully accommodate learners' diverse needs. ............110 |
| Skill 8.3 | Identify appropriate criteria for use in evaluating, modifying, and integrating curricula. ............114 |
| Skill 8.4 | Apply knowledge of procedures for involving and leading stakeholders in curriculum development, implementation, and evaluation. ............116 |
| Skill 8.5 | Demonstrate knowledge of the relationships between Oklahoma's Priority Academic Student Skills and local curricula. ............117 |
| Skill 8.6 | Analyze issues and procedures related to the development of curricula to meet the needs of all students. ............118 |
| Skill 8.7 | Demonstrate knowledge of strategies for infusing diversity awareness into the curriculum. ............119 |
| Skill 8.8 | Apply knowledge of current research in curriculum development and strategies for developing an inclusive curriculum that reflects the diversity of the classroom, the community, the nation, and the world. ............123 |

**COMPETENCY 9.0 UNDERSTAND HOW TO APPLY PRINCIPLES OF INSTRUCTION AND INSTRUCTIONAL LEADERSHIP TO PROMOTE THE SUCCESS OF ALL STUDENTS ............ 126**

Skill 9.1 Apply knowledge of strategies for helping school personnel apply best practices and sound educational research to improve instructional programs. ............ 126

Skill 9.2 Demonstrate knowledge of principles and techniques associated with various instructional methods, including technology-based methods. ............ 127

Skill 9.3 Examine the significance of student differences for instructional planning and implementation. ............ 131

Skill 9.4 Describe methods of assessing student learning and achievement and examine the role of student assessment for instruction and program evaluation. ............ 131

Skill 9.5 Examine how various staffing patterns, student grouping arrangements, behavior management practices, class scheduling formats, school organizational structures, and facility designs affect teaching and learning. ............ 132

Skill 9.6 Identify strategies for using resources within the community to enhance education and promote achievement ............ 133

Skill 9.7 Describe how to use technology and information systems to enrich the school's curriculum and instruction. ............ 134

## COMPETENCY 10.0 UNDERSTAND STRATEGIES FOR PROMOTING PROFESSIONAL GROWTH AND DEVELOPMENT AND STRATEGIES FOR CREATING A POSITIVE SCHOOL CULTURE FOR LEARNING. ...... 136

Skill 10.1 Demonstrate knowledge of research-based professional development that includes authentic problems and tasks, mentoring, coaching, conferencing, and other techniques for promoting adult learning and developing new knowledge and skills in the workplace. ...... 136

Skill 10.2 Identify procedures for working collaboratively with school personnel to develop and implement comprehensive professional growth plans. ...... 138

Skill 10.3 Recognize how to evaluate professional development programs to ensure that they advance the school's vision of learning. ...... 139

Skill 10.4 Recognize the importance of encouraging reflective practice for one's self and staff, including reflection on the role that one's own attitudes, biases, and preconceptions play in interactions with students, colleagues, and others. ...... 142

Skill 10.5 Demonstrate knowledge of principles and procedures for effective personnel evaluation and developmental supervision. ...... 143

Skill 10.6 Describe how to create a personal development plan that reflects commitment to life-long learning and best practices and that takes advantage of varied resources for continuing professional development. ...... 147

Skill 10.7 Analyze strategies for creating and maintaining a positive school culture that draws on the diversity of the school community and fosters the belief that all children can learn and succeed. ...... 148

**COMPETENCY 11.0 UNDERSTAND PRINCIPLES OF ORGANIZATIONAL MANAGEMENT, BUDGETING, RESOURCE UTILIZATION, FINANCIAL MANAGEMENT, AND TECHNOLOGY USE ................................. 149**

Skill 11.1 Examine ways to apply knowledge of organizational development and data management to optimize learning for all students. ........ 149

Skill 11.2 Analyze ways to apply long-range planning procedures and problem-solving skills to promote effective and equitable resource allocation that focuses on teaching and learning. ......................... 150

Skill 11.3 Identify characteristics of school budgets, stages in the budgeting process, and strategies for working effectively with stakeholders to develop the school budget .......................................................... 152

Skill 11.4 Apply knowledge of effective procedures for managing scarce resources and creative strategies for seeking new resources to support student learning, including grant money and other nonbudgetary resources. ............................................................ 155

Skill 11.5 Identify basic principles of financial and cost accounting, methods for financial record keeping and reporting, and effective procedures for managing activity funds. ........................................................ 157

Skill 11.6 Demonstrate knowledge of current technologies and information systems designed to facilitate management, business, and scheduling practices. ................................................................. 157

**COMPETENCY 12.0 UNDERSTAND PRINCIPLES OF HUMAN RESOURCE PLANNING AND MANAGEMENT. ............................ 161**

Skill 12.1 Demonstrate knowledge of procedures and legal requirements (e.g., EEOC, ADA) for recruiting, screening, and selecting personnel. ............... 161

Skill 12.2 Analyze issues of equity and diversity in human resource management. ............... 164

Skill 12.3 Examine the relationship between personnel practices and quality and justice in the workplace. ............... 166

Skill 12.4 Apply knowledge of skills and procedures for supervising and evaluating school personnel. ............... 167

Skill 12.5 Apply knowledge of procedures for disciplining and dismissing staff in accordance with due process. ............... 168

Skill 12.6 Identify requirements and effective practices in situations involving contract negotiation and management and employee grievances. ............... 172

# TEACHER CERTIFICATION STUDY GUIDE

**COMPETENCY 13.0 UNDERSTAND HOW TO MANAGE THE SCHOOL'S PHYSICAL PLANT AND AUXILIARY SERVICES TO ENSURE A SAFE AND EFFECTIVE LEARNING ENVIRONMENT.** ................................................................... 173

Skill 13.1 Identify the features of a safe and effective learning environment. ................................................................................ 173

Skill 13.2 Examine strategies for ensuring the safety of students and school personnel and for addressing suspected problems related to safety. .................................................................................... 174

Skill 13.3 Identify procedures for crisis planning and for responding to crises. ............................................................................... 174

Skill 13.4 Demonstrate knowledge of public school safety, security, and emergency procedures. ........................................................ 175

Skill 13.5 Identify procedures for monitoring and evaluating the operation, use, maintenance, and efficiency of school facilities. ........... 175

Skill 13.6 Identify legal issues related to the operation and maintenance of school facilities ............................................................... 176

Skill 13.7 Demonstrate knowledge of regulations, issues, and procedures related to purchasing, food services, transportation services, information management services, and health services in the school. ..................................................................................... 177

**Sample Test** ................................................................................................ 179

**Answer Key** ................................................................................................ 193

**Sample Questions with Rationale** ............................................................ 194

# TEACHER CERTIFICATION STUDY GUIDE

## Great Study and Testing Tips!

*What* to study in order to prepare for the subject assessments is the focus of this study guide but equally important is *how* you study.

You can increase your chances of truly mastering the information by taking some simple, but effective steps.

## Study Tips:

**1. Some foods aid the learning process.** Foods such as milk, nuts, seeds, rice, and oats help your study efforts by releasing natural memory enhancers called CCKs (*cholecystokinin*) composed of *tryptopha*n, *choline*, and *phenylalanine*. All of these chemicals enhance the neurotransmitters associated with memory. Before studying, try a light, protein-rich meal of eggs, turkey, and fish. All of these foods release the memory enhancing chemicals. The better the connections, the more you comprehend.

Likewise, before you take a test, stick to a light snack of energy boosting and relaxing foods. A glass of milk, a piece of fruit, or some peanuts all release various memory-boosting chemicals and help you to relax and focus on the subject at hand.

**2. Learn to take great notes.** A by-product of our modern culture is that we have grown accustomed to getting our information in short doses (i.e. TV news sound bites or USA Today style newspaper articles.)

Consequently, we've subconsciously trained ourselves to assimilate information better in neat little packages. If your notes are scrawled all over the paper, it fragments the flow of the information. Strive for clarity. Newspapers use a standard format to achieve clarity. Your notes can be much clearer through use of proper formatting. A very effective format is called the *"Cornell Method."*

> Take a sheet of loose-leaf lined notebook paper and draw a line all the way down the paper about 1-2" from the left-hand edge.
>
> Draw another line across the width of the paper about 1-2" up from the bottom. Repeat this process on the reverse side of the page.

Look at the highly effective result. You have ample room for notes, a left hand margin for special emphasis items or inserting supplementary data from the textbook, a large area at the bottom for a brief summary, and a little rectangular space for just about anything you want.

**PRINCIPAL COMMON CORE**

**3. Get the concept then the details.** Too often we focus on the details and don't gather an understanding of the concept. However, if you simply memorize only dates, places, or names, you may well miss the whole point of the subject.

A key way to understand things is to put them in your own words. If you are working from a textbook, automatically summarize each paragraph in your mind. If you are outlining text, don't simply copy the author's words.

*Rephrase* them in your own words. You remember your own thoughts and words much better than someone else's, and subconsciously tend to associate the important details to the core concepts.

**4. Ask Why?** Pull apart written material paragraph by paragraph and don't forget the captions under the illustrations.

Example: If the heading is "Stream Erosion", flip it around to read "Why do streams erode?" Then answer the questions.

If you train your mind to think in a series of questions and answers, not only will you learn more, but it also helps to lessen the test anxiety because you are used to answering questions.

**5. Read for reinforcement and future needs.** Even if you only have 10 minutes, put your notes or a book in your hand. Your mind is similar to a computer; you have to input data in order to have it processed. *By reading, you are creating the neural connections for future retrieval.* The more times you read something, the more you reinforce the learning of ideas.

Even if you don't fully understand something on the first pass, *your mind stores much of the material for later recall.*

**6. Relax to learn so go into exile.** Our bodies respond to an inner clock called biorhythms. Burning the midnight oil works well for some people, but not everyone.

If possible, set aside a particular place to study that is free of distractions. Shut off the television, cell phone, and pager and exile your friends and family during your study period.

If you really are bothered by silence, try background music. Light classical music at a low volume has been shown to aid in concentration over other types. Music that evokes pleasant emotions without lyrics is highly suggested. Try just about anything by Mozart. It relaxes you.

**7. Use arrows not highlighters.** At best, it's difficult to read a page full of yellow, pink, blue, and green streaks. Try staring at a neon sign for a while and you'll soon see that the horde of colors obscure the message.

A quick note, a brief dash of color, an underline, and an arrow pointing to a particular passage is much clearer than a horde of highlighted words.

**8. Budget your study time.** Although you shouldn't ignore any of the material, *allocate your available study time in the same ratio that topics may appear on the test.*

# TEACHER CERTIFICATION STUDY GUIDE

## Testing Tips:

**1. <u>Get smart, play dumb</u>. Don't read anything into the question.** Don't make an assumption that the test writer is looking for something else than what is asked. Stick to the question as written and don't read extra things into it.

**2. <u>Read the question and all the choices *twice* before answering the question</u>.** You may miss something by not carefully reading, and then re-reading both the question and the answers.

If you really don't have a clue as to the right answer, leave it blank on the first time through. Go on to the other questions, as they may provide a clue as to how to answer the skipped questions.

If later on, you still can't answer the skipped ones . . . ***Guess.*** The only penalty for guessing is that you *might* get it wrong. Only one thing is certain; if you don't put anything down, you will get it wrong!

**3. <u>Turn the question into a statement</u>.** Look at the way the questions are worded. The syntax of the question usually provides a clue. Does it seem more familiar as a statement rather than as a question? Does it sound strange?

By turning a question into a statement, you may be able to spot if an answer sounds right, and it may also trigger memories of material you have read.

**4. <u>Look for hidden clues</u>.** It's actually very difficult to compose multiple-foil (choice) questions without giving away part of the answer in the options presented.

In most multiple-choice questions you can often readily eliminate one or two of the potential answers. This leaves you with only two real possibilities and automatically your odds go to Fifty-Fifty for very little work.

**5. <u>Trust your instincts</u>.** For every fact that you have read, you subconsciously retain something of that knowledge. On questions that you aren't really certain about, go with your basic instincts. **Your first impression on how to answer a question is usually correct.**

**6. <u>Mark your answers directly on the test booklet</u>.** Don't bother trying to fill in the optical scan sheet on the first pass through the test.

*Just be very careful not to miss-mark your answers when you eventually transcribe them to the scan sheet.*

**7. <u>Watch the clock</u>!** You have a set amount of time to answer the questions. Don't get bogged down trying to answer a single question at the expense of 10 questions you can more readily answer.

**PRINCIPAL COMMON CORE**

# TEACHER CERTIFICATION STUDY GUIDE

**SUBAREA I.**                      **SCHOOL VISION AND LEADERSHIP**

**COMPETENCY 1.0**     **UNDERSTAND HOW TO FACILITATE THE DEVELOPMENT AND ARTICULATION OF A SCHOOL VISION THAT PROMOTES LEARNING FOR ALL STUDENTS.**

**Skill 1.1**     **Demonstrate knowledge of techniques for collaborating with other administrators, teachers, students, parents/guardians, community members, and state and federal agencies to develop a school vision of learning that promotes the success of all students.**

All staff need and deserve to be treated with respect, whether they are part of the teaching staff or the custodial staff. Staff members need to know that the administration is there to help in any situation and will do so in confidence if need be.

Administrators should not show favoritism to any one teacher or give more attention to one more than the other. Aspects of dealing with members of the staff include:

- Interpersonal communication
- Retention of staff
- Civility
- Reward and recognition
- Developing teams
- Establishing trust
- Managing stressful situations
- Supporting staff in times of change

When a new administrator comes into a school, he/she has to develop a sense of trust with the staff. They need to know that the administrator will support them in cases of problem students or if problems arise with parents. Staff that do an exceptional job need to be recognized and this should be done at a staff meeting. However, the administrator should look for exemplary teaching or behavior in all staff, but at the same time rewards and recognition should not be handed out frivolously.

Developing teams is something that will take time, but the administrator has to make sure that the members of the team do get along. Teams with members that cannot work together will not function effectively.

An administrator also has to be able to manage stressful situations without panicking or becoming distraught. This will let the teachers know they have a leader on whom they can depend. At the same time, the administration has to support the school district in bringing in policies and programs with which the teachers may not agree. Therefore there will be times when teachers who are used to doing something the same way all the time will be forced to change. Change is not easy, which is what the administrator has to realize. The teachers should be coached to take small steps leading to change.

Effective communication strategies can include the practices of good communication as well as the specific transmission methods.

Practices
- Think first. This applies to both preparation before a formal written or oral presentation and to pausing to gather your thoughts before impromptu speaking.

- Stay informed. Never speak or write off-the-cuff or attempt to discuss matters beyond your scope of knowledge. Stay abreast of education issues, especially in leadership and supervision. Read journals and participate in professional organizations. Keep a notebook of newsletters, clippings, and resource lists that can be highlighted and used to add credibility to your communication.

- Assess your audience. Know the addressed person or group's interests and attitudes. Show respect for their points of view by your tone and pace as well as your volume and posture when speaking. Demonstrate a genuine liking for people by a willingness to share your ideas and solicit their responses.

- Focus attention on your message, not on yourself. A little nervousness about communicating well is normal even for practiced writers/speakers. Familiarity with your topic, the ability to develop clear, complete sentences, and the use of concrete examples will enhance delivery.

- Speak/write correctly. Use of proper grammar, usage, and sentence structure will allow listeners/readers to concentrate on what you say, rather than on distracting language errors.

- Be concise. Get to the point and then quit. Use words and sentences economically. Being unnecessarily long-winded is a sure way to lose your audience.

- Use delivery techniques to your advantage. In written communication, be sure to state the main idea, give examples or explanations, and link the ideas in a logical manner. In oral communication, use eye contact to establish sincerity and hold listener attention. Use body language to add enthusiasm and conviction to your words, but avoid expansive or repetitive movements that can distract. Modulate the pitch and volume of your voice for emphasis.

- Listen thoughtfully to feedback. In face-to-face communication, be aware of nonverbal cues that suggest either active listening or boredom.

Transmission methods
- Written (for internal audience)
  ⇒ Daily announcements for students and faculty
  ⇒ Student newspapers
  ⇒ Superintendent's monthly newsletter to faculties
  ⇒ Reports of school board meetings
  ⇒ Memorandums from all levels, downward or laterally
- Written (for external audience)
  ⇒ Principal's newsletter to parents
  ⇒ Annual reports
  ⇒ News releases
- Oral (for internal audiences)
  ⇒ Daily announcements or other student broadcasts over intercom or closed circuit television
  ⇒ Meetings of committees of students, parents, teachers, and administrators
  ⇒ Faculty meetings
  ⇒ Student government or club meetings
  ⇒ Pep rallies
- Oral (for external audience)
  ⇒ Video-taped promotions of schools or school-related events
  ⇒ Direct telephone contacts with parents
  ⇒ Student presentations—concerts, plays, content area fairs, awards ceremonies
  ⇒ Radio and television programs to promote school events or discuss education issues

In any organization or business, more than half of any administrator or supervisor's time is spent communicating with others. Good communication is essential to any educational organization. The more effective the communication process, the more successful the education process. The roles of the administrator as goal setter, task organizer, employee motivator, decision-maker, and public relations agent are facilitated by her ability to manage the communication process effectively.

Communication is the exchange of information (message) between a sender and a receiver. The process involves six steps:

1. Ideating - development of the idea or message to be communicated

2. Encoding - organization of the idea into a sequence of symbols (written or spoken words, nonverbal cues, or medium) to convey the message

3. Transmitting - delivery of the encoded message through a medium (face-to-face, telephone, written statements, video or computer products)

4. Receiving - claiming of the message by the receiver, who must be a good reader/listener, attentive to the message's meaning

5. Decoding - the receiver's translation of the message

6. Acting - action taken by the receiver in response to the message (ignore, store, react). Feedback to the sender that the message has been received and understood is what makes communication reciprocal.

Educational leadership training programs often explain the communication process in terms of sources and channels. The main source elements are expertise, credibility, composure, and dynamism. The ability to incorporate these elements into idea presentation results in the most persuasive communication.

The means of message transmission are referred to as channels. The characteristics of channels are such elements as the need to use different media for different audiences, the need to use recognizably respected channels, the need to select mass media that serve different purposes, and the recognition of personal channels as more effective than mass media in changing opinions.

Direction of Communication (Formal)

1. Downward - the transmission of information from people at higher levels to people at lower levels (superintendents to principals, principals to faculty and staff)

2. Upward - the transmission of information (usually feedback) from people who are at lower levels to people who are at lower levels (principals to directors of instruction, department heads/team leaders to principals)

3. Lateral (horizontal) - transmission of information between people on the same level in the organizational structure ( assistant superintendent of instruction to assistant superintendent of facilities)

4. Diagonal - direct transmission of information between people at different levels in the hierarchy (usually reserved for instances when information cannot go through proper channels in a timely fashion—special reports from principals that go directly to the superintendent or assistant superintendents for transmission to the state)

A fifth form of communication exists apart from direction or formal practice—the grapevine. In actuality, the majority of information transmitted by employees laterally is carried through the grapevine. Its face-to-face informality transmits information rapidly.

Administrators should be aware of the operation of the school grapevine and incorporate its positive aspects into the communication structure. The negative aspect of unsubstantiated rumor-passing will be overridden if the administrator

- keeps employees informed about matters relevant to school or district and about issues that impact the employees' jobs

- provides employees the opportunity to express attitudes and feelings about issues

- tests employees' reactions to information before making decisions

- builds morale by repeating positive reactions/comments made by employees to higher level administrators or the community and vice versa

Teaching professionals do not like the feeling that they are being kept in the dark or are getting only partial or untimely information. Telling teachers in a faculty meeting that the district is going to reduce the faculty at their school before transfer provisions have been established will create distrust. It may seem an open gesture on the principal's part, but the timing is wrong.

Barriers to Communication

- The communication process requires that the sender and receiver have a common frame of reference. Because we all interpret information based on previous experience and cultural background, receivers may interpret the ideas in messages differently than the sender intended. For example, information, delivered during contract negotiations, is interpreted differently by union representatives than by district contract negotiators. These distorted perceptions arise because the participants are operating from different frames of reference. To make the communication effective, all parties must realize the specific goal of the talks is to spend funds in the most educationally sound manner, not to deprive either group of its just desserts.

- Filtering is a barrier that occurs during transmission of information from one level to another. It may be intentional or unintentional. In downward communication, it may be the omission of some of the message or improper encoding for the intended audience. Administrators frequently deliver information only on a need-to-know basis or deliver only positive information, fearing that negative information will damage the decoding process. This succeeds only in causing the receivers to be confused as to the message's intent or to feel patronized. In upward communication, employees may limit information to those facts that shed favorable light on their personal performance because of previous experience with inconsistent or arbitrary evaluations.

- Another barrier results from improper listening skills. The receiver must heed the entire message, decode it non-judgmentally, and seek clarification of any unclear points. This happens best when the sender creates a non-threatening environment in which the listener can practice non-evaluative listening.

- Biases against race, gender, or status can prejudice receivers against a message. Senders can suggest bias by words, nonverbal clues, and attitudes. A male principal with chauvinist attitudes may alienate female teachers; a male teacher who resents a female principal may tune her out.

Overcoming these barriers becomes an administrative responsibility. To establish effective communication, the supervisor should

- establish trust by sincerely correlating her message and behavior. Never being available after stating the existence of an open-door policy will not create trust.

- listen carefully and provide open channels for feedback. Avoid giving non-verbal cues that contradict the message.

- understand and respect employees' needs, interests, and attitudes. Allow discussion, even disagreement. The important thing is that employees know they are being heard.

- time information delivery properly. Timing affects the manner in which employees perceive the message. Avoid leaking partial information. Transmit accurate information in time for employees to provide feedback.
- use appropriate media for transmitting the message. Written or face-to-face communication is necessary when the message is of concern to a single receiver or when the message is of immediate concern to a group with common interests. Oral or video presentations are appropriate for delivery of information that affects a department or faculty, such as safety measures or reporting abuse.

The educational leader must be adept in the many skills of communication.

**Knowledge of the effect one's behavior and decisions have on other individuals and on the culture and climate of groups and organizations**

Because communication is a process in which a person or group learns another's ideas, attitudes, and beliefs, the process becomes a prime focus of supervisory behavior. If a positive interaction is to occur, the educational leader must understand the cause/effect relationship between her actions and the reactions of others.

Positive Behaviors

Show an interest in the work of others.
- Cause: Assistant principals and principals should take note of student and teacher performance and offer assistance as indicated. Superintendents should exhibit knowledge of work of teachers, administrators, and students by first-hand observation.
- Effect: Workers at all levels will recognize the consideration given to their achievements and will feel more comfortable in seeking help to solve problems.

Be knowledgeable of job requirements for all personnel and give praise.
- Cause: Supervisors must evaluate performance on job descriptors. Focus on good performance; avoid being overly critical. Pass on compliments to higher level management.
- Effect: Employees respond with better performance when supervisors show the ability to note specific facets of the employee's work.

Exhibit pleasing personality traits.
- Cause: Being courteous, fair, and honest and having high integrity are desirable because supervisors serve as role models for the type of behavior expected of everyone in the system.
- Effect: Workers in the system will strive to emulate desirable personality traits. Members of the community form an opinion of the system based on the personalities of educational leaders that they meet at school functions or in other community organizations.

Stand by convictions.
- Cause: Supervisors should formulate strong beliefs, state them unequivocally, and support them despite opposition.
- Effect: Students, teachers, and other leaders do not respect fence-sitters. They may not always agree with the stated beliefs, but they will defend the right to express them.

Show confidence in employees' abilities and allow self-direction.
- Cause: Supervisors at all levels must recognize the professional qualities of other professionals. Allow subordinates to work flexibly within prescribed guidelines.
- Effect: Employees will become confident decision makers, capable of completing their jobs without constant supervision.

Be firm in following school and district guidelines for student discipline.
- Cause: School administrators should consistently adhere to discipline policy. Show no favoritism, but be fair. Principals should receive support from superintendent and school board.
- Effect: Students will know that their misdeeds will be dealt with efficiently. Teachers will see more effectiveness in classroom management.

Exhibit a sense of humor.
- Cause: A sincere sense of humor—not sarcasm or facetiousness—encourages an amiable environment for communication. It can be used to release tension and to foster the relaxed climate in which comfortable exchange can occur.
- Effect: Employees recognize a supervisor's ability to establish rapport by not taking herself or the demands of her position too seriously. An occasional shared laugh at some absurdity puts the situation in proportion and creates a climate in which all parties can view the issue in proper perspective.

The principal competency of *organizational sensitivity* relates to the principal's awareness of the effect of behavior and decisions on others. The objectives for evaluation include:

- using tactful oral and written responses to persons within and outside the school.

- informing members of the school community of information that is or could be relevant to them.

- considering the position, emotions, and attitudes of others when organizing, planning, and making decisions.

**Skill 1.2    Analyze the use of data-based research strategies (e.g., analysis of student assessment results, student and family demographic data, and data on community needs) to develop a school vision of learning.**

The evaluation of students is a very important aspect of the teaching and learning process. Periodic testing assesses learning outcomes based on the objectives established for learning and it provides information at various stages in the learning process to determine future learning needs such as periodic reviews, re-teaching, and enrichment. As the end process, the evaluation of students' performance measures the level of goal attainment, which is operationalized through the learning activities planned by the teacher. At varying stages of the teaching and learning process, the intended outcome must be measured and the level of goal attainment is established in order to proceed with this continuous cycle of student evaluation.

Evaluation and measurement are often used interchangeably to imply the same process. However, while closely related, they should be differentiated. *Evaluation* is identified as the process of making judgments regarding student performance and *measurement* is the actual data collection that is used to make judgments of student performance. Evaluation is related to student performance when the focus is on how well a student carries out a given task is measured or when a student work or product is the focus of the measurement.

The purpose of the student evaluation will determine the type of process to use. Diagnostic evaluation, formative, and summative evaluations are the three types of student evaluations most commonly used. *Diagnostic evaluation* is provided prior to instruction to identify problems, to place students in certain groups, and to make assignments that are appropriate to their needs. While it is important to address the specific needs of students, teachers must be cautious of the ramifications of grouping children in homogeneous groups versus heterogeneous groupings. It may appear time effective to group and work with children of like situations, yet often it fails to foster students' intellectual and social growth and development. In fact, it has been proven that children in mixed groups benefit from the diversity within the group. *Formative* evaluation is used to obtain feedback during the instructional process. It informs teachers of the extent to which students are really learning the concepts and skills being taught. The information obtained through the formative process should lead to modification in the teaching and learning process to address specific needs of the students before arriving at the end of the unit. Formative evaluation is designed to promote learning. Therefore, it must be done frequently using the specific objectives stated for learning outcomes. *Summative evaluation* is used to culminate a unit or series of lessons to arrive at a grade. It is the sum of all the accomplishments of the student over a specified period of learning. Knowing the content studied and having the specific skills required to score well on tests are two different endeavors which require not only learning content, but also following form. Often, standardized tests are considered to be summative evaluations.

Therefore, it is also the responsibility of teachers to train the students in test taking skills with regard to following directions, managing time effectively, and giving special attention to the type of tests and the skills required.

Regardless of the type of assessment, educators must gather and analyze the information they yield to determine problem areas. The problem areas uncovered should be discussed with the students collectively and individually and also be presented as items for discussion at teacher conferences with parents. Whether diagnostic, formative or summative, the evaluation of student performance should be a continuous process.

The accuracy of student evaluation is essential. The accuracy is related to consistency of measurement, which is observed through reliability and validity of the instruments used to measure student performance as well as usability of the instrument.

*Validity* is the extent to which a test measures what it is intended to measure. For example, a test may lack validity if it was designed to measure the creative writing of students, but it is also used to measure handwriting even though it was not designed for the latter.

*Reliability* refers to the consistency of the test to measure what it should measure. For example, the items on a true or false quiz, given by a classroom teacher, are reliable if they convey the same meaning every time the quiz is administered to similar groups of students under similar situations. In other words, there is no ambiguity or confusion with the items on the quiz.

*Usability* is another factor in the evaluation process, which refers to practical considerations such as scoring procedures, level of difficulty, and time to administer the test. The usability of a test will be questionable if the scoring procedures had to be changed to accommodate local financial circumstances or if the allotted time for the test had to be reduced because of other circumstances.

With the purpose of assessment instruments being one of data gathering, it is important to use various forms of information gathering tools to assess the knowledge and progress of students. Standardized Achievement Tests have become a central component of education today, particularly due to *No Child Left Behind*. The widespread use of standardized achievement tests to provide information for accountability to the public has driven many teachers to teach to the test and embrace more objective formats of teaching and learning. Although these tests are very limited in what they measure, too often they are used to make major decisions for which they are not designed.

Standardized achievement measurements can be norm-referenced or criterion-reference. In *norm-referenced* measurements the performance of the student is compared with the performance of other students who also took the same test.

The original group of students who took the test establishes the norm. Norms can be based on age, sex, grade level, geographical location, ethnicity, or other broad combination of classifications.

Standardized norm-referenced achievement tests are designed to measure what a student knows in a particular subject in relation to other students of similar characteristics. The test batteries provide a broad scope of content areas coverage so that it may be used on a larger scale in many different states and school districts. However, they do not measure the goals and content emphasized in a particular local curricula. Therefore, using standardized tests to assess the success of the curriculum or teachers' effectiveness should be avoided (McMillan, 1997).

Norm-reference standardized achievement tests produce different types of scores that are useful in different ways. The most common types of scores are the percentile rank or percentile score, grade equivalent score, stanine, and percentage of items answered correctly. The percentile score indicates how the students' performance compares to the norming group. It tells us that the percentage of the norming group was outscored by a particular student taking the test. For example, a student scoring at the eightieth percentile did better than 80% of the students in the norming group. Likewise, 20% of the norming group scored above the particular student and 80% scored below. The scores are indicative of relative strengths and weaknesses. A student may show consistent strengths in language arts and consistent weakness in mathematics as indicated by the scores derived from the test. Yet one could not base remediation solely on these conclusions without a closer item analysis or a closer review of the objectives measured by the test. The grade equivalent score is expressed by year and month in school for each student. It is used to measure growth and progress. It indicates where a student stands in reference to the norming group. For example, a second grade student who obtained a grade equivalent score of 4.5 on the language arts section of the test is really not achieving at the fourth grade five month level as one may think. The 4.5 grade equivalence means that the second grader has achieved at about the same level of the norming group who is in the fifth month of the fourth grade, if indeed such a student did take the test. However, when compared to other second graders in the norming group, the student is about average.

A point of consideration with grade equivalence is that one may never know how well the second grader might do if placed in the fourth grade or how poorly the second grader might do if given the fourth grade test as compared to other second graders in the norming group.

Another type of standard score for standardized testing is the stanine, which indicates where the score is located on the normal curve for the norming group. Stanines are statistically determined but are not as precise as percentile ranking because it only gives the area in which the score is located, but not the precise location. Using stanines to report standard scores is still found to be practical and easy to understand for many parents and school personnel. Stanines range from one to nine (1-9) with five being the middle of the distribution.

Finally, achievement test scores can be reported by percentage of items answered correctly. This form of reporting may not be very meaningful when the items in a particular area are few. This makes it difficult to determine if the student guessed well at the items, was just lucky at selecting the right answers, or indeed chose the correct responses.

*Criterion-Referenced Standardized Achievement Tests* are designed to indicate the student performance that is directly related to specific educational objectives, thus indicating what the student can or cannot do. For example, the test may measure how well a student can subtract by regrouping in the tens place or how well a student can identify the long vowel sound in specific words. Criterion reference tests are specific to a particular curriculum, which allows the determination of the effectiveness of the curriculum, as well as specific skills acquired by the students. They also provide information needed to plan for future student needs. Because of the recognized value of criterion-referenced standardized achievement tests, many publishers have developed tailor-made tests to correlate with state and districts' general goals and specific learning objectives by pulling from a test bank of field-tested items. The test scores are reported by percentage of items answered correctly to indicate mastery or non-mastery.

*Aptitude tests* are another standardized form of testing that measure the cognitive ability of students. They also measure potential and capacity for learning. While they do not test specific academic ability, the ability level is influenced by the child's experiences in and out of the academic setting. Whether broad in measurement of the child's ability or focused, aptitude tests are used to predict achievement and for advanced placements of students.

*Teacher-made* tests are also evaluative instruments designed by classroom teachers to measure the attainment of objectives. While they may lack validity, they serve the immediate purpose of measuring instructional outcomes. Teacher-made tests should be constructed to measure specific objectives, but they also take into account the nature of the behavior that is being measured. Among teacher-made tests are multiple choice, essay, quizzes, matching, alternative choices (yes/no, agree, disagree, and the like), and completion (fill in the blanks).

*Portfolio assessment* is fast becoming a leading form of teacher assessment, in which the student and teacher collect sample work in a systematic and organized manner to provide evidence of accomplishments and progress toward attaining specific objectives.

Certainly, testing is very important in the assessment of students' progress, but there are other sources of information that can be used for assessment. For example, conferencing can provide factual information for effective assessment, while the cumulative records of a child may also provide factual information for cognitive and psychomotor assessments. Other information sources may include interviews, diaries, self-assessment, observation, simulations, and other creative forms.

**Skill 1.3** **Demonstrate knowledge of strategies for developing a school vision based on relevant educational theories, models, and practices, including an understanding of the goals for learning in a pluralistic society, the needs of diverse learners, the nature of schools as interactive social and cultural systems, and the dynamics of social and organizational change.**

There are many different learning theories and learning processes. Listed below are some of the most common and recent learning theories and processes.

### Behaviorism
Behaviorism is a theory of animal and human learning that only focuses on objectively observable behaviors and discounts mental activities. Behavior theorists define learning as nothing more than the acquisition of new behavior. Behaviorists identify conditioning as a universal learning process. Classic conditioning is when a natural reflex responds to a stimulus (Pavlov's dogs). Behavioral or operant conditioning occurs when a response to a stimulus is reinforced or rewarded. Behaviorism is often used by teachers when they reward or punish student behaviors.

### Constructivism
Constructivism is the belief that by reflecting on our experiences, we construct our own understanding of the world we live in. Each of us generates our own "rules" and "mental models," which we use to make sense of our experiences. Learning, therefore, is simply the process of adjusting our mental models to accommodate new experiences. Constructivism eliminates standardized curriculum and customizes curriculum to students' prior knowledge. Teachers focus on open-ended questions and dialogue among students.

### Brain-based Learning
This theory is based on the structure and function of the brain. As long as the brain is not prohibited from fulfilling its normal processes, learning will occur. People often say that everyone can learn. Yet the reality is that everyone does learn. Every person is born with a brain that functions as an immensely powerful processor. Traditional schooling, however, often inhibits learning by discouraging, ignoring, or punishing the brain's natural learning processes. Teachers design learning around student interests and make learning contextual.

## Multiple Intelligences

This theory of human intelligence, developed by psychologist Howard Gardner, suggests there are at least seven ways that people have of perceiving and understanding the world. Gardner labels each of these ways a distinct "intelligence"-- a set of skills allowing individuals to find and resolve genuine problems they face. Gardner suggests his list of intelligences may not be exhaustive, he identifies the following seven: *Verbal-Linguistic*--the ability to use words and language, *Logical-Mathematical*--the capacity for inductive and deductive thinking and reasoning, as well as the use of numbers and the recognition of abstract patterns, *Visual-Spatial*--the ability to visualize objects and spatial dimensions, and create internal images and pictures, *Body-Kinesthetic*--the wisdom of the body and the ability to control physical motion, *Musical-Rhythmic*--the ability to recognize tonal patterns and sounds, as well as a sensitivity to rhythms and beats, *Interpersonal*--the capacity for person-to-person communications and relationships, and *Intrapersonal*--the spiritual, inner states of being, self-reflection, and awareness.

Other learning theories include Piaget's Developmental Theory, Neuroscience, Learning Styles, Right Brain/Left Brain and Observational Learning.
Three processes are central to learning. They are: reflection, negotiation and collaboration. When students are able to use the three processes, they not only learn much more effectively, but they also gain valuable thinking and communication skills that will stand them in good stead in their lives outside school. The processes work well together. When students negotiate, they reflect on their learning: when they collaborate, they negotiate with other students. A learning program that gets students actively using all three processes is likely to work best.

The two most common motivational theories talked about in education are intrinsic and extrinsic motivation.

**Intrinsic motivation** is when a person is motivated by internal factors, as opposed to external. Intrinsic motivation drives people to do things because they are fun or because they believe they are a good or right thing to do. Intrinsic motivation is a much stronger motivator than extrinsic motivation. Subject areas that become a student's passion are intrinsic motivators. Much learning at a young age is intrinsically motivated as children love school and learning new ideas and concepts. This motivation returns when students are older and have developed deeper knowledge and understanding of specific skills and concepts.

**Extrinsic motivation** is motivation by external factors. It drives people to do things for tangible rewards or pressures, rather than for the fun of it. Students are often trying to please parents, be eligible for sports, or earn high marks for college admission. These are all examples of extrinsic motivators. Extrinsic motivation is often the impetus for learning during adolescence as students develop ambivalence toward school and learning.

**Skill 1.4** **Recognize the value of reflecting on the current status of the school and using that knowledge to inform the process of defining educational goals.**

The decision-making process includes a matrix of specialists who provide Administrative direction in the school community. The Superintendent is the CEO of school communities who hires Principals to effectively lead school communities. Principals must report to Secondary Executive Directors who are charged with the professional development of school leaders in the area of school budgets, hiring and firing practices, evaluation of school staff, community liaison communication, PTSA (Parent Teacher Student Association) collaborations, student program development and a list of other duties as assigned.

The Administrative team in schools can consist of the Principal, Assistant Principals, Deans, Activity/Athletic Directors and Security who are all integrally involved in the decision-making processes that impact school communities. Decision making in schools are relegated to the specific areas designated by school Districts. Districts are the ultimate decision makers in the school communities and each District has the active input from the School board members.

Administrators must understand that there are various types of formal decision making processes that are implemented in school communities. Consensus is used by staff to actively vote on proposal of programs and curriculum diversity. In consensus, the majority vote is used to determine if most of the staff is in favor of a proposal or implementation. Using a show of hands or written ballots provides the designated Union representative with a quantitative score to present to staff after a vote. The role of the Administrator is to insure that the vote is accurate and carries a majority input of voters from the staff.

Other decision making include Instructional Council votes that determine if proposal or curriculum designs are implemented during the current or next school year. These votes are composed of Department Chairs for each academic core and program areas who meet bimonthly to deal with issues such as registration, curriculum, staffing and budget. The Administrator/Principal is in charge of facilitating effective and representative decision making by the Instructional Council.

The Building Leadership Team is composed of staff volunteers, parent volunteers, and a student leader, who provides a decision making process on the building facilities and overall expectations of the academic subject area. Administrators are instrumental in organizing decision making input from this leadership team and bringing it back to the Instructional Council and the staff community.

Administrators engage in decision making processes daily. During District requests for interview teams, Administrators must understand the expectations of them to make both subjective and objective decisions in hiring the best candidates for the job positions for staffing or Administrative jobs. There are many venues for decision making for Administrators, so it is part of their responsibility to have active knowledge of those impacting the school community.

**Skill 1.5   Demonstrate knowledge of strategies and procedures for ensuring that the school vision addresses the diversity of learners and community needs.**

Once school principals have an understanding of the important issues affecting teaching and learning, they must be able to deal with them using existing legal guidelines. These guidelines exist with the sole purpose of protecting the rights of students and staff.

The No Child Left Behind Act, NCLB, is one such guideline designed to helps schools improve by focusing on accountability for results, freedom for states and communities, proven education methods, and choices for parents. Some important terms associated with NCLB include adequate yearly progress (AYP), standardized assessments, and Title I.

Today in our countries' schools there are over 6 million eligible children with disabilities. The Individuals Disability Education Act, IDEA, was enacted in 1975 to make sure that children with disabilities had the opportunity to receive a free appropriate public education, just like other children. Among other things IDEA is in place to improve accountability, expand services, simplify parental involvement, and provide earlier access to services and supports for students with disabilities. There is a continuous goal of educating students with special needs in the least restrictive environment.

During the 2001-2002 school year, nearly one in 12, almost 4 million public school children, received special assistance to learn English. This number continues to steadily increase. These students, like all others, are protected by Title VI (of the Civil Rights Act). This act states "school systems are responsible for assuring that students of a particular race, color, or national origin are not denied the opportunity to obtain the education generally obtained by other students in the system". Additionally, a section of the U.S. Equal Educational Opportunities Act (EEOC), the federal agency responsible for interpreting and enforcing Title VI, adds that states are mandated also to protect and help students "overcome language barriers that impede equal participation by its students in its instructional programs."

Maintaining confidentiality is of the utmost importance in the school setting. If students, parents, or staff members feel as though important information can be kept confidential, this can promote more active participation in the school community.  One existing law that deals with confidentiality in the schools is FERPA. FERPA, the Family Educational Rights and Privacy Act, is a Federal law that governs the disclosure of student education records.

As principals we are aware that a school with a variety of races, ethnicities, and learning differences can provide extraordinary academic and social opportunities to the entire school community. Diverse schools offer opportunities not always available in other settings. When knowledge can be shared not only by teachers and textbooks, but also by fellow students with a variety of life experiences and cultures, learning takes on a whole new meaning. For example, classroom discussions with students from varying backgrounds can be rich and challenging, fostering critical thinking skills. Students learn there are different perspectives on global issues, motivating them to study and more thoughtfully define their own views.

It is also important to make sure that everyone feels safe and comfortable in school.  Try to make students and parents feel welcome and included in every aspect of the school community.  Invite members of diverse groups to share their stories or cultures with others.

School principals must learn to recognize and respect the diversity in their school.  The key for effective school leaders in a diverse school is to face any obstacles early on, tackle them with energy and creativity, and build a school culture based on a foundation of respect and high expectations.  Creating awareness amongst the entire school community is an important step in the success of a diverse school.  When doing this, principals should ensure that community stakeholders know that diversity is recognized and valued in their schools.  Principals should offer resources, such as professional development, to help teachers and parents become more culturally aware.  Additionally, principals should provide an environment where all stakeholders are treated fairly and equitably.

## Skill 1.6 Demonstrate knowledge of strategies for articulating the school vision throughout the development process.

Developing a school vision or renewing one that already exists is something that every administrator should take seriously. Even if a school vision has existed for years, it needs to be looked at on an annual basis to make sure that it is still addressing the needs of the school as determined by a thorough analysis of data. The main focus in building a school vision is that the school is a place where all children will be academically successful.

In communities where the demographics are constantly changing, strategies will include looking at the needs of the students on a yearly basis. This includes analyzing test results to determine where improvements may be made in teaching and learning, and communication with parents. Determining the school culture is a strong point in this strategy as it brings the school and the community together. When teachers and parents see that they have a voice in what happens in the school, vision building no longer becomes a boring process, but one in which they will take an active role.

The vision of a school needs to include a plan for addressing student and family conditions. Teams of teachers can deal with separate issues and then bring the results to the whole staff. In schools, where there is only a small staff, this can be a collaborative effort by all. The administrator has to let the teachers and parents know that their ideas are valued in order to build relationships and work toward consensus. Teachers need to be empowered in their classroom and be allowed to conduct action research on issues important to them and their students' learning. Collaborative dialogue allows teachers to share these individual findings and determine how they may contribute to the collective vision of the building.

A school-wide discipline or character education plan is often part of the vision creating consistency throughout the building. When the plan is imparted to parents and they have had voice in the decisions, they are more likely to support the disciplinary efforts of the school.

At the beginning of each school year, the administrator should set aside meeting time for the teachers to take a new look at the school vision and set goals for the coming year. At the same time, teachers can set their own professional development goals in relation to the main goals of the school.

If administrators approach the school vision utilizing the Understanding by Design model, they will start out with a final vision of what they want their schools to look like. Then they determine benchmarks for assessing achievement towards that goal. It may take years to achieve the final vision, but by regularly reviewing and renewing the school vision, change will occur.

Teachers are encouraged to engage in self-reflection to ensure that they are helping students achieve the state standards. Self-reflection is also a necessary part of the role of the administrator. It is of no use to the school to build a vision and then forget about it for the rest of the year. The vision should be regularly used as programs and initiatives are evaluated. Administrators should engage in self-reflection as part of their role as instructional leaders and agents of change within the school setting. One learns a great deal about his/her own practice through reflection. When an administrator self-reflects on a regular basis, it is then that he/she can determine strengths and weaknesses and develop a focus for future goals and changes.

An administrator should set professional goals at the beginning of a school year and continually refer back to them making certain that school improvement is taking place. Developing relationships with teachers, staff and parents is an important part of this process. Keeping a diary or journal of dialogue with colleagues helps in the reflection process. Administrators should also stay abreast of the latest educational and school reform research in order to keep current with what is happening in the world of education.

By realizing that school reform is not just about changing how teachers teach, administrators are better able to forge a new identity in the school setting. Self-reflection can take many forms, such as:

- Setting time aside each week to reflect on the events of the week as they relate to the school goals.
- Journaling the strengths and weaknesses of individual lessons.
- Reflecting on relationships with teachers in order to better help these teachers in the classrooms.
- Reflecting on relationships with parents in order to help the students in the school.

One of the main responsibilities of an administrator is managing the budget of the school. Reflecting on the school vision can directly impact on how the monies available are spent. For example, the focus could be on sending teachers to professional development opportunities or on buying more resources for the individual classrooms. The administrator can also self-reflect with regards to the professional goals of the teachers. Since the role of the administrator is to be visible in the classrooms, he/she can see how teachers are practicing and changing their instructional methods. Self-reflection on what is seen in the classroom will help when discussing the goals and what the teacher needs to meet them. This is also true of the evaluation of new teachers. Before any decision is made on any recommendation for the teacher, the administrator needs to engage in self-reflection about the teacher and his/her successes or failures. When failures occur, the self-reflection will help decide future help for the teacher and students. Administrators should also self-reflect on situations they experience, allowing them to continuously improve as the building leader.

**Skill 1.7** **Demonstrate knowledge of communication techniques, including the use of technology, symbols, ceremonies, stories, and other activities, for conveying the school vision to staff, parents, students, and community members.**

Traditionally, interpersonal influence related to the managerial motivation elements—need for power and need for achievement. The successful traditional educational leader was recognized as an effective communicator if he or she possessed the skills of persuading subordinates of the validity of striving toward challenging goals. Measuring leadership success in these terms resulted in some assumptions that current research has shown to inhibit effective communication.

- The leader's ideas/goals are viewed as best for the institution. This assumption fosters an authoritative style which communicates downward and discounts the value of ideas generated by employees. Honest feedback is discouraged.

- The setting of goals is the responsibility of an individual or administrative group, not the result of collegial collaboration. This assumption reflects the leadership attitude that employees lack the professional knowledge to participate in the decision making process.

Post-World War II studies of the social organization of work environments revealed that greater communication restraints existed in businesses with rigid social structures that encouraged stereotypical role perceptions. The emphasis on hierarchical status creates low-quality or non-existent communication between persons who feel inferior to those in power and authority figures who perceive themselves as superior.

The development of instructional leadership models in the 1970s was based on traditional assumptions that effective school leaders were firm disciplinarians who set high expectations of employee performance. They set the goals that staff and faculty were expected to meet; task orientation was tantamount regardless of anxiety levels.

Studies of human dynamics in the 1980s and 90s led to total quality management in business and industry, a concept that has many names in education. Facilitative leadership seems to most accurately apply. This leadership model stresses that productive work environments depend on interpersonal relationships that are high in collaboration and empowerment of all persons involved in the education process.

The needs for power and achievement become shared criteria. The leadership role focuses on involving employees in the solving of problems that lead to improved performance and higher levels of achievement. Similar to cooperative learning models of classroom management, facilitative leadership requires improved communication based on the perceptions of senders and receivers. It also recognizes behavior and emotions as communication tools.

**Sender Perceptions**

1. Open communication is sharing, not persuading. Although favorable presentation of an idea necessitates the persuasive technique of analyzing the audience's biases, interests, and emotions, the object is not to refute any conflicting ideas based on these receiver elements but to use them as a means to better understand the issues that evolve from the idea as it is decoded. Encouraging the discussion of issues from all perspectives results in better decoding and appropriate action. The outcome will be the arrival at truth, i.e. a mutually acceptable position, not the imposition of convincing.

2. Open communication results from relating to, not controlling, others. Exhibiting positive behaviors reflects a leader's ability to constantly assess the consequences of his words and behaviors against the ideas and actions of others. Behavior is recognized as communication as much as language is.

The non-verbal messages inherent in behavior must be as conscientiously encoded as language if the message is to be properly decoded. Because the receiver decodes emotionally as well as cognitively, the sender must recognize that the listener may not react appropriately if he does not understand the expected type of response or if he feels anxiety which blocks an appropriate response. Misinterpretation of the message may result from the lack of experience with the sequential nature of behavior communication—antecedent, behavior, consequence.

For example, if in their experience with a former principal, a faculty has become accustomed to being patronized, they may not recognize sincere praise. They may view praise, especially general praise, as condescension. They may respond with signals of disbelief because that reaction was acceptable in the old pattern of behavior. The principal's sensitivity to this barrier to communication (filtering) may need to develop another means of transmission (another medium or sender) until the teachers learn the skill of accepting praise based on trust of the sender and his delivery method.

3. Open communication relies on reciprocal trust. Supervisors must deliver consistent verbal and non-verbal messages, exhibit empathy for the values and ideas of others, demonstrate sincere commitment to the school's vision and the work of the staff and students, be honest in information sharing; and be accessible to all members of the school community.

4. Use vocabulary and complete sentence structures that lead to appropriate interpretation of the message. Select words and symbols that are understood by all or can be explained with alternate word choice. Avoid making incomplete statements into which listeners are expected to fill in the blank. Encourage questioning for clarification.

5. Use feedback as a means to evaluate the effectiveness of communication. Concentrate on listening non-judgmentally to listener reactions. View disagreement as a tool for analyzing the clarity of presentation. Ask focused questions that give the listener the opportunity to ask for additional information.

Use perception checking and behavior description as a means of eliciting understanding from listeners' perceived feelings or observable behavior.

**Receiver Perceptions**

1. Seek understanding, not judgment. Do not argue points of disagreement. Try to understand what the sender is saying. Identify specific points of agreement and disagreement. Paraphrase areas of agreement to determine if interpretation is correct. Point out areas of disagreement for further examination and discussion.

2. Practice active listening skills. Recognize that receiver decoding skills are affected by feelings and perception about the sender that hinder receipt of the message. As receivers ask questions or paraphrase your message, focus on their ideas, ask specific questions to reveal their level of attentiveness, and avoid drawing heated emotional responses. Avoid defensive or attacking responses. Remember that open communication is based on reciprocal trust.

The principal competency of *self-presentation* relates to the ability to convey a message effectively and to share ideas in a non-evaluative manner.

The principal should

- communicate ideas (his own and others') in clear, informative way in both one-on-one and group situations
- stimulate others to ask questions about their own issues
- present himself in a way that is not viewed as controlling or demanding or conformity

Included in the realm of self-presentation are the qualities of good grooming, a pleasant speaking voice, and a likable personality. The more things employees can find to commend, the better the working relationship.

Effective communication relies on the ability of the supervisor, especially the school principal, to project a positive self-image and to instill in others the feelings that foster self-esteem.

Self-concept (a person's concept of what he is within the organization or social structure) results from his perceptions of what he would like to be, what he wants others to think he is, and what he thinks others already think he is. A mature employee must have an awareness of and control of self to satisfy the psychological need for acknowledgment of worth. The supervisor contributes to this satisfaction by modeling positive behaviors that create respect and trust. He or she enhances the staff's individual and group self-concept through encouragement, constructive criticism, and non-threatening discipline.

**Encouragement**
Use the techniques of successful coaches.
- Demonstrate patience and caring. When you are introducing new ideas or information, give the staff members on the school team the sense that you are constantly taking into consideration what is best for the school, the teachers, the support staff, and the students. Referring often to the school's vision and the objectives to achieve that mission will keep team efforts focused and give members the sense of the role each of them plays in the organization.
- Take time to explain and demonstrate and give learners ample time to practice. Even professionals cannot be expected to grasp new concepts and perform with improvement until they have had plenty of time to implement the new skills. Suggest that they observe experienced teachers who exhibit mastery of the expected skills.
- Offer praise and advice. Be cautious that praise is sincere and advice is warranted and wanted.
- Provide support and positive reinforcement. During the improvement process, make sure to note specific elements of success. Focus on those successes, not on mistakes.
- Challenge people to do their best. We often settle for less than we are truly capable of. Help team members see an ultimate goal and the steps to its achievement, then, encourage them toward the goal.
- Encourage enjoyment and appreciation of work. Work is drudgery when the workers do not believe in the product and in their own ability to turn out the best product. The coach has to help the team members realize that the reward of the work is doing it. This means that everyone on the team must have the goal clearly in mind, have the ability to strive for the objectives that lead to the goal, and participate in activities that are relevant to the goal's accomplishment.

## Constructive Criticism

- Lace criticism with deserved, specific, positive praise. To achieve this goal, the supervisor must be prepared to recognize individual differences shaped by societal values and professional attitudes. Planning for constructive criticism requires personal knowledge of performance in the work setting and understanding of each person's interests and emotions. Then, channeling staff members creative energies into productive participation reinforces their sense of worth. Make a point to note the value of their contributions orally or in writing. The collective self-concepts of the individuals in the school community then contribute to the image of the school.

- Encourage improved performance in a relaxed atmosphere. Severe criticism is threatening and non-productive. It forces the criticized individual or group into a defensive posture. Supervisors should therefore provide opportunities for employees to critique their own performance and offer strategies for improvement.

## Non-threatening Discipline

Use effective communication strategies when the need for disciplining employees arises.

- Improving performance requires putting interventions in place in a timely manner, that is, as soon as the problem is diagnosed.

- Criticize performance, not the person. Be sure that your personal judgments do not influence your opinions and actions.

- Maintain emotional stability by offering caring support in a courteous manner and voice.

- Address specifics, not generalities. Have your facts straight and adhere to the prescribed method for handling each situation.

- Protect the confidentiality of the diagnosis and interventions.

## Consensus Building

Consensus building is an ideal decision making tool to use in planning and policy decision making. Consensus reaching is an art that can be time consuming and requires the commitment of all team members. In order to reach consensus all team members must accept and agree to support the decision at hand. All members may not agree or like the decision, but consensus is met when all members can commit to the decision. Consensus building requires the establishment of group norms and relationship building among the team.

All parents have deeply personal reasons to support the school's efforts: they want their child to do well in school. Some parents will have strong opinions about how the principal should run a school; if they were star students they will want the principal to replicate their school experiences. But many parents have memories of their own schooling that are less than positive, and these memories hamper their involvement in the school. Principals must constantly communicate the school's vision, so that parents understand what the school is trying to accomplish. Uninformed parents and community members can derail your improvement efforts.

Educating the parents and community about the school's programs, goals and results is a key responsibility of the school principal, but such communication will be different for every school building and school community. Your parents are as diverse as your student population, with varying degrees of understanding and prior knowledge. Communicating in a variety of ways will enable you to reach your goals of parent and community involvement. Fullan writes about the power of three- teachers, parents and students working together. Involving parents is an unleashed force to school improvement that we must tap.

Successful principals share leadership as they reach out to their parents and community and work hard to expand the professional capacity of the teachers to develop a coherent professional community. Effective leaders are energy creators, creating harmony, forging consensus, setting high standards, and developing a "try this" future orientation. They are forever hopeful and cause everyone in the school's community to share this hope.

Cognitive theory suggests that there are two personal factors to consider in relation to motivation (Eggen & Kauchak, 1997). Those factors are expectations and beliefs. When there is the expectation that one can succeed at a task, and value to achieving that task is attached, then a feeling of self-efficacy emerges. In organizations then, leaders may ask what can be done to help bring about emotions of self-efficacy in its members. The Humanistic perspective views motivation as attempts by people to reach their potential (Eggen & Kauchak, 1997). Motivation proceeds from internal mechanisms acting to cause individuals to achieve, grow and develop, and reach their potential.

Incentives and rewards are used by an organization to influence individuals' motivation to be productive members in the organization. Of importance in any work environment are the environmental factors present, those things that tend to make the workplace enjoyable and those things that tend to make the workplace distasteful. Administrators' attentions to the factors, (which will permeate the workplace and, subsequently, have impact on the motivation of organizations' members to accomplish tasks) have a bearing on the fulfillment of organizational goals. Because individuals have needs, desires, likes, and dislikes and these are related to their motivation, an understanding of this and how it relates to work is important for the leadership function.

Currently, educational policy has relied on the idea of external motivation to improve instructional quality. *No Child Left Behind* operates largely on the principle that rewards and punishments will increase motivation levels of teachers, principals, and students. While growth targets are incremental, when they are not met, schools and staff may, for example, be transferred to other schools in the district. We may not know until 2014, when all students are expected to be fully proficient, how effective external motivation is for improving the learning of all students across the country.

Schools are social systems. As a social system, the school consists of four key elements: the structural, the individual, the cultural, and the political (Hoy & Miskel, 1997). Structure is recognized as the formal bureaucratic expectations promulgated by the organization to achieve its goals. The individual is viewed in terms of personal needs and the capabilities required in order to exist in the organization and to contribute to fulfilling its goals. Culture is defined as the shared work expectations or the attitude and climate about work and the organization (Deal and Kennedy, 1982, describe culture as "the way things are done around here."). Politics is the system of power relations that emerge from the context of the organization's interacting parts. These interdependent parts contribute to the operations of the school. The behavior of the organization is directly related to the interaction of these elements. As a social system, schools are also open systems, meaning that they are influenced by organizations and structures external to the immediate school environment.

The conceptualization of schools as social systems suggests that conflict is possible. There are, within organizations, at least two roles for individuals: the first, the role that the individual carves according to personal idiosyncrasies, and second, the role that the organization imposes because of the specified goals that are to be accomplished. The bureaucratic roles imposed by the organization upon the individual can be inconsistent with the roles the individual perceives as a member in the organization and with the personal role the individual desires to have.

Co-existent with the formal organization is the informal organization. Members of an organization bring with them a number of characteristics, such as values, needs, and motives (Hoy & Miskel, 1987). These attributes play out in the atmosphere of the organization. The informal organization is a network of interpersonal relations that form over a period of time due to the interaction of members within an organization. As individual opportunities to engage in social settings emerge, group members begin to behave according to desirable and acceptable norms that grow out of group interactions. Hoy and Miskel (1987) identified three important functions of the informal organization. Those functions are to serve as a vehicle for communication, to serve as a means of cohesion, and to protect the integrity of individuals. Groups in organizations develop personalities, mores, customs, and traditions to sustain them in the organizational environment. These elements give identity to the group and define group behavior.

Inevitably, problems occur in schools. How those problems are addressed and the quality of the problem-solving episode determines the longevity of the proposed solution and the probable reoccurrence of the same or similar difficulty. Hersey and Blanchard (1988) identified four group problem-solving modes. They are the (a) Crisis Mode, (b) organizational problem solving mode, (c) interpersonal problem solving mode, and (d) routine procedural mode. Using the situational leadership model, which emphasizes task behavior and relationship behavior, they described how each mode is used to resolve organizational problems. When the crisis mode is used for problem solving, it requires high task behavior and low relationship. When the organizational mode is applied, high task and high relationship behavior takes place. The interpersonal mode suggests a high relationship and low task behavior. The routine mode uses low task and low relationship behavior.

Parnes, Noller, and Biondi (1977) developed a five-step model for problem solving. Their model provided for (a) fact finding, (b) problem finding, (c) idea finding, (d) solution finding, and (e) acceptance finding. Fact finding centers on gathering information related to a situation. The problem finding step identifies the problems and sub problems. Idea finding employs techniques to create ideas about the problem. The solution finding step uses criteria to evaluate the ideas. Acceptance finding is the stage where a plan of action is developed to address the problem.

Negotiation has become a central component of managing group conflict and improving the dynamics of groups. For example, good leaders use "win-win" tactics that leave both sides of a conflict with an understanding that a decision was made in the best interest of both parties. Many other negotiation tactics have been found to be highly successful, and descriptions are available all over the Internet.

**Skill 2.2** **Identify procedures for implementing the school vision, including procedures for initiating change and for overcoming obstacles to change.**

Change is always easier to talk about than it is to accomplish. Yet change must be a consistent element of organizational vitality. Determining when to change and what to change in the organizational milieu presents difficulties for a leader. People resist change for a variety of reasons. Perhaps the most prominent barrier to change is the threat it poses to individual roles and the perceived security individuals have in an organization. Human beings resist change almost instinctively. Regardless of the way a certain task is being performed, individuals engaged in performing it are familiar with the details and comfortable using the existing format. Change is viewed as disruptive because members of an organization have devoted energy and resources to accomplishing certain tasks in prescribed ways. To alter the methodology used to accomplish the tasks engenders threat to competency—given a new way of doing it, individuals are not sure they can accomplish the task. Change entails the prospect of discarding the old way of doing something for a new way of doing a task. So much has been invested in the old way that it is very difficult to acknowledge another method. As well, there is a legitimacy of the old versus the unknown qualities of the new.

Change entertained for the organization should be well thought through. Several points are illustrative and serve as advice for a change agent. The change that is to be introduced should not be done abruptly, but rather mentioned and discussed over a period of time preceding its intended implementation. Considerable support for the change should be marshaled so that it has sufficient sustaining forces in the organization. Details regarding the specific goals that are to be addressed by the change are important.

Furthermore, when change is top-down, or driven entirely be a school principal, for example, change is viewed as a threat. Successful change comes from allowing teachers in a school to be central in the decision-making and implementation process. While studies of decentralized decision making (or site-based management) are mixed on the impact of involving teachers in management decisions, in general principle, top-down imposed change causes more anxiety and is less effective at actually effecting real and significant change.

Doll (1996) discusses the process of change from three different perspectives. First, change is viewed as technical; that is, an innovation can be designed carefully and implemented into an organization with needed technical assistance.

Second, change is political, meaning that there are special interests of individuals at work in the planning of change. The third is cultural. Each planned change has potential for disturbing or altering the cultural context.

The Northwest Regional Educational Laboratory used a modified version of the five classic steps in the change process in a plan called the *research utilizing problem solving process.* Those steps are (a) identifying a need for change, (b) diagnosing the situation in which change is to take place, (c) considering alternative courses of action, (d) testing the feasibility of a plan for change, and (e) adoption, diffusion, and adaptation of successful change effort. This plan presents one approach to the change process that concentrates primarily on the initiation phase of a change process.

The change process is further complicated when there is no (or very little) existing support structure for the change or innovation to be introduced in the organization. Generally, a different kind of support system is necessary to maintain the change once it is introduced. It is important for a school leader to be aware and to begin to develop a support system for change in the school environment. Teachers are the ones expected to implement innovations and sustain change in the school. For change to be successful, attention must be given to them and their emotional and professional needs regarding change. If teachers' emotional and professional needs are neglected, the change or innovation will quite likely create difficulty. Change occurs best in a non-punitive, pressure-less, supportive environment. School leaders who foster change on this basis increase the likelihood of change becoming legitimized in the school.

### Skill 2.3 Demonstrate knowledge of procedures for defining educational goals related to the school vision.

No matter what goals are set in a school, the ultimate goal is to increase the level of achievement for all students. Sometimes these goals are expressed in terms of students achieving a specific score on standardized tests, whereas in others they may involve increasing student attendance or parental involvement. Along with these larger goals, there may be intermediate goals such as providing suitable professional development or purchasing resources.

Just as teachers use goals and benchmarks to guide their instruction, administrators can also set benchmarks to help them assess how well the school is achieving the goals. Student assessment is usually the guiding principle for knowing whether or not the school is performing as it should academically. Therefore, a comprehensive analysis of the figures is necessary to determine where success has been achieved and where more work needs to be done.

Under each goal, there should be a list of short-term goals, who is responsible for them and by when. Regular review of these will be the basis for assessing the larger goals in the school growth and improvement plan. However, as each milestone is reached, it is necessary to revisit the goals, determine needs and set more goals. Achieving school growth is an ongoing process because the school will never reach a point where it does not have more growing to do in terms of teaching and learning.

Current research on school growth and development as well as instructional methodologies should be part of all goals. When these are at the forefront of teachers planning and they are taking small steps to improve student learning and their knowledge of the different ways students learn, the goals will eventually be achieved.

Assessment of the school goals also requires the participation of other stakeholders, such as parents and community members. Specialists working with the school, such as guidance counselors and mental health workers who are from the community, rather than the school, should also be involved in the assessment process. They can provide valuable information about specific students that will help identify special needs that must be considered.

**Skill 2.4** **Analyze the use of data-based research strategies to monitor school improvement efforts, evaluate the school's progress toward achieving its goals and vision, ensure accountability, and make needed adjustments.**

See Skill 1.2

**Skill 2.5** **Analyze the use of management techniques and group processes to define roles, assign functions, delegate effectively, facilitate teamwork and collegiality, encourage innovation and autonomy, and determine accountability for attaining goals related to the school vision.**

All leaders must have the capacity to plan. The ability to plan is an essential skill in today's high pressure and ever-changing school environment. It serves the very practical function of assisting administrators to organize their work and to project solutions to problems. Making a determination about what to plan for precedes the activity of planning.

In schools, there is a need to plan the curriculum, to plan for students, and to plan for teachers. The aspect of planning emerges from problems in the environment. Problems are identified and defined. Planning is attached to goals and objectives that are to be achieved. Who participates in the planning process is also crucial to receiving a quality and dynamic plan for implementation.

The essential foundation of planning begins with the identification of needs. A need is identified as a measurable discrepancy between what currently exists and a desired outcome. Planning is an important tool for administrators to cope with changes in the environment. There is a way of decision making wherein the decision-maker acts before thinking. Planning, however, is a commitment to think before acting, which prevents administrators from potentially being embroiled in a set of negative consequences. Planning can be defined as a conceptualization of activities to reach an objective. Planning has anticipated and unanticipated consequences. Planning, like decision making, often occurs in the absence of all the necessary information. In fact, the current drive for "strategic planning" has many critics who argue that too much attention on planning blinds school personnel from actually accomplishing their plans. Yet, planning is much too important not to do, because no planning is worse than poor planning.

Plans develop from the process of planning. The planning function entails an agreement on long term and short term goals that move the school from where it is to where stakeholders want it to be (Kaiser, 1996). Schools need to have a strategic plan that details what the school wants to accomplish over a period of time. Planning in schools is based on student enrollments, staffing projections, curriculum needs, and the vision established by stakeholders.

Administrators engage in the planning process as a means of accomplishing desired objectives and accommodating future events, which can impact the school positively or negatively. Schools, being open systems, are dependent on their external environments and are subject to the uncertainties that exist in that environment. Planning by administrators can be to identify potential support to accomplish school goals and to identify those elements that can have a negative influence on the functioning of the school.

A leader must be in charge. The community of learners expects an ultimate source of authority. They insist that equity exists and that decisions will be reached in an effective and timely manner. The "buck stops" with the principal who is responsible for what happens and what does not happen in the school. Examples of being "in charge" include determining who does what and when in clearly stated written or oral communication, designating persons responsible for given duties, handling security measures, safeguarding the internal accounts, and ensuring safety at all school events. Lately, the principal has taken on a stronger role in instructional leadership. To be a proactive instructional leader, the principal must take care to ensure that teachers understand expectations and are provided with the materials and training they need to be successful teachers.

The principal accepts responsibility for what goes wrong and shares what goes right with those who made it happen. The principal understands his or her role in assuming responsibility for all required tasks and ensures that they are accomplished in a timely manner. To achieve this end of being "in charge," the principal must determine the barriers and ways to overcome them, avenues to achieve the goals, and how to best use available human and material resources to best advantage or how to secure additional resources to achieve the goals.

The bottom line is that the principal must accept the responsibility for what happens. In this process, the principal must change behavior based upon prior experiences and successes or errors. The process requires continuous evaluations and reflections on what worked and why, as well as what did not work and why not. Through this process, the principal corrects past behavior and continues to grow and develop within a collegial environment. Although someone else on the faculty and staff may have created the problem, the principal is still responsible and must handle the bad situation. For example, if a child were illegally paddled and the parent is very angry, the principal must apologize. State school policy indicates she or he will investigate, take appropriate action, and inform the parent of what the investigation revealed and what was done by the principal to close the case in an equitable manner.

School leaders must often be forceful and feel confident about decisions made. Such leaders do not require confirmation from others although they may discuss the situation(s) with fellow administrators, supervisors, or teachers as a means of sharing and acquiring other approaches for future use. Good leaders get all the facts possible on all sides of an issue prior to making a decision unless it is a life and death situation that requires immediate action for the safety and life of people. After getting all possible facts, the principal can use best principles of management to make the correct decision and to stick with the decision unless new evidence becomes available to change the original decision. An example of this decision-making activity is for the principal to deny a dance after an important football game because the students failed without just cause to live up to their attendance agreement the six weeks prior to the game. The forceful principal maintains this decision despite parental and student discontent.

To be especially proactive, principals must clearly delineate expectations for all stakeholders. Responses must be consistent yet fair. It is particularly important that principals "manage by walking around," a common phrase to describe a leader who is visible, knows what is going on, and does not hide in his or her office.

Planning has long been recognized as a key factor in getting the work of a school done. Mandates from superiors, desires of subordinates and others in the learning community, and a vision are but a few of the reasons that a school principal realizes the importance of planning. To develop a plan, the principal must organize all who are to be involved in the planning process.

In designing a plan, the school leader must adhere to meeting established deadlines, developing a flow of activities, identifying resource allocations, and ascertaining evaluation strategies. The deadlines must be for today or for a longer period time. Tasks to be accomplished must be prioritized with identification of persons who are to accomplish each. The principal plans for such tasks as student achievement, accreditation, co-curricular activities, master schedule, parent organizations, student trips, and school special events. Managerial competencies are required to get each of these tasks accomplished.

Prior to developing a plan, the principal has to identify what needs to be done and procedures to accomplish the task. Consultation with others in determining assigned and unassigned tasks is best accomplished through early involvement of others who are involved or will be involved with the tasks. The tasks may involve changing an existing situation or creating a new one to benefit the students.

Planning includes the flexibility to reorder plans as unexpected activities occur to enable the school to reach its goals. The principal is also able to see when and from whom help is needed to achieve the goals in a timely manner. Effective communication competencies are required to act in proactive ways to accomplish tasks identified in plans.

Schools never have enough resources to meet all the demands placed upon them. Technology is expensive and places tremendous demands on the budget. The proactive principal understands this and makes a plan to maximize available resources. These resources include relocation, renovation, new construction, and allocation of such resources as computer quantity and location, audio-visual equipment quantity and quality, media resources and space, meeting rooms, teacher and staff offices, multi-purpose rooms, classrooms, laboratories, cafeterias, playgrounds, physical education indoor and outdoor space, and auxiliary spaces.

Some problems within a school are related to the larger community and require knowledge beyond the school. For example, if drugs are allegedly being sold a few blocks from a school and students are supposedly making purchases during the lunch hour, all information should be obtained and the community should be involved. Community involvement is critical in making a decision on how to handle this problem.

Prior to reaching a decision, the principal must gather as much information as possible from the community and the school. All potential data sources must be identified and information obtained there from. During the data gathering process analysis of the information and needs to explore other sources must be explored. This process must be systematic and include such information as the source(s) of the original information, potential data sources, ways to obtain the data, means to analyze the data, who to involve and when, and how to make the decision to create the fairest and best solution(s).

Organizational goals are accomplished in school through and with others. The principal's ability to delegate is crucial to meeting goals in the organization. Routine and non-routine assignments must be delegated with clearly stated tasks, expected outcomes, and timelines for accomplishment. The kind of work that is delegated includes such areas as developing the basketball schedule, establishing the orientation program and agenda for kindergarten parents, preparing for an accreditation visit, and developing an assembly.

In delegating responsibility, it is important to ascertain the steps needed to achieve the tasks with persons designated to accomplish the tasks. In site-based management, the principal and staff involved act in a collegial manner and determine what is needed and how best to achieve it. Increasingly, schools are using this model of management.

Delegation of responsibilities is often treated less as a method of relieving leaders of their busy schedules and more of a method of encouraging collective ownership for schools. Often, when teachers feel that they have a stake in their school's whole success (through completing tasks outside of the classroom), they are more energized in the classroom.

Additionally, the idea of teacher leadership has become a new way to encourage collaboration and peer control of school quality. The more principals can involve school staff in important decisions, plans, and activities, the more the teachers will see the school with a "birds-eye view," causing them to notice the wider implications of their classroom practices.

## COMPETENCY 3.0 UNDERSTAND HOW TO PROMOTE COMMUNITY COLLABORATION AND INVOLVEMENT IN SUPPORTING THE SCHOOL VISION OF LEARNING

### Skill 3.1 Analyze varied strategies for encouraging the involvement of staff, students, parents/guardians, and community members in supporting the school vision.

Communication in schools is a critical component to their proper operations. Parents need to communicate information to teachers and other school staff members; students need to communicate to teachers and administrators; administrators need to communicate to parents, community members, students, and district leaders; and teachers need to communicate to students, parents and administrators. With so many groups and so few methods of direction communication (after all, how often can a teacher leave his or her classroom to make phone calls?), it is imperative that principals find and provide stakeholder access to a variety of communication tools. Additionally, principals must utilize a wide variety of communication techniques in order to effectively convey their messages.

While email, for example, is a great communication tool, it ceases to be effective if responses are not given in a timely manner, or if responses are short or terse, lacking in emotional character. Indeed, there are a variety of techniques that can be used in person-to-person communication, small meetings, large group information sessions, electronically, or informally. The techniques are explained below:

*Active listening.* Even when the ultimate goal for communication is to send a message from the speaker to the audience, the speaker must demonstrate that he or she is attentive to audience needs and reacts to concerns and questions. Speakers can be active listeners by re-phrasing questions, summarize stated ideas, and purposely integrate audience concerns into the message.

*Personal.* There is nothing worse than listening to someone who has a prepared speech, no emotion, and little personality or humor. Even with a serious topic, principals can insert a sense of humanity into any speech or communicative act. It helps people feel comfortable and open.

*Focusing on nonverbal cues.* Facial expressions, posture, gestures, and eye contact all make a huge difference in communicating ideas effectively. It is especially important that principals continuously look interested, informed, and proactive as they present information to people.

*Balanced.* Principals who carefully consider the needs of all groups are most effective. Principals, therefore, should seek to treat each group fairly and speak about each group with respect.

Overall, communication strategies help to convey messages in formal and informal situations. New principals can pay close attention to these strategies; eventually, they will become internalized, as many experienced principals do these things naturally.

Public information management is a systematic communication process between an educational organization and its public, both within and outside the schools. It is the exchange of two-way information, designed to encourage public interest in and understanding of, education. The principal competency *concern for image* in the consensus management area specifies that a principal shows concern for the school's image through impressions created by students and staff and manages both these impressions and public information about the school by (1) advertising successes and (2) controlling the flow of negative information.

To be effective, communication between school leaders and the public must be open, honest, and unbiased. The attitudes of parents and members of the community at large have been adversely affected by reports in the decline of American education and media coverage which appears to focus on negative perceptions. Despite the general perception of poor public education, the majority of parents surveyed nationally expressed satisfaction with their children's schools and teachers. The most positive feedback resulted when parents felt that their concerns were being heard and addressed and that they were involved in the decision-making process.

Public relations must be carefully organized. Information deliverers must have accurate information, understand their roles in the disseminating of the information, and provide appropriate channels for feedback. The public must perceive that they are being given complete, timely information by officials who respect their feelings and sincerely want feedback. They must have an established frame of reference, i.e. know the schools' vision/mission statements, goals and objectives, and legislative issues that affect local education.

Public Relations Process

1. Public information management requires analyzing the community attitude toward educational issues. The required school improvement surveys conducted each spring in many schools provide not only feedback on the issues but priorities for addressing them. Public workshops and meetings allow community members to become involved in learning about budget, discipline, and academic issues. Information gathering should be structured to obtain the most scientific results, i.e. ensuring a representative sampling by mailing surveys rather than entrusting their delivery and return to students.
2. The planning phase requires setting specific goals and designing the campaign to achieve the goals. During this phase, educational leaders should determine the audiences, forums, and time frames in which their message(s) will be delivered to the public. Presentations to senior citizens concerning a tax increase may require a different slant than a presentation to people who have children in the schools. Issues that require voter decisions should be presented with ample time for study and cooperative decision-making or at least discussion.
3. Following the communication process is equally important whether information is delivered internally or externally. Student groups are a segment of the internal public and should be treated with the same open respect as elements of the community at large. The information campaign must be encoded with specific audiences in mind. Especially important is selection of the media (transmission methods) to convey the message. [Specific strategies are outlined in 2.0.] First-approach media are usually in the form of newsletters to parents, press releases, annual reports—any written document that can be distributed to the intended audiences. Follow-up transmissions include open houses, school committee or school board meetings, education fairs—any face-to-face communication that brings the public and school representatives together for a two-way exchange.
4. Finally, school/district officials must evaluate the results of the public relations effort. Some evaluation is immediate, as in the defeat of a candidate or the passage of a bond issue. Periodic evaluations in the form of brief questionnaires in school newsletters, telephone surveys, or written assessments at the end of public meetings can help test the public's understanding and the level of community support.

Other Considerations

1. Schools must establish good relationships with the media. When there are more complaints in the "Letters to the Editor" section of the newspaper that there are news articles about school events, there is obviously a poor interaction between media and the schools.

   Of course, there are several reasons for the amount of educational coverage provided by various media.

   - Small, hometown newspapers give broader coverage to local issues/events. They may devote a whole page or section to school/classroom events.
   - Newspapers have to evaluate the "newsworthiness" of stories. Local spelling bees get better coverage than Mrs. Clarke's debate class's mock trial because one spelling bee winner in each district will compete nationally. Most newspapers consider a story of vandalism or fire at a school or a union walkout to be more newsworthy than a piece about students working at an animal shelter. Large city newspapers and television stations focus more on national and state news and regrettably often focus on educational issues that have negative or sensational impact.
   - Local radio and television stations may be a better venue for school news; interviews with school officials, teachers, or students; or debates on education issues that have local impact.

2. School/district publications—newsletters, information brochures, handbooks, annual reports—may be more useful in providing a positive link with the community.

3. Displays of student work in public places—malls, building lobbies, and business waiting rooms—provide visual evidence of student achievement.

## Establishing a Good Relationship with the Media

Educational leaders need to apply the communication process to public information management.

1. Ideating - Create messages that reflect understanding of the audience (the general public) and the nature of different media (newspapers, radio, television). Ask editors and producers to provide information concerning the types of material they consider newsworthy. Be available when asked to meet with reporters. Make sure press releases meet the space and time constraints of news copy.

2. Encoding - Speak in plain English, avoiding educational jargon. If you must use terms such as "block scheduling" or "outcome-based education," be sure you can define, explain, or give examples that can be easily understood. Remember the receiver for whom you are encoding the message.

3. Transmitting - Be open and honest with reporters. Assume a cooperative, rather than an adversarial, posture. Be prepared to provide specific, accurate information or to direct the reporter to the person(s) who can give solid answers to his questions. Refusing to answer may only lead to the reporter getting information from an unreliable source.

Having followed these steps, the receiver should be able to decode your message and feel free to give feedback.

Organization Development is a values-based approach to systems change. The goal is to build the capacity to achieve and sustain a new desired state that benefits the organization and community around it. Organizational Development is an evolving field of practice grounded in a set of core values and principles that guide behavior and actions.

The key values include: **respect and inclusion**- equitably values the perspective and opinions of everyone; **collaboration**- builds collaborative relationships between the practitioner and the client while encouraging collaboration throughout the client system; **authenticity**- strives for authenticity and congruence and encourages these qualities in their clients; **self-awareness**- commits to developing self-awareness and interpersonal skills. OD practitioners engage in personal and professional development through lifelong learning: **empowerment**- focuses efforts on helping everyone in the client organization or community increase their autonomy and empowerment to levels that make the workplace and/or community satisfying and productive.

Organizational Development draws from multiple disciplines that inform an understanding of human systems, including applied behavioral and physical sciences. It approaches communities and organizations as open systems, acting with the knowledge that change in one area of a system always results in changes in other areas, and change in one area cannot be sustained without supporting changes in other areas of the system. Organizational Development continuously reexamines, reflects and integrates discoveries throughout the process of change in order to achieve desired outcomes. In this way, the client members are involved both in doing their work, and in dialogue about their reflection and learning in order to apply them to achieve shared results. It intervenes in organizational or community processes to help bring about positive change and help the client work toward desired outcomes

Organizational Development involves proactive inquiry and assessment of the internal environment in order to discover and create a compelling need for change and the achievement of a desired future state of the organization or community. Some methods include survey feedback, assessment tools, interviewing, focus groups, story telling, process consultation and observation. Mary Eggers and Allan Church led an initiative to develop Principles of Practice and a definition of Organizational Development, to provide guidance for the practice of Organizational Development. They were asked to produce a document that would serve as a ruler for current practitioners to assess their practice, a compass for training and development of practitioners, and one guideline for clients to evaluate the internal and external consultants they intend to hire. Building on the work of the Values and Advocacy Initiative, they solicited input from a diverse segment of practitioners and leaders in the field of Organizational Development

**Skill 3.2    Identify strategies for drawing on the diversity of the community to improve educational programs, meet diverse student needs, and support the school vision.**

With the rapidly changing population demographics of the United States and the significant growth of diverse multicultural groups, schools and education professionals are being challenged as to how to provide the best comprehensive educational and support services to their increasingly diverse student population. (Sanchez, 1995)

An important element of a successful diverse school is the belief that all children, of every background, can and should succeed. In order to make this happen schools must offer challenging academic programs, set high expectations, and identify ways to support students who are struggling to meet those expectations.

In any school, equally as important as academics are the lessons of tolerance and respect for differences. Students and parents should be encouraged to share their unique life experiences in the classroom and after school.

Schools also need to build community support by keeping the entire school community aware of what's really happening inside the school.

The value of respect for each individual must be at the foundation of the school's management. The creation of a positive school climate takes commitment and hard work. In the end it will pay off as we prepare students for the global community that awaits them. (Kugler, 1999)

Today's classrooms are more ethnically diverse than ever before. For students from different ethnic backgrounds or recent immigrants to the country, going to school may be a traumatic experience. This will have implications for teaching and learning in the classroom. Teachers and administrators must be more culturally sensitive than ever before in order to meet the needs of these students. Some of the factors that could affect learning include language, cultural values, dress codes, learning styles and family preferences.

In order to meet the needs of a culturally diverse classroom, the administrator has to have a repertoire of tactics when dealing with both students and parents. Teachers need to employ different instructional techniques and it is the administrator's responsibility to find the appropriate professional development for these teachers.

When teachers read books aloud in the classroom, they must ensure that they have a cultural mix befitting the cultural diversity of the class. They must also make sure the information is accurate and up to date.

Administrators may have to make allowances for students missing school because of various religious observances and provide the appropriate support for the families. They also have to be cognizant of food restrictions for some students when hosting hot dog days or sports days. These students need to know that they are an accepted part of the school setting and provisions for special accommodations should be in place.

Bulletin boards, signs and posters throughout the school celebrating cultural diversity is another way to help students feel welcome. This is often easier for teachers to do than to delve into the curriculum to make sure that everything is culturally correct. However, it is important for teachers to explain any facts that are not accurate. Having students of different ethnicities make presentations to the class or the school will help to improve relationships within the school.

The most important factor is for both the administration and the teachers to be aware of the ethnic differences when speaking and listening. In most cultures there is a unique method to communication and if the staff is not aware of the method, it could cause problems for the students involved.

## Skill 3.3 Identify strategies for collaborating with community agencies to integrate health, social, cultural, and other services in the schools to address student needs.

The superintendent of a school district is responsible for ensuring that there are enough teachers in all the schools to deliver the curriculum. The staff of the district office, which includes coordinators for various subjects, report to the superintendent about their work with the schools in the jurisdiction. This staff coordinates the professional development for the district and provides individual administrators with the flexibility to provide professional development for which they deem there is a need in a school.

The school district also allocates the funds the administrator needs to conduct the day to day business of the school and provide the resources that the teachers and students need. The district staff is also responsible for ensuring that all teachers have adequate training in new programs and that the administration of the school evaluates new teachers.

Many districts have developed policies to allow more participation by parents in the workings of the school through School Councils. Regularly planned meetings with administrators are part of the annual calendar as are monthly parent meetings.

The district staff is instrumental in collecting assessment data and in developing goals to help address any identified gaps. While it is the administrator's responsibility to ensure that all teachers develop professional goals, the administrator also has to have professional goals and these are sent to the superintendent.

Outside agencies have a role to play in determining and enforcing educational accountability. Police, for example, can come into the school to give presentations of many different sorts to help in the development of citizenship or cultural diversity. Leaders of all cultures in the community should also be part of the overall school community, coming into the school on a regular basis to consult with the administration, teachers and students. Health care professionals, such as nurses, social workers, and mental health workers have an important role to play in ensuring that the school is accountable for the success of all students.

The school, the school district and outside agencies in the community should have a partnership with the education of the students at the core of the relationship.

# TEACHER CERTIFICATION STUDY GUIDE

**Skill 3.4** **Demonstrate knowledge of community relations techniques that make effective use of varied media to help support the school vision.**

See Skill 3.1

**Skill 3.5** **Identify outreach strategies for involving business, religious, political, and service organizations in supporting the school vision.**

School principals and administrators should recognize that counselors and social service providers are key in creating a positive environment in the school, and dealing with concerns and often crises. They may have significant roles in developing effective discipline plans, enlisting parent support, helping teachers with classroom management and helping students perform to their potential.

There are various social service agencies and resources available for students and schools, depending on the school district. Social services available to public school students include health services and emotional counseling services, family help services, special services for students with mental or physical disabilities, testing services, behavior intervention services and self-help programs.

Administrators should learn about the available resources from social service agencies and become familiar with referral processes and procedures. It is important to work in collaboration with the school counselor and specialized personnel on those issues.

Dr. James Comer, professor of child psychiatry at Yale University, stated that "No significant learning takes place without a significant relationship." Principals should be aware of this insight as they seek to create productive relationships in the school community regardless of the socioeconomic, ethnic or educational background of the stakeholders. Community groups, such as churches, businesses, and daycares, who are engaged in the education process, are invaluable partners, increasing the likelihood that children will be successful in meeting the learning goals of the school.

**PRINCIPAL COMMON CORE**

A principal should seek out diversity on school committees so that all stakeholder groups are giving feedback about the school. When recruiting volunteers, principals should make conscious decisions to reach out to underrepresented groups. This can be done with personal phone calls, a willingness to meet at unusual times and places to accommodate work schedules, or simply asking input, even if it has to be by phone. Realizing that some people in your school community have had negative personal school-related experiences can make you more sensitive to the barriers to involvement. Principals must also realize that community members and parents are often impacted by the mental and physical fatigue stemming from economic stress. When you assume that the lack of involvement means a lack of caring, you push people away instead of drawing them into your school.

Here are some things that you can do to begin to build strong relationships with the diverse groups in your school community:

**Take steps to ensure that your staff knows your clientele.** Tour the community with your staff so that they see where the students live and what resources may be available in the community.

**Treat all visitors to your building with a high level of professionalism.** Be willing to accommodate their preferences concerning day and time for meeting, then arrive on time and be well-prepared. Schools lose credibility with parents and the community when they appear to not know what is happening with a child and/or they have no idea of what to do about it. When confronted with a problem, do not be afraid to admit mistakes. If you mess up, always apologize.

**Administrators must ensure that all communication with the community is clear and effective.** Lack of communication and miscommunication account for nearly 80% of problems or conflicts. You can develop key communicator email lists to get word out quickly if there is a school problem, event or need that involves the community. Utilize neighborhood newsletters and local newspapers to get the facts out about the school. Don't assume that everyone knows what you are trying to accomplish with your students. Make sure that language barriers are not an issue. Be aware of written or verbal language that is overloaded with educational verbiage.

**Make the effort to find out what the community groups are thinking and feeling.** This can be done by regularly using short surveys that address very specific topics. Make a few phone calls or visits each week to randomly ask how they think things are going at the school. Be sure to include a diverse population on your site council or school improvement team.

**Find out what the school can do to support community efforts as well.**
Local restaurants may need seasonal decorations that your art classes can provide. A nursing home in the area may enjoy a holiday concert from your school choir. Local churches may need help with a variety of service projects. Older students may be able to assist with babysitting at community functions. When your school contributes to the needs of the community, you will find the community groups more willing to involve themselves in the success of the school.

**Ask the school staff to be visible in the community.** When the school staff frequents restaurants or churches, ask them to identify themselves to the people in charge. Knowing that some of the customer base comes from the local school will increase interest and participation in school events and programs by the community group.

**Don't be afraid to ask for help.** When you've invested time in building relationships with community groups, when you've actively sought their input, then you can ask for help without hesitation. Employees of local businesses may be able to come at lunch and tutor at-risk children. Donations may be given that will provide students with school supplies or other needed items. Healthcare services may be provided at low cost to families in need. Always remember to follow up with a letter of thanks for the support you receive. Involving the students in the displays of gratitude add the personal connection that will keep the community continually involved in the school.

**Skill 3.6** **Analyze the use of community relations models, marketing strategies, and data-driven decision making to develop educational partnerships among schools, businesses, community organizations, government agencies, and higher education institutions.**

See Skill 3.5

## Skill 3.7 Describe ways to support the involvement of families in the education of their children.

All parents have deeply personal reasons to support the school's efforts: they want their child to do well in school. Some parents will have strong opinions about how the principal should run a school; if they were star students they will want the principal to replicate their school experiences. But many parents have memories of their own schooling that are less than positive, and these memories hamper their involvement in the school. Principals must constantly communicate the school's vision, so that parents understand what the school is trying to accomplish. Uninformed parents and community members can derail your improvement efforts.

Educating the parents and community about the school's programs, goals and results is a key responsibility of the school principal, but such communication will be different for every school building and school community. Your parents are as diverse as your student population, with varying degrees of understanding and prior knowledge. Communicating in a variety of ways will enable you to reach your goals of parent and community involvement. Fullan writes about the power of three- teachers, parents and students working together. Involving parents is an unleashed force to school improvement that we must tap.

Successful principals share leadership as they reach out to their parents and community and work hard to expand the professional capacity of the teachers to develop a coherent professional community. Effective leaders are energy creators, creating harmony, forging consensus, setting high standards, and developing a "try this" future orientation. They are forever hopeful and cause everyone in the school's community to share this hope.

Public information management is a systematic communication process between an educational organization and its public, both within and outside the schools. It is the exchange of two-way information, designed to encourage public interest in and understanding of, education. The principal shows concern for the school's image through impressions created by students and staff and manages both these impressions and public information about the school by (1) advertising successes and (2) controlling the flow of negative information.

To be effective, communication between school leaders and the public must be open, honest, and unbiased. The attitudes of parents and members of the community at large have been adversely affected by reports in the decline of American education and media coverage which appears to focus on negative perceptions. Despite the general perception of poor public education, the majority of parents surveyed nationally expressed satisfaction with their children's schools and teachers. The most positive feedback resulted when parents felt that their concerns were being heard and addressed and that they were involved in the decision-making process.

Principals should seek input from parents in systematic and planned ways. Annual surveys, parent informational nights, and parent advisory committees allow principals to receive valuable input on a variety of topics. Principals benefit from opportunities to learn about the perception of the school out in the community and what issues might impact the school's progress. Public relations must be carefully organized. Information deliverers must have accurate information, understand their roles in the dissemination of the information, and provide appropriate channels for feedback. The public must perceive that they are being given complete, timely information by officials who respect their feelings and sincerely want feedback. Developing a key communicator email list is a new method that many principals use to disperse information immediately. Each parent can receive the information and not have to rely on rumors or gossip from the neighborhood. This ability to communicate quickly and effectively with key members of the community is especially important when a crisis situation develops at a school. Having a key communicator email keeps parents informed and prevents them from hearing about an issue from a biased media presentation.

Research has proven that when schools and parents work together, children receive higher grades and test scores. A key responsibility of the principal is to continually provide opportunities for parents/caregivers to be involved in the education of their children.

Training the school staff on how to communicate with parents is the place to begin. Teachers must understand that parents want to hear positive information about their child and not just phone calls about negative behavior or academic failure. Teachers should also be discouraged from using educational jargon that parents may not understand. Principals should check the reception area of the school to see how parents are treated when they arrive at the school. If everyone at the school shows appreciation for parents who are trying to be involved, then parent involvement will increase.

Finding and removing barriers to parent involvement is important to a school's success. Here are some ideas that will increase opportunities for parent involvement in a school:

1. Offer incentives for parents to attend meetings. Giving away food, books, and other door prizes helps to increase attendance.
2. Have students perform at school meetings. All parents like to see their children on stage and will attend meetings for that reason.
3. Call parents and give them a personal invitation to a meeting.
4. Provide rides to meetings for parents lacking transportation.
5. Open a Parent Center. Stock it with parenting books and other resources so that parents will have a place to increase their own knowledge and to network with other parents.
6. Hold parent workshops. Topics such as working with your ADHD child, computer literacy and how to read with your child will increase student success and parent involvement.
7. Ask teachers to provide several opportunities each year for parents to come to school, and look at a portfolio of their child's work. The teacher can circulate and answer questions. Parent and child can also work on skills or projects together with the teacher present to assist, explain or clarify the expectations.

**Skill 3.8    Describe ways to acknowledge that families have the best interests of their children in mind.**

See Skill 3.7

# TEACHER CERTIFICATION STUDY GUIDE

**COMPETENCY 4.0    UNDERSTAND THE SIGNIFICANCE OF DIVERSITY FOR THE SCHOOL'S VISION OF LEARNING AND WAYS TO EXERCISE LEADERSHIP IN SUPPORTING AND VALUING DIVERSITY.**

**Skill 4.1    Examine ways to use the experiences and perspectives of members of the school community with diverse backgrounds to help achieve the school vision and meet the learning needs of all students.**

Developing a school vision or renewing one that already exists is something that every administrator should take seriously. Even if a school vision has existed for years, it needs to be looked at on an annual basis to make sure that it is still addressing the needs of the school as determined by a thorough analysis of data. The main focus in building a school vision is that the school is a place where all children will be academically successful.

In communities where the demographics are constantly changing, strategies will include looking at the needs of the students on a yearly basis. This includes analyzing test results to determine where improvements may be made in teaching and learning, and communication with parents. Determining the school culture is a strong point in this strategy as it brings the school and the community together. When teachers and parents see that they have a voice in what happens in the school, vision building no longer becomes a boring process, but one in which they will take an active role.

The vision of a school needs to include a plan for addressing student and family conditions. Teams of teachers can deal with separate issues and then bring the results to the whole staff. In schools, where there is only a small staff, this can be a collaborative effort by all. The administrator has to let the teachers and parents know that their ideas are valued in order to build relationships and work toward consensus. Teachers need to be empowered in their classroom and be allowed to conduct action research on issues important to them and their students' learning. Collaborative dialogue allows teachers to share these individual findings and determine how they may contribute to the collective vision of the building.

A school-wide discipline or character education plan is often part of the vision creating consistency throughout the building. When the plan is imparted to parents and they have had voice in the decisions, they are more likely to support the disciplinary efforts of the school.

At the beginning of each school year, the administrator should set aside meeting time for the teachers to take a new look at the school vision and set goals for the coming year. At the same time, teachers can set their own professional development goals in relation to the main goals of the school.

**PRINCIPAL COMMON CORE**

If administrators approach the school vision utilizing the Understanding by Design model, they will start out with a final vision of what they want their schools to look like. Then they determine benchmarks for assessing achievement towards that goal. It may take years to achieve the final vision, but by regularly reviewing and renewing the school vision, change will occur.

No matter what goals are set in a school, the ultimate goal is to increase the level of achievement for all students. Sometimes these goals are expressed in terms of students achieving a specific score on standardized tests, whereas in others they may involve increasing student attendance or parental involvement. Along with these larger goals, there may be intermediate goals such as providing suitable professional development or purchasing resources.

Just as teachers use goals and benchmarks to guide their instruction, administrators can also set benchmarks to help them assess how well the school is achieving the goals. Student assessment is usually the guiding principle for knowing whether or not the school is performing as it should academically. Therefore, a comprehensive analysis of the figures is necessary to determine where success has been achieved and where more work needs to be done.

Under each goal, there should be a list of short-term goals, who is responsible for them and by when. Regular review of these will be the basis for assessing the larger goals in the school growth and improvement plan. However, as each milestone is reached, it is necessary to revisit the goals, determine needs and set more goals. Achieving school growth is an ongoing process because the school will never reach a point where it does not have more growing to do in terms of teaching and learning.

Current research on school growth and development as well as instructional methodologies should be part of all goals. When these are at the forefront of teachers planning and they are taking small steps to improve student learning and their knowledge of the different ways students learn, the goals will eventually be achieved.

Assessment of the school goals also requires the participation of other stakeholders, such as parents and community members. Specialists working with the school, such as guidance counselors and mental health workers who are from the community, rather than the school, should also be involved in the assessment process. They can provide valuable information about specific students that will help identify special needs that must be considered.

**Skill 4.2** **Demonstrate knowledge of strategies for creating an atmosphere in the school that encourages respect, sensitivity, and appreciation for all people.**

Parents, teachers and administrators want to provide safe and caring schools where students feel safe and protected. The Virtues Project (Popov, Popov and Kavelin) is one such way that administrators can help engender an atmosphere encouraging students to be respectful and sensitive of people of all cultures and races and to develop a respect for these cultures. In developing character and citizenship, teachers reinforce the positive character traits in the classroom. The teachers model the characteristics and teach students about them by integrating them into all subjects and interactions with students. This is not taught as a separate subject, but is infused into all facets of the curriculum.

Some schools may feel they have specific issues that need to be dealt with, such as bullying or racial tensions. They may focus their resources toward dealing with these issues, whereas other schools might take a larger focus and deal with all aspects of character education.

Bullying is an issue that faces all schools and all grades. One strategy that has worked in many schools is to start a peer mediation program. This is usually one class of students who may need help with bullying or has students that are more sensitive to the needs of others. The students are taught the negative effects of bullying and prevention strategies. Students sign up to be part of the mediation team and wear a vest or some other insignia to identify them to students while on the playground or in the school building. When a student who is being bullied reports to the mediator, the teacher is then informed of the situation and can deal with it. Presentations and plays about bullying can also be part of the school assemblies throughout the year.

In any character building program some of the values that are stressed include:

- Respect
- Initiative
- Responsibility
- Perseverance
- Honesty
- Courage
- Empathy
- Integrity
- Fairness
- Optimism

By concentrating on one virtue a month and making this the focus of the school assembly, the students will gradually internalize the virtue and display it in their actions towards others. Some schools arrange the instruction by grade levels, with specific grades being responsible for specific virtues.

**Skill 4.3    Analyze factors involved in working effectively with diverse groups within the school and community.**

The administrator of any school is charged with ensuring that the programs, services and personnel are in place to meet the needs of all the students in the school. This means ensuring that the teachers are in place for all grade levels or in the case of junior high and high schools, teachers are in place for all subjects. It is also the responsibility of the administrator to ensure that the teachers are suited to these grade levels and subjects with the proper training.

In addition to ensuring that programs are in place to meet the needs of the students that are struggling, there should also be programs in place to meet the needs of the gifted and talented students. In most cases, schools do not have the budget needed to hire special teachers, nor should these students be segregated from their peers. Therefore, teachers in the classrooms should provide challenging experiences and activities that meet the learning outcomes and yet meet the needs of students that are exceeding the objectives.

Special education for struggling students involves having the personnel in place to meet their specific needs. In classrooms, teachers should provide extra support for the students, but there should also be personnel who can pull the students out of class to give them extra instruction in the areas with which they are experiencing difficulty. Testing procedures should also be in place so that the teachers can determine exactly what the problems are and how best to address them. For most schools, these testers are educational psychologists and reading specialists who come to the school on a regular basis and meet with the students, teachers and parents. These ancillary services also include mental health workers, home-school liaison personnel, health professionals and the police who come to the school to meet with the students and help them through times of difficulty.

Student activities in school should be aligned with the state standards. They also include after school activities to provide the students with physical education skills or field trips to points of interest during the school day.

The role of the principal has indeed changed over the past ten years. Prior, principals were the managers of the school building: They made sure all aspects were working together according to specification. They ensured that activities were safe and cost effective, that all students had places to go during the day, that students were behaving properly, and that teachers had the resources they needed to teach.

Lately, there has been a shift to thinking of principals as instructional leaders. They are expected to be thoroughly aware of each classroom, the instructional styles of each teacher, and the learning outcomes of all students. In summary, they are held responsible for the quality of instruction and the depth of learning at their schools.

With this shift of responsibilities, though, comes a dilemma for most school leaders: Should they focus on instruction at the expense of all other areas they know to be effective in the development of student growth, as well as the refinement of a positive school culture? Or do they try to balance both demands—which takes much more time, cost, and effort?

Most principals would argue that both are necessary, no matter the cost. They realize that students, their families, and teachers need to see that all students' needs are met on a variety of levels. Schools are ideal places to provide various athletic, creative, and intellectual activities. Furthermore, these activities provide schools with a greater sense of community.

How do principals balance those two disparate roles, as well as facilitate the development, implementation, evaluation, and refinement of student services and activity programs to fulfill academic, developmental, social, and cultural needs? First, principals must focus on the school's mission. Most schools think beyond test scores and student achievement in their mission statements. For example, a school that says that its mission is to prepare students to succeed in a changing world will ultimately acknowledge that achievement is important. However, such a school will also offer students opportunities to succeed socially, physically, and creatively. As school needs are identified in order to reach those broad goals, principals can help select faculty to participate; they can also set aside money. As they allocate school resources—money, personnel, time, and space—they must be very careful to ensure that students are treated fairly and equally. In this day and age, directing significant resources to the football team—and few resources to the chess team—may be seen as highly unfair.

In addition to activities, principals must ensure that student services are nimble and responsive to needs that may arise at random times. For example, a highly bureaucratic student services office may not respond quickly when emergencies arise and students—en masse—need counseling. Such offices also need to pay close attention to the requests of parents. Principals can help to assure this by instituting planning sessions and regular meetings to review policies, procedures, and school goals. Such staff should play critical roles throughout the campus so that they see the concerns and needs of teachers, as well as students when they are in academic and athletic environments.

**Skill 4.4** **Examine cultural, social, and economic factors affecting students and society.**

It is not only the teachers in the classroom that directly impact a student's success or failure. Peers, parents and the community at large have a direct influence on the student's performance in school. These forces shape the student's attitude toward school. In families where education is seen as being important, students will be encouraged to do well in school. In families where the parents have had bad experiences with school, the children will likely internalize the parental attitudes and bring them to the classroom. While many students appreciate the value of succeeding in school and graduating, they are skeptical of the value of what they are learning, therefore they do not place much emphasis on the content in the curriculum.

Children in primary and elementary grades generally love school and try to do well. Students, who are struggling, however, find the content difficult and many of them give up. These students are often stigmatized because of the difficulty and perceive themselves as being unsuccessful. This leads to even further difficulties if appropriate supports are not in place in school.

Many intermediate and high school students are employed after school, some have to and other by choice. These students may have to work to help support their families and therefore do not have enough time to devote to their schoolwork to help them succeed. Administrators and teachers should be aware of these cases and work with the families and students to help ease the burden.

The classrooms of this country are much different today than they once were. It is possible to have students from many different countries in one room and this presents a different set of problems. There may be students learning English, those running from political situations in their home countries or even students who have experienced racial or religious prejudice. The administrator must be aware of all these factors so that the classroom can function so that all students learn.

**Skill 4.5** **Analyze the implications of diversity for education.**

See Skill 4.1

**Skill 4.6** **Demonstrate knowledge of ways to work with others in the school community to address prejudice and ensure that all students have an equal opportunity for educational success.**

With the rapidly changing population demographics of the United States and the significant growth of diverse multicultural groups, schools and education professionals are being challenged as to how to provide the best comprehensive educational and support services to their increasingly diverse student population. (Sanchez, 1995)

An important element of a successful diverse school is the belief that all children, of every background, can and should succeed. In order to make this happen schools must offer challenging academic programs, set high expectations, and identify ways to support students who are struggling to meet those expectations.

In any school, equally as important as academics are the lessons of tolerance and respect for differences. Students and parents should be encouraged to share their unique life experiences in the classroom and after school.

Schools also need to build community support by keeping the entire school community aware of what's really happening inside the school.

The value of respect for each individual must be at the foundation of the school's management. The creation of a positive school climate takes commitment and hard work. In the end it will pay off as we prepare students for the global community that awaits them. (Kugler, 1999)

Today's classrooms are more ethnically diverse than ever before. For students from different ethnic backgrounds or recent immigrants to the country, going to school may be a traumatic experience. This will have implications for teaching and learning in the classroom. Teachers and administrators must be more culturally sensitive than ever before in order to meet the needs of these students. Some of the factors that could affect learning include language, cultural values, dress codes, learning styles and family preferences.

In order to meet the needs of a culturally diverse classroom, the administrator has to have a repertoire of tactics when dealing with both students and parents. Teachers need to employ different instructional techniques and it is the administrator's responsibility to find the appropriate professional development for these teachers.

When teachers read books aloud in the classroom, they must ensure that they have a cultural mix befitting the cultural diversity of the class. They must also make sure the information is accurate and up to date.

Administrators may have to make allowances for students missing school because of various religious observances and provide the appropriate support for the families. They also have to be cognizant of food restrictions for some students when hosting hot dog days or sports days. These students need to know that they are an accepted part of the school setting and provisions for special accommodations should be in place.

Bulletin boards, signs and posters throughout the school celebrating cultural diversity is another way to help students feel welcome. This is often easier for teachers to do than to delve into the curriculum to make sure that everything is culturally correct. However, it is important for teachers to explain any facts that are not accurate. Having students of different ethnicities make presentations to the class or the school will help to improve relationships within the school.

The most important factor is for both the administration and the teachers to be aware of the ethnic differences when speaking and listening. In most cultures there is a unique method to communication and if the staff is not aware of the method, it could cause problems for the students involved.

There are many issues facing administrators when dealing with students, teachers and parents. Every situation needs to be looked at individually, which means the administrator may be accused of not treating everyone equally. Each situation brings with it special circumstances which need to be considered before rendering a decision. For example, when dealing with an unruly student, the administrator has to look beyond the student's actions to determine the cause. Many students bring a lot of baggage with them when they come to school in the morning and quite often this baggage is the reason for their problems. By building relationships with students, administrators and teachers are better able to recognize these factors.

The same thing applies to teachers. There may be family problems and the teacher may need to take time off or be able to share personal information. Teachers need to know that they are respected as individuals and that their administrator will listen to them, whether it is social, to complain or to seek advice.

The administrator must be cognizant of any signs and patterns of discrimination in the school. Subtle signs of discrimination include racial jokes and slurs. There may be minority groups that do not fit in with the other students and are visibly segregated in the corridors. Sometimes, this transfers to groups in the classrooms and teachers need to be cognizant of how they group the students to together. Name calling is another sign of discrimination and if the situation is not handled immediately, tensions will intensify and violence could result.

A shortage of role models in some schools for certain populations sometimes leads to tension. When the diversity of the staff represents the student body, it helps to put the students at ease and to give them someone to talk to with whom they can feel comfortable.

For some students who are learning to speak English, they feel at a disadvantage when they are placed in a regular classroom. The supports must be there to help them with the language, and whenever possible, the instruction of new ideas should be in the student's first language until he or she is able to understand the concept.

Discrimination of any kind evokes responses of anger, sadness and fear. Administrators should be visible during recess and lunch time talking with the students and noticing any actions which may be inappropriate. The administrator must get to know the students so that it is easy to determine when they are exhibiting any of these behaviors.

Gender discrimination is another aspect of discrimination in schools that teachers and administrators must watch for. Today, education is guaranteed for everyone, but in some culturally diverse families, education for girls is not viewed as being as important as it is for boys. Here the school staff will have to work with the families as well as the students in an effort to change these views while still being sensitive to the culture.

### Skill 4.7 Demonstrate knowledge of strategies for infusing diversity awareness into the curriculum.

Infusing diversity awareness into the curriculum is known as global citizenship. There are several advantages to this approach of teaching and learning.

- Students come to have more respect for cultures other than their own and to appreciate the value of these other cultures.
- Students learn about the developing countries of the world and the problems faced by the people living there.
- Students become more responsible for the environment and for the interdependence shared by all cultures.
- Students have a better outlook on what they can do to bring peace to the world.

Through global education, the school can increase the students' knowledge of international organizations and the work that they do. This will help to instill in them a sense of global responsibility as a citizen of the world, rather than only their own small part of the world.

The Internet is an excellent resource for teachers to aid them in developing such a curriculum. Administrators should ensure that all classes have access to computers and the Internet, either by having computers in all classrooms or providing access to a computer lab within the school. This education goes hand in hand with safe and caring schools because when students are taught to respect and empathize with other cultures they develop a sense of their own self-worth. Problem solving strategies are essential as part of the curriculum with the teachers posing real world problems to the students and helping them work through the problems to arrive at a suitable solution.

Cooperative learning is an aspect of learning about diversity awareness as students work together. The literature in the classroom should also reflect the cultural diversity and it should be accurate in its facts and illustrations. Above all, the teaching and learning should be respectful of all the stakeholders – teachers, students and parents.

Students will learn how to make connections between their own lives and those of others in various parts of the world. They will come to understand that all human beings have the potential for greatness, but that not all have the same opportunities. By looking at the issues facing the world through several different perspectives, students will have a better understanding of justice, human rights and their own responsibilities.

**Skill 4.8　　Identify policies and strategies to help students and staff learn how to function effectively in a multilingual, multicultural, and economically diverse society.**

As the influx of immigrants continues, schools now have students from more countries of the world than ever before. These students speak different languages and have different religious beliefs and cultural expectations that students may not be familiar with. While it is important for teachers to have the same high expectations for these students as they have for others, when they are placed in the regular classroom, they may feel that they cannot keep up with the work and this translates into frequent absences and poor performance in school. Teachers must be cognizant of the factors that can affect these students' learning success and make changes to their instructional techniques to accommodate them.

Culturally diverse students cannot unlearn everything they have learned in their own culture up to this point and it would be ludicrous for administrators or teachers to expect them to immediately adapt to new circumstances. Therefore teachers and administrators need to be aware of the cultural implications of having these students in the school and develop methods to teach them so that they can experience success. For some cultures, oral traditions may be very important and children learn by talking and discussing. For others, they have been taught to be silent and this should not be interpreted as a lack of understanding or disrespect on the part of the student.

Students may have been in a culture where they were afraid to speak out because of political situations and therefore do not actively participate in the classroom. When new students come into the school, the administration and the teachers should not only read the records they bring with them, but should research the specific culture the students come from. Interview the students and let them tell about their lives. Making sure the parents feel comfortable in the school setting is also very important so that they can support the student at home.

# TEACHER CERTIFICATION STUDY GUIDE

**COMPETENCY 5.0**     **UNDERSTAND HOW TO SUPPORT THE SCHOOL VISION BY USING HUMAN RELATIONS SKILLS AND COMMUNICATION SKILLS TO SOLVE PROBLEMS AND FACILITATE DECISION MAKING.**

**Skill 5.1**     Analyze the use of communication skills and public relations techniques in disseminating information to the public and engaging the community in dialogue to support the school vision.

See Competency 1.0

**Skill 5.2**     Demonstrate knowledge of techniques for facilitating communication with and among members of the school community.

See Skill 3.1

**Skill 5.3**     Apply knowledge of skills for listening and speaking effectively in small- and large-group contexts.

See Skill 1.1

**Skill 5.4**     Identify procedures to promote collaborative decision making and creative problem solving in various school situations.

See Skill 2.5

**Skill 5.5**     Demonstrate knowledge of various theories of conflict resolution and appropriate application of these models to specific communities.

"Problems are only opportunities in work clothes."
    --Henry J. Kaiser

Most decision making models include the following steps:
- identifying the problem
- gathering information
- developing alternatives
- selecting an alternative
- implementing the alternative
- periodically evaluating the alternative

Once a decision has been made the next step would be to analyze and evaluate it, asking what measures were effective, what we have learned, and whether we should continue. A principal is responsible for the effects of decisions, so it is your job to make sure it works. If it doesn't then principals should work with the staff to "unmake" and improve the decision.

Once you identify that a decision needs to be made, you begin gathering relevant information and identifying alternatives. Two possible paths of action usually become apparent, but if you use your imagination and other information you may be able to construct even more than two. Try to avoid either/or thinking; usually there are more than two options. As you weigh the evidence and consider these alternatives, use your emotions to imagine what it would be like if you carried each alternative action out to the end. You must evaluate whether the identified problem would be helped or solved by each action path. Try to consult more than one source of information so that you are sure that your information is not biased. Eventually you are able to place the available alternatives in priority order. Once you have weighed all the evidence you are ready to make the decision. You may want to think through the worst outcome and decide if you could live with that. Remember that all decisions are tentative and you can change your mind. There is probably never one right choice, and few decisions are totally wrong.\

School leaders are required to make quick decisions and react to numerous problems and situations throughout every school day. Some days it seems as though all principals can do is wait for what and who is going to come at them next. In the process, they feel like someone who has the responsibility to lead, but hasn't been given the authority to think, decide, and take action.
Principals are encouraged to be proactive, and not reactive, by anticipating and intervening positively when confronted with an expected or unexpected situation, especially a negative or difficult one. Proactivity is one of the most popular management buzzwords to come from the 1990's. Stephen Covey, who has "be proactive" as the first of his famous "7 Habits of Highly Effective People", defines proactivity as more than merely taking the initiative, but focuses on "response-ability" - the ability and freedom to choose our response to a stimulus. Look at the model below, which show the difference between reactive thinking where a stimulus gives rise to an immediate response, and proactivity where there is sufficient space between the stimulus and the response for a choice of response to be made.

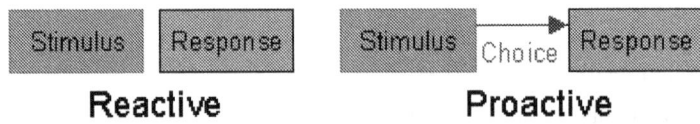

       **Reactive**                 **Proactive**

The key to this model is recognizing and using the space between stimulus and response to make responsible choices by calling upon self-awareness, imagination, conscience and independent will. Proactive leadership springs from awareness that we are not a product of our systems, or our environments. Those things powerfully influence us, but we can choose our responses to them. The two marks of proactive leadership are the ability to anticipate and meet the future and the ability to respond intentionally and freely.

A leader must be in charge. The community of learners expects an ultimate source of authority. They insist that equity exists and that decisions will be reached in an effective and timely manner. The "buck stops" with the principal who is responsible for what happens and what does not happen in the school. Examples of being "in charge" include determining who does what and when in clearly stated written or oral communication, designating persons responsible for given duties, handling security measures, safeguarding the internal accounts, and ensuring safety at all school events. Lately, the principal has taken on a stronger role in instructional leadership. To be a proactive instructional leader, the principal must take care to ensure that teachers understand expectations and are provided with the materials and training they need to be successful teachers.

The principal accepts responsibility for what goes wrong and shares what goes right with those who made it happen. The principal understands his or her role in assuming responsibility for all required tasks and ensures that they are accomplished in a timely manner. To achieve school goals, the proactive principal will determine the barriers and ways to overcome them, avenues to achieve the goals, how to best use available human and material resources to best advantage and how to secure additional resources to achieve the goals. The reactive principal will blame others and engage in faultfinding, responding according to emotions and feelings, focusing on circumstances or people over which they have no control.

The bottom line is that the principal must accept the responsibility for what happens. In this process, the principal must change behavior based upon prior experiences and successes or errors. The process requires continuous evaluations and reflections on what worked and why, as well as what did not work and why not. Through this process, the principal corrects past behavior and continues to grow and develop within a collegial environment.

Good leaders get all the facts possible on all sides of an issue prior to making a decision unless it is a life and death situation that requires immediate action for the safety and life of people. After getting all possible facts, the principal can use best principles of management to make the correct decision and to stick with the decision unless new evidence becomes available to change the original decision. There are many times when a leader must react, of course. In fact, if you can't react you can't be successful. However, if your predominant leadership stance is reacting, you are not going to find leading very productive or satisfying. Today's effective school leaders look at their responsibilities holistically, not as a series of tasks and responses to emergencies.

Principals can also serve as a support for the decision making committee by clarifying issues, gathering resources and supplying information, so that the teachers and parents see, hear and talk about the influences on the school and its achievement. Principals should also provide data from multiple sources so the committee can consider many alternatives

**Skill 5.6    Demonstrate knowledge of strategies for applying group process skills and for using research-based data to build consensus and resolve conflicts.**

See Skill 1.8

## COMPETENCY 6.0 UNDERSTAND HOW SCHOOL LEADERSHIP AND THE SCHOOL VISION RELATE TO THE LARGER POLITICAL, SOCIAL, ECONOMIC, CULTURAL, LEGAL, AND ETHICAL CONTEXT OF EDUCATION

### Skill 6.1 Examine how an understanding of the larger political, social, economic, and cultural context of education informs the development of effective policies and practices to benefit the school and its students.

Program effectiveness can only be measured through the process of evaluation. Program evaluation is the process of collecting and analyzing data to discover whether the design, development or implementation is producing the desired outcomes. The data gathering and analyses also carry the purpose of making informed decisions about the program. It may lead to changing or eliminating aspects of the program.

The CIPP (Content, Input Process Product) model developed by Daniel Sufflebeam is an example of program evaluation. In a three-step process, information is provided for decisions, including delineating the information to be collected, obtaining the information, and providing the information to others. These steps must then correspond with four distinct types of evaluation: content, input, process and product evaluations (Onstein and Hunskin 1993). *Content Evaluation* is concerned with the environment of the program in terms of needs and unmet needs. *Context evaluation* constitutes the diagnostic stage of the evaluative process. It provides baseline information related to the entire system of operation. *Input Evaluation* is concerned with providing information and determining how to utilize resources to attain the goals of the program. It focuses on whether the goals and objectives for the program are appropriate to the expected outcome or if the goals and objectives are stated appropriately. It also takes into account whether the resources to implement specific strategies are adequate, whether or not the strategies are appropriate to attain the goals, or if the time allotted is appropriate to meet the objectives set forth for the program.

*Process Evaluation* focuses on decisions regarding curriculum implementation. It is concerned with whether the activities planned are being implemented and with the logistics of the total operation so that procedures are recorded as they occur and monitoring is continuous to identify potential problems. The continuous process of identifying potential problems leads to decisions to make corrections before or during the implementation of the program. For example, it might be necessary to establish special planning sessions or teacher in-service at specific grade levels to work on modification of some of the strategies established for the program because of problems uncovered. Process evaluation is also known as the piloting process prior to the actual implementation of a school-wide or district-wide program (Ornstein and Hunskin, 1993). Finally, *Product Evaluation* takes into account whether the final product or curriculum is accomplishing the goals or objectives and to what degree.

At this point decisions must be made regarding the continuation, termination or modification of the program. Since the evaluation process is continuous, the evaluators may, at this point in the cycle, link specific actions back to other stages or make changes based on the data collected. The data obtained may very well indicate the need to delay full implementation of the program until such time that corrections are made, or it may lead to the decision that the program is ready for large scale implementation.

In summary, the main purpose of the evaluative process is to diagnose strengths and weaknesses, and to provide feedback to make appropriate decisions for programs and schools. The data collection for the evaluation process originates from a number of sources, including classroom observation, interviews and discussions with students, discussion with teachers and parents, testing and measurement data, information from pupil services or guidance services, and surveys of the school and school community.

Systematic assessment of school needs may range from grade level surveys of needs to school-wide surveys. This practice is insignificant, unless careful attention is given to a cohesive set of goals that are developed jointly with administrators, teachers, parents, and members of the school community to address specific needs. It is important that the instrument gathers pertinent information related to students' needs and the program situation at the school. Once the instrument is administered and the results are quantified, analyzed, and interpreted, the direction to follow is then determined.

When the purpose of the needs assessment is for program development, goal statements are carefully stated and established, and goals are prioritized and linked to performance outcomes of the learner. High priority goals are placed into a plan of implementation with specific strategies delineated. However, if the purpose of the assessment is for a progress check then the assessment instrument should reflect statements concerning activities and functions of the students and the staff, as well communication between the various levels. The systematic assessment of school needs should go beyond surveys to include cumulative folder content, anecdotal records, test results, interviews, classroom sociograms, direct teacher observation, and other means deemed appropriate.

Change is, generally, desirable for growth and development, but not all reasons for change are plausible. In many instances, the acceptance of change is dependent on concrete measures of comparison between the existing and the desired programs. Such comparison might be done through the Purvus Discrepancy Evaluation Model in which program standards and performance must first be determined, then both performance and standards are compared to determine if indeed there are discrepancies. The discrepancy between standards and performance is established throughout every aspect of the program including the design, installation, processes, products and cost.

While change is necessary, it will not occur just because someone has the knowledge for a bright idea that may very well be beneficial and may work beautifully. Change will occur when the individuals at all levels in the organization recognize that there is a need for it. It takes effective leadership and open two-way communication to initiate the change process. Problem solving, support, and continuous assessment of the process are also important aspects of promoting change.

The process of educating students is accomplished through instruction that is designed to attain specific objectives that are reflected in the educational aims and goals. Change occurs because people such as principal, curriculum leaders, teachers, parents, staff, and students work together by accepting their roles as agents of change. The organizational pattern and climate must be transformed in order to accept change.

**Skill 6.2** **Recognize how economic and political factors shape a community and affect the opportunities available to children in particular schools.**

The economic situation of a community has a direct impact on the school that the students attend. For rural communities, where there is usually only one school, the wealth of the community will determine what extracurricular opportunities are open to the children. The economics of the families also impacts the learning as many of the children may come to school without breakfast or lunch. The parents may not have the money needed to buy school supplies for the children and then this duty falls to the school to make sure students have everything they need to perform well in school. When the majority of families are not in a good financial position, there is a good chance that this is a fact of life in the community. Therefore the businesses in the community are not in a financial position to offer much support to the school.

In urban areas, students from needy families often have jobs after school because they have to contribute to the family finances. This affects their learning because they do not have time to do homework or studying. They may often drop out of school as soon as possible to earn more money. Principals need to look at how the bulk of the school families earn their living and how the instruction offered in the classroom relates to these jobs. The jobs of the parents and their level of education also affects the students. Parents may not see how important education is and may not have access to the resources to help the children at home. It is important to relate the school environment to that of the economic environment so that students can see the relevance of staying in school.

The size and strength of the economic situation of the community will affect how much money the school has to spend on resources and activities for the students. Schools with fewer numbers of students will not receive the same amount of grant money from the state and federal governments and if the financial situation of the families is not a good one, then this makes it hard to raise money through fundraising activities. If parents spend all their time working, it is also difficult to obtain volunteers in the school. Activities that involve parental participation may also have to be held at times that best suits the parents.

Politics, too, affects the opportunities that schools can offer to students. Government policy determines how much money schools receive in operating grants. A change in politics can affect this money in that it may be deflected from education to other more pressing projects and situations. There is also politics involved in parental decisions to send their children to one school or the other. The results of achievement tests are political in some ways in that schools with higher results are more likely to attract more students as parents deem them to be better schools.

In addition to choosing a school for their children, parents also have the option of homeschooling their children or sending them to a charter school. A charter school is a private school that still follows the state mandated curriculum, but there may be religion taught in this school or it may be geared to students for whom the public school system does not work well. These schools still receive the grant money from the government, but the employees are usually not unionized. Parents who can afford to do so can also send their children to private schools.

**Skill 6.3　Recognize the importance of communicating regularly with all members of the school community, including representatives of diverse community groups, concerning trends, issues, and policies affecting the school.**

Teachers who take the time to get to know students will find that developing student learning plans for academic performance is an easier task when communication about testing data is shared and evaluated with the student. Students can share if they were truly engaged in taking the pre-assessment for an Algebra class or simply filling in the blanks due to a falling out with a friend during the period that preceded your math class. Having authentic communication can help facilitate authentic assessment that can help both teacher and student create clear expectations for academic and behavioral performances in classrooms.

*Working with parents, caregivers, and others*

Research proves that the more families are involved in a child's educational experience, the more that child will succeed academically. The problem is that often teachers assume that involvement in education simply means that the parents show up to help at school events or participate in parental activities on campus. With this belief, many teachers devise clever strategies to increase parental involvement at school. However, just because a parent shows up to school and assists with an activity does not mean that the child will learn more. Many parents work all day long and cannot assist in the school. Teachers, therefore, have to think of different ways to encourage parental and family involvement in the educational process.

Quite often, teachers have great success within involving families by just informing families of what is going on in the classroom. Newsletters are particularly effective at this. Parents love to know what is going on in the classroom, and this way, they'll feel included. In newsletters, for example, teachers can provide suggestions on how parents can help with the educational goals of the school. For example, teachers can recommend that parents read with their children for twenty minutes per day. To add effectiveness to that, teachers can also provide suggestions on what to do when their children come across difficult words or when they ask a question about comprehension. This gives parents practical strategies.

Parents often equate phone calls from teachers with news about misbehaviors of their children. Teachers can change that tone by calling parents with good news. Or they can send positive notes home with students. By doing this, when negative phone calls need to be made, teachers will have greater success.

Teachers can also provide very specific suggestions to individual parents. For example, let's say a student needs additional assistance in a particular subject. The teacher can provide tips to parents to encourage and increase deeper understandings in the subject outside of class.

When you find it necessary to communicate (whether by phone, letter, or in person) with a parent regarding a concern about a student, allow yourself a "cooling off" period before making contact with the parent. It is important that you remain professional and objective. Your purpose for contacting the parent is to elicit support and additional information that may have a bearing on the student's behavior or performance. Be careful that you do not demean the child and do not appear antagonistic or confrontational. Be aware that the parent is likely to be quite uncomfortable with the bad news and will respond best if you take a cooperative, problem solving approach to the issue. It is also a nice courtesy to notify parents of positive occurrences with their children. The teacher's communication with parents should not be limited to negative items.

According to Campbell, Campbell and Dickinson (1992) "Teaching and Learning Through Multiple Intelligences," "The changing nature of demographics is one of the strongest rationales for multicultural education in the United States." The Census Bureau predicts a changing demographic for the American population and school communities which will include a forecast between 1990 and 2030, that "while the white population will increase by 25%, the African American population will increase by 68%, the Asian-American, Pacific Island, and American Indian by 79%, and the Hispanic-American population by 187%." Reinforcing the learning beyond the classroom must include a diversity of instructional and learning strategies for any adult role models in a student's life.

Mentoring has become an instrumental tool in addressing student achievement and access to learning. Adult mentors work individually with identified students on specific subjects areas to reinforce the learning through tutorial instruction and application of knowledge. Providing students with adult role models to reinforce the learning has become a crucial instructional strategy for teachers seeking to maximize student learning beyond the classroom. Students who work with adult mentors from culturally diverse backgrounds are given a multicultural aspect of learning that is cooperative and multi-modal in personalized instruction.

The interpersonal use of technology provides a mentoring tutorial support system and different conceptual learning modalities for students seeking to understand classroom material. Technology provides a networking opportunity for students to find study buddies and peer study groups, along with free academic support to problem-solve and develop critical thinking skills that are imperative in acquiring knowledge and conceptual learning. Distance Learning is a technological strategy that keeps students and teachers interactively communicating about issues in the classroom and beyond. Students will communicate more freely using technology to ask teacher or adult mentors clarity questions than they will in a classroom of peers and the typical insecurities that typify teenage development and learning acquisition.

Connecting with community resources will also provide viable avenues of support in helping students who need additional academic remediation access learning. There are a diversity of programs that are offered through the local Universities and community agencies that connect college students or working adults with subject areas and classrooms in need of additional student interns/adult volunteers to support the academic programs in school communities.

The support of the parent is an invaluable aid in the educational process. It is in the best interests of child, parent, and teacher for there to be cooperation and mutual support between parent and teacher. One of the teacher's professional responsibilities is to establish and maintain effective communication with parents. A few basic techniques to pursue are oral communication (phone calls), written communication in the form of general information classroom newsletters, notes to the parent of a particular child, and parent-teacher conferences.

Teachers should share with parents items of interest, including but not limited to, classroom rules and policies, class schedules and routines, homework expectations, communication procedures, conferences plans, and other similar information. Much of this can be done in a newsletter format sent home early in the school year. It is imperative that all such written communications be error free. It is a good idea to have another teacher read your letter before you send it out. Good writing and clear communication are learned skills and require time and effort to develop.

When you find it necessary to communicate (whether by phone, letter, or in person) with a parent regarding a concern about a student, allow yourself a "cooling off" period before making contact with the parent. It is important that you remain professional and objective. Your purpose for contacting the parent is to elicit support and additional information that may have a bearing on the student's behavior or performance. Be careful that you do not demean the child and do not appear antagonistic or confrontational.

## *Conferences*

### Parent conferences

The parent-teacher conference is generally for one of three purposes. First, the teacher may wish to share information with the parents concerning the performance and behavior of the child. Second, the teacher may be interested in obtaining information from the parents about the child. Such information may help answer questions or concerns that the teacher has. A third purpose may be to request parent support or involvement in specific activities or requirements. In many situations, more than one of the purposes may be involved.

### Planning the conference

When a conference is scheduled, whether at the request of the teacher or parent, the teacher should allow sufficient time to prepare thoroughly. Collect all relevant information, samples of student work, records of behavior, and other items needed to help the parent understand the circumstances. It is also a good idea to compile a list of questions or concerns you wish to address. Arrange the time and location of the conference to provide privacy and to avoid interruptions.

### Conducting the conference

Begin the conference by putting the parents as ease. Take the time to establish a comfortable mood, but do not waste time with unnecessary small talk. Begin your discussion with positive comments about the student. Identify strengths and desirable attributes, but do not exaggerate.

As you address issues or areas of concern, be sure to focus on observable behaviors and concrete results or information. Do not make judgmental statements about parent or child. Share specific work samples, anecdotal records of behavior, etc., which demonstrate clearly the concerns you have. Be a good listener and hear the parent's comments and explanations. Such background information can be invaluable in understanding the needs and motivations of the child.

Finally, end the conference with an agreed plan of action between parents and teacher (and, when appropriate, the child). Bring the conference to a close politely but firmly and thank the parents for their involvement.

## After the conference

A day or two after the conference, it is a good idea to send a follow-up note to the parents. In this note, briefly and concisely reiterate the plan or step agreed to in the conference. Be polite and professional; avoid the temptation to be too informal or chattcoy. If the issue is a long term one such as the behavior or on-going work performance of the student, make periodic follow-up contacts to keep the parents informed of the progress.

### *The School Community*

Local school boards are often charged with spending the public money on schools. They have the fiscal responsibility to manage the local schools' money in such a way that the schools are able to meet their educational goals and requirements (such as the standards set by No Child Left Behind). Local school boards are generally made up of locally elected officials.

A district superintendent is the chief officer of the school district over which he or she supervises. The superintendent's job is to implement the policies set by the Board of Regents and to advocate for his district when necessary.

A school principal is head of the individual school. He or she is under the supervision of the superintendent. The principal handles disciplinary actions for students in the school and may also discipline teachers for minor infractions. For major violations, the principal will consult with the superintendent, who may in turn go to the Board of Regents.

Boards of Cooperative Educational Services (BOCES) were created under the Intermediate School District Act in 1948. BOCES allow small school districts to combine their financial power to share costs of services and programs that no one small district would be able to afford on its own. BOCES are voluntary. A district is free to buy their own services separate from others if it feels it can get a better deal that way.

Unions and other professional organizations allow teachers to work together and develop professionally. These organizations also help keep teachers up-to-date on current educational standards and developments. Unions in particular often work to make sure teachers receive fair wages and that when a teacher is facing charges for an alleged crime, he or she receives adequate legal counsel. Unions tend to be active in lobbying the legislature on behalf of the teaching community.

Parent organizations, such as a PTO or PTA, allow parents to have access to their children's schools and gives them a voice when school-based decisions are being made. These organizations also allow parents and teachers to work together on behalf of the students.

## Working with the Greater Community

Students who feel like they belong in their school communities may feel more motivated to succeed academically than students who simply feel like a number among the thousands of students. Parents and community members who are actively involved in PTSAs and community after school support groups will find that students actually appreciate having their support and involvement in school activities and governance.

Community support provides additional resources for classrooms and school communities on limited District budgets. Additional grant sources from local PTSAs and educational organizations continue to provide financial resources for teachers seeking to provide maximal learning opportunities for students.

The community is a vital link to increasing learning experiences for students. Community resources can supplement the minimized and marginal educational resources of school communities. With state and federal educational funding becoming increasingly subject to legislative budget cuts, school communities welcome the financial support that community resources can provide in terms of discounted prices on high end supplies (e.g. computers, printers, and technology supplies), along with providing free notebooks, backpacks and student supplies for low income students who may have difficulty obtaining the basic supplies for school.

Community stores can provide cash rebates and teacher discounts for educators in struggling school districts and compromised school communities. Both professionally and personally, communities can enrich the student learning experiences by including the following support strategies:

- Provide programs that support student learning outcomes and future educational goals
- Create mentoring opportunities that provide adult role models in various industries to students interested in studying in that industry
- Provide financial support for school communities to help low-income or homeless students begin the school year with the basic supplies
- Develop paid internships with local university students to provide tutorial services for identified students in school communities who are having academic and social difficulties processing various subject areas.
- Providing parent-teen-community forums to create public voice of change in communities
- Offer parents without computer or Internet connection, stipends to purchase technology to create equitable opportunities for students to do research and complete word.doc paper requirements.
- Stop in classrooms and ask teachers and students what's needed to promote academic progress and growth.

Community resources are vital in providing that additional support to students, school communities and families struggling to remain engaged in declining educational institutions competing for federal funding and limited District funding. The commitment that a community shows to its educational communities is a valuable investment in the future. Community resources that able to provide additional funding for tutors in marginalized classrooms or help schools reduce classrooms of students needing additional remedial instruction directly impact educational equity and facilitation of teaching and learning for both teachers and students.

When community institutions provide students and teachers with meaningful connections and input, the commitment is apparent in terms of volunteering, loyalty and professional promotion. Providing students with placements in leadership positions such as the ASB (Associated Student Body); the PTSA (Parent Teacher Student Association); School Boards; neighborhood sub-committees addressing political or social issues; or government boards that impact and influence school communities creates an avenue for students to explore ethical, participatory, collaborative, transformational leadership that can be applied to all areas of a student's educational and personal life.

Community liaisons provide students with opportunities to experience accountability and responsibility so that students learn about life and how organizations work with effective communication and teams working together to accomplish goals and objectives. Teaching students skills of inclusion, social and environmental responsibility and creating public forums that represent student voice and vote foster student interest and access to developing and reflecting on individual opinions and understanding the dynamics of the world around them.

When a student sees that the various support systems are in place and consistently working as a team to effectively provide resources and avenues of academic promotion and accountability, students have no fear of taking risks to grow by becoming a teen voice on a local committee about "Teen Violence" or volunteering in a local hospice for young children with terminal diseases. The linkages of community institutions provide role-models of a world in which the student will soon become an integral and vital member, so being a part of that world as a student makes the transition easier as a young adult.

*Respecting Diversity*

Teachers today will deal with an increasingly diverse group of cultures in their classrooms. And while this is an exciting prospect for most teachers, it creates new challenges in dealing with a variety of family expectations for school and teachers.

First, teachers must show respect to all parents and families. They need to set the tone that suggests that their mission is to develop students into the best people they can be. And then they need to realize that various cultures have different views of how children should be educated.

Second, teachers will have better success when they talk personally about their children. Even though teachers may have many students, when they share personal things about each child, parents will feel more confident that their child will be "in the right hands."

Third, it is very important that teachers act like they are partners in the children's education and development. Parents know their children best, and it is important to get feedback, information, and advice from them.

Finally, teachers will need to be patient with difficult families, realizing that certain methods of criticism (including verbal attacks, etc.) are unacceptable. Such circumstances would require the teacher to get assistance from an administrator. This situation, however, is very unusual, and most teachers will find that when they really attempt to be friendly and personal with parents, the parents will reciprocate and assist in the educational program.

*In Summary*

Part of being an effective teacher is to not only get your students to grow educationally, but to allow oneself to also continue to grow. Working with other members of the school community—peers, supervisors, and other staff—will give you the grounding you need to increase your skills and knowledge sets. Identifying possible mentors, teachers you respect and whom you would like to emulate, is one step. Search out other teachers who have had an amount of success in the area you wish to learn more about. Ask them questions and for advice on brushing up your lesson plans. Talk to your supervisor or the principal when you are having difficulties, or when you want to learn more. They may know of development training seminars, books, journals, or other resources that might help you. Teachers should remember that they are part of a team of professionals, and that their personal success is part of a greater success that everyone hopes to achieve.

**Skill 6.4** **Identify ways to advocate for policies and programs at the local, state, and federal levels that promote equitable learning opportunities and success for all students, regardless of socioeconomic background, ethnicity, gender, disability, or other individual characteristics.**

Disparity with relation to ethnicity, socioeconomic background, gender, disabilities or other individual characteristics should not be allowed to hinder the learning opportunities available to all students or their success within the school setting. The principal of any size school should be in tune with what is happening at the local, state and federal levels in order to advocate for all monies available for education.

Local, state and federal governments do allocate funds for school districts to help provide needed services for children with disabilities under IDEA. In addition, there are grants for schools that offer early childhood education programs so that all children are able to start Kindergarten on an equal footing and continue to do so during the early years of their education.

Lobbying the elected representatives for policies and programs is one way of reaching out to the governments for equitable learning opportunities. When lobbying for a new program in school or a new governmental policy, it is important to have all the research to accompany the proposal. This will show the representative how the program will be beneficial to the students and where it has worked well in the past. However, it is very little use in the principal taking on such a task alone. The whole school staff must be involved in the lobbying effort as well as the parents.

Inviting representatives of the local, state and federal governments to the school is also effective in showing these people where the needs of the school lie. When they visit the classes, and talk to the students and teachers, they will have a much better idea of how useful such a new policy or program will be for the education of the children. However, the principal should not arrange for a public forum at this time where the parents are present and may become verbally abusive to the invited guest.

Other tactics for getting policies and programs for the school include:
- Letter writing campaigns
- Inviting the media into the school so that the issue gets coverage on TV, radio and in the newspaper
- Writing letters to the editors of the newspapers
- Lobbying local businesses and community groups for support
- Presentations to various groups
- Involvement of the Parent Council

**Skill 6.5** **Analyze community norms and values and explain how they relate to the role of the school in promoting social justice.**

"It takes a village to raise a child". The norms and values of a community are often reflected in the way the students treat one another and the teachers at a school. It is the duty of a school to uphold democratic rights by establishing fundamental moral values that are important for all citizens to have. It is this background in social justice that is at the core of schools in order to create just and caring students.

The administration of a school handles all the problems that teachers deem are too large for them within the confines of the classroom. Some of the students that are sent to the Principal's office may not have a sense of justice when it relates to other students. Some of this may come from the family background. For example, a student raised in a home where racial prejudice is the norm will not act appropriately with ethnic minorities in the classroom or the school in general. When the principal sees that this is the norm in the school, then it is time to take steps to correct the prevalent behavior as well as the thoughts and feelings.

Bullying is another issue that plagues the schools of the 21st century often resulting in extreme situations for students and teachers. The school should have clear rules for bullying, prejudice and other types of unjust behavior. Both the students and their parents need to be made aware of these rules and the consequences for breaking them. When there is a discrepancy between the home and the school over these rules, it may be necessary to have a meeting with the parents.

The school also has access to outside agencies who can help with issues of social justice. Counselors can help with students who are experiencing problems and can help guide them in the right direction.

Issues related to social justice should be infused in the curriculum. When students are faced with real life problems in the classroom, they are better able to cope with social issues outside the school. Students need to have opportunities to explore the rights, viewpoints and responsibilities of others through discussion in the classroom. A study of social issues will also help to strengthen students' reasoning abilities. The United Nations Charter of Rights and Freedoms is a resource that can be used for teaching social justice.

# TEACHER CERTIFICATION STUDY GUIDE

**Skill 6.6**     **Recognize how the Oklahoma and U.S. Constitutions; district policies; and statutory, common, and case law regulate the behavior of students, staff, and administration in the schools.**

In the United States, education is primarily a state and local responsibility. Business, churches and communities can establish schools. However, it doesn't matter who establishes a school because there are state standards that all schools must use in developing the curriculum for each subject and grade level. The Federal government is able to make policy decisions and directives only for programs which it is funding (Title 1, Reading First, etc.). The state government is the primary legal decision making authority and founder of public school districts. It is States and communities, as well as public and private organizations of all kinds, that establish schools, develop curricula, and determine requirements for enrollment and graduation. The structure of education finance in America reflects this predominant State and local role. Of an estimated $909 billion being spent nationwide on education at all levels for school year 2004-2005, about 90 percent comes from State, local, and private sources.

School districts also have a board of directors or trustees who determine the school district's budget and oversee the operation of the schools within the district. Schools receive the money to operate from the state, but each school also has a budget. Schools can also engage in fundraising for various events. Each school usually has a parent council, which helps the school to keep operating. These councils provide parents with a voice in what takes place in the school. The administration also presents the budget to this council and the council does have to approve all fund raising ventures.

The duties of local school boards include:

- Adopt rules and regulations governing teachers and students in all schools
- Determine the budget for each school
- Hire teachers
- Establish the standards for the curriculum and choose the textbooks
- Serve as adjudicators in the dismissal of teachers and students

**Skill 6.7** **Demonstrate knowledge of the system of public school governance and strategies for working effectively with local governing boards.**

A school does not just rely on the school board and the teachers for support. There are many outside agencies involved in the operation of a school. Local law enforcement may visit the school to make presentations to the students designed to keep the students safe. They also want to make their presence known as people who are there to help if the students need it. They take on the role of teachers in helping students to learn the proper way to behave both inside and outside the school. This allows local officers to build relationships with students and the school community further benefiting the community.

Health professionals, such as school nurses, speech pathologists, social workers and mental health professionals are also part of the school system. They come into the school on a regular basis or as they are needed to help both students and teachers.

Informally, the parents and businesses of the community have a role to play within a school. Parents want to know what is happening in the school and this can be done through the parent council. However, parents are also visible in the school as volunteers helping teachers in the classroom or serving as chaperones for field trips and events. Businesses show their support for the school by providing funding for events or support for school projects. There are also organizations in the community that provide extra resources for the students and teachers, such as museums which allow teachers to take their students there on field trips. Some of these organizations take their material directly into the school for presentations to all the students. Additional organizations provide enrichment or extra-curricular opportunities for students such as athletics, fine arts, mentoring, tutoring, and community education programs for parents and families.

Public information management is a systematic communication process between an educational organization and its public, both within and outside the schools. It is the exchange of two-way information, designed to encourage public interest in and understanding of, education. The principal shows concern for the school's image through impressions created by students and staff and manages both these impressions and public information about the school by (1) advertising successes and (2) controlling the flow of negative information.

To be effective, communication between school leaders and the public must be open, honest, and unbiased. The attitudes of parents and members of the community at large have been adversely affected by reports in the decline of American education and media coverage which appears to focus on negative perceptions. Despite the general perception of poor public education, the majority of parents surveyed nationally expressed satisfaction with their children's schools and teachers. The most positive feedback resulted when parents felt that their concerns were being heard and addressed and that they were involved in the decision-making process.

Principals should seek input from parents in systematic and planned ways. Annual surveys, parent informational nights, and parent advisory committees allow principals to receive valuable input on a variety of topics. Principals benefit from opportunities to learn about the perception of the school out in the community and what issues might impact the school's progress. Public relations must be carefully organized. Information deliverers must have accurate information, understand their roles in the dissemination of the information, and provide appropriate channels for feedback. The public must perceive that they are being given complete, timely information by officials who respect their feelings and sincerely want feedback. Developing a key communicator email list is a new method that many principals use to disperse information immediately. Each parent can receive the information and not have to rely on rumors or gossip from the neighborhood. This ability to communicate quickly and effectively with key members of the community is especially important when a crisis situation develops at a school. Having a key communicator email keeps parents informed and prevents them from hearing about an issue from a biased media presentation.

In addition, the school must also consider who other stakeholders may be. Local religious leaders, business owners, neighborhood associations, key communicators, and day cares are all important members of the school community. These organizations should have representation on school committees and be members of the school improvement process. Strong relationships with these groups will benefit the school with additional support in the form of funding and programs, as well as support for the school and initiatives such as referendums.

See also Skill 6.6

**Skill 6.8** **Recognize how to demonstrate honesty, integrity, impartiality, fairness, sensitivity to student diversity, respect for confidentiality, and ethical behavior in interactions with members of the school community.**

## *Diversity Awareness*

Equity in the learning community addresses the following issues:

- Equal Access
- Equal Treatment
- Equal Opportunity to Learn
- Equal Outcomes

Equal Access requires that there be no impediment (physical, cultural, intellectual, social, economic, etc.) or bias which restricts some students from access which is available to others.

Equal Treatment ensures that no student is valued above or below the others. Physical, intellectual, cultural, economic or other criteria may not be applied in determining how a student is treated. Equally high academic expectations are afforded all students, with the assurance that this objective is achievable and will be supported by the teacher and the educational system.

Equal Opportunity to Learn requires that every student have equal access to all resources, physical and intellectual as well as equal instruction and support from the classroom teacher and staff.

Equal Outcomes requires that instruction and evaluation are structured to ensure all students acquire the skills being taught.

While equal treatment and equal access for all individuals is mandated under various state and federal statutes, not every issue has necessarily been considered and addressed. There can be difficulties with interpretation of these statutes. There may be inconsistencies between the letter of the law and the intent of the law. Significant differences in the implementation and conduct of policy and procedure within institutions can also hamper the effectiveness of the laws and the intent with which these statutes were created. Equity may not be fully achieved if practices are instituted or changed, superficially, only to comply with statutory regulations rather than internalized and embraced by the entire learning community as an opportunity to improve the educational system.

In an educational environment, from the classroom throughout the entire school system, there should be no such impediments to achieving equity. The primary responsibility of the educator is to ensure that all aspects of the educational process, and all information necessary to master specified skills, are readily accessible to all students. There should be no conflict between laws mandating equity and educational philosophy. Policies, practices and procedures instituted to comply with (or surpass the requirements of) these laws support our educational objectives. By creating, internalizing and practicing the values of an academic culture with high expectations for all students and inclusion of all students in every aspect of the educational process, we provide for equity in education and fulfill our primary responsibility as educators.

When diversity is promoted in learning environments and curriculum, both students and teachers are the beneficiaries of increased academic success. Using classrooms as vital resources for cultural and ethnic inclusion can assist students in contributing cultural norms and artifacts to the acquisition of learning. Teachers are able to create global thinkers by helping students identify cultural assumptions and biases that may direct the type of social and academic groupings that occur in the classroom and influence the type of thinking and construction of learning that happens within a classroom. For example, if a student is struggling in math, a teacher can examine the cultural aspect of learning math. For some students, math is insignificant when socioeconomic issues of poverty and survival are the daily reality of existence. When students see parents juggling finances, the only math that becomes important for them is that less is never enough to keep the lights on and mortgage paid.

When there is equity pedagogy, teachers can use a variety of instructional styles to facilitate diversity in cooperative learning and individualized instruction that will provide more opportunities for positive student experiences and academic success. Empowering the school culture and climate by establishing an anti-bias learning environment and promoting multicultural learning inclusion will discourage disproportionality and unfair labeling of certain students.

Teachers can use various toolkits of assessing integration and incorporation of ethnic and cultural inclusion in classroom. Effective promotion should translate into increased academic success and opportunities for all students. Looking at diverse or homogenous groupings in the classroom can provide teachers with opportunities to restructure cooperative learning groupings and increase diverse student interactions, which can provide increased improvements for school communities.

Using culture grams to help students understand different cultures and research cultural diversity is a useful tool for helping teachers profile student's learning styles and engagement in the classroom. Students can use technology to network how students in other cultures and in other states learn. The ability to communicate with other learners provides another way of compiling and categorizing cultural profiles that may assist teachers in identifying learning styles and how students acquire learning. An interesting aspect of using culture grams is the manner in which it helps students connect to other cultures and their perceptions of students who identify with different cultures.

*Permanent Records*

The student permanent record is a file of the student's cumulative educational history. It contains a profile of the student's academic background as well as the student's behavioral and medical background. Other pertinent individual information contained in the permanent record includes the student's attendance, grade averages, and schools attended. Personal information such as parents' names and addresses, immunization records, child's height and weight, and narrative information about the child's progress and physical and mental well being is an important aspect of the permanent record. All information contained within the permanent record is strictly confidential and is only to be discussed with the student's parents or other involved school personnel.

The purpose of the permanent record is to provide applicable information about the student so that the student's individual educational needs can be met. If any specialized testing has been administered, the results are noted in the permanent record. Any special requirements that the student may have are indicated in the permanent record. Highly personal information, including court orders regarding custody, is filed in the permanent record as is appropriate. The importance and value of the permanent record cannot be underestimated. It offers a comprehensive knowledge of the student.

The current teacher is responsible for maintaining the student's permanent record. All substantive information in regard to testing, academic performance, the student's medical condition, and personal events are placed in the permanent record file. Updated information in regard to the student's grades, attendance, and behavior is added annually. These files are kept in a locked fireproof room or file cabinet and cannot be removed from this room unless the person removing them signs a form acknowledging full responsibility for the safe return of the complete file. Again, only the student's parents (or legal guardians), the teacher or other concerned school personnel may view the contents of the permanent record file.

The permanent record file follows the student as he/she moves through the school system with information being updated along the way. Anytime the student leaves a school, the permanent record is transferred with the student. The permanent record is regarded as legal documentation of a student's educational experience.

The contents of any student records should be indicative of the student's academic aptitude and/or achievement. The information contained should never be in any way derogatory or potentially damaging. It is important to keep in mind that others who view the contents of the records may form an opinion of the student based on the information in the student's record or file. Anyone who places information in a student's record must make every effort to give an accurate reflection of the student's performance while maintaining a neutral position as to the student's potential for future success or failure.

The most essential fact to remember in regard to students' records is that the information within is confidential. Although specific policies may vary from one school or district to another, confidentiality remains constant and universal. Teachers never discuss any student or his/her progress with anyone other than the student's parents or essential school personnel. Confidentiality applies to all student information whether it is a student's spelling test, portfolio, standardized test information, report card, or the contents of the permanent record file.

The significance of the student's records is not to be taken lightly. In many instances, teachers have access to a student's records before she actually meets the student. It is important for the teacher to have helpful information about the student without developing any preconceived biases about the student. Careful regard must be given to all information that is added to a student's file without diluting the potential effectiveness of that information. It is also important to be cognizant of the fact that the primary function of student records is that they are intended to be used as a means of developing a better understanding of the students' needs and to generate a more effective plan for meeting these needs.

### *Confidentiality & Students' Rights*

The student's permanent record is kept in the file in the main office and is to be kept locked. The files on each child are confidential and are not to be released to anyone other than the student, if he/she is old enough, the parent or the teacher/administrator. Some of these files contain information about the family situation and also contain court orders regarding custody or abuse issues. Teachers should familiarize themselves with each student's file so they will know when certain parents are not allowed to have access to the child. Under the Privacy Act, the information contained in these files is confidential and private

When children change schools, they are not permitted to take the files with them to the new school on their own. The only way the receiving school can gain access to the file is to submit a written request and the file is them sent through the mail. While the request can be faxed to the school, none of the information within the permanent record can be faxed to the new school.

### *Acting With Respect For all Students*

It is the duty of teachers to show respect for all students in the school and to model this behavior for the students. This includes respect for the students' languages, cultures and histories. Teachers should model this behavior by treating students, parents and staff with respect and by not accepting a lack of respect for any of these groups. Consistency, contradiction and balance are important in helping to translate this into specific classroom behaviors. The students, parents and staff of a school need to know that the principal and the teachers are honest, fair and trustworthy. The principal needs to be impartial when dealing with the teachers, parents and students and the teachers also need to follow this in their dealings within the school.

Consistency is important in order to be seen as fair and impartial. There should be a set of school rules with consequences if these rules are broken. Allowing one student to get away with breaking the rules can be seen as being unfair to another student who gets punished for doing so. However, there are always extenuating circumstances that could affect the consequences.

It is important to establish rules and explain them to students along with the reasons why the rules are in place. Acting towards others in a respectful manner means that one knows when to act in a certain way and when that behavior is not acceptable. Sometimes adults do not behave in the same manner they expect from students. This results in students feeling confused. Therefore, the principal and teachers must be aware of any contradictions that exist and take steps to correct them.

Students and parents should always hear the truth about their education and learning. Glossing over problems in school and then giving the student a poor grade on the final report will give both the student and the parent the impression that the teacher is not a person of integrity. The same applies to students whop misbehave in school. Parents need to know what is happening and the student needs to know why this behavior cannot continue.

## SUBAREA II. INSTRUCTIONAL LEADERSHIP

**COMPETENCY 7.0 UNDERSTAND HOW TO USE KNOWLEDGE OF HUMAN DEVELOPMENT, LEARNING AND TEACHING THEORIES, EDUCATIONAL RESEARCH, AND BEST PRACTICE TO PROMOTE THE SUCCESS OF ALL STUDENTS.**

**Skill 7.1 Recognize the characteristics and stages of physical, cognitive, and social/emotional development and their educational significance.**

Students are at varying stages of development in any grade. The administrator of the school should have knowledge of the developmental stages that children go through so as to be knowledgeable about the curricular outcomes and types of learning activities teachers can plan. This includes the Intellectual, social and emotional development, physical development and spiritual and moral development.

Intellectually Kindergarten students are curious and eager to learn. They are interested in books and stories and love to be actively involved. They are lively and constantly in motion, but depending on their individual circumstances, they may not be very well developed socially and emotionally. The spiritual and moral development of children before they come to school also depends on the family situation. At this stage, children need a lot of extra support with literacy and numeracy.

As students progress through the grades, teachers and administrators are able to see growth in all areas. The administrator knows that although elementary grade children like to think they are grown up, they still act their age and do childish things. The instruction that the teachers provide in the classroom should include a lot of modeling. At this instructional level, students so not remember directions and do need to have them written down. They are still active because they are still growing, so it is common to find them racing around. They need time to get to the gym or outdoors. By this time most of the students have become fluent readers, but there may still be some students in the classroom who are struggling. When students have problems with reading, it also transfers over to problems in study subjects.

At the junior high level, students are not quite so active in the classroom and teachers can engage them in frank discussions in the classroom. They do like to experiment so discipline problems tend to increase in this age group. Junior high students are pretty much independent in their study habits, but there will be groups of students who do need to be prodded into getting the work done. At the same time, there will be students who still need support.

In the high school years, students become more independent learners. By this time, struggling students can choose to take different courses, but supports are still provided in school.

**Skill 7.2** **Analyze how sociological, linguistic, cultural, and other factors may affect students' development and needs and the implications of these factors for instruction.**

Schools are complex social systems, involving a diverse range of students and teachers. Principals have success at running schools when they can find ways to ensure that all students' sociological, linguistic, and cultural concerns are attended to. Let's deal with each of these issues separately.

**Sociological issues** are highly important at schools, mainly because schools deal directly with children, who at different stages of development undergo significant emotional and physical changes. As we have seen with school shootings, gang activity, and other tragedies that occur on school grounds, schools have many issues to deal with beyond student achievement. Namely, schools must be places where students feel safe, accepted, and valued. Particularly at some of the more challenging phases of student development, such as adolescence, schools must focus on ensuring that bullying does not take place. When principals reiterate messages to schools about the importance of keeping the campus safe, secure, and welcoming for all students, the message eventually sinks in to all stakeholders that mean, discriminative, dangerous, and illegal activities are not tolerated under any circumstance.

**Linguistic issues** are critical in a population that is increasingly diverse. Students come from many cultures and often speak different languages at home. While bilingual and English Language Learner programs deal directly with the academic issues of second language learners, the school culture must be positioned to deal with such issues, as well. Often, the message that students get at school is that in classrooms (where bilingual support is provided), second language learners are valued. But, when they get out of the classroom and try to participate in the life of the school (activities, governance, athletics, etc.), they are not valued. This incongruity does a huge disservice to these students as they then feel separate from the school culture. Principals must make sure that all second language learners feel like they are part of the whole school at all times. Working with activities directors, support personnel, and faculty encourages this.

Finally, **cultural issues** are important in multiple ways. Most importantly, teachers must be sensitive to students' cultural biases and assumptions in the classroom. Culturally-relevant instruction is a concept that has become very important to public schooling over the last few years. It suggests that because students come from different cultures, they will learn things in different ways. Teachers, therefore, must be attentive to students' background knowledge, culture, religion, sexual orientation, etc. Even if some information is not known, teachers need to be aware that all students will see information in different ways. While a final standard for each academic area must be met, there are many ways for students to learn and come to understand that information. Principals can model that behavior with teachers, as well as continually encourage teachers and students to consider thoughts from others' perspectives.

**Skill 7.3** **Examine ways to apply research-based knowledge of human development, learning, motivation, and best practice instruction to optimize learning for all students.**

The principles of cognitive, moral, and social/emotional development of learners in the school community must be recognized and understood in order to develop effective teaching and curriculum designs that grow each learner.

The earliest cognitive theorist, Jean Piaget discovered that children develop along prescribed cognitive and social/emotional development continuums at different ages. In creating a cognitive construct in understanding the application of situational impacts, a child thinks differently from the pre-adolescent through the adolescent years. During the school age years, a child's cognitive development and responses to his or her environment are congruent with how much the child understands the differing situations that occur each day.

According to Piaget, children construct knowledge through a gradual interaction with their environment. As children are presented with vast amounts of information from their environment, they attempt to incorporate this information into existing constructs that contain previous knowledge and learning schematics. Children adjust their schematics in order to make sense out of new experiences using old applications of knowledge. Piaget calls a child's adjustment and ability to incorporate new schemes into existing schematic foundations, "assimilation." A child's ability to adjust new schemes in order to better understand the application of knowledge, Piaget calls "accommodation."

In Piaget's cognitive development theory, a child's cognitive development is characterized through distinctive thinking processes called sensorimotor, preoperational, concrete operational, and formal operational. The correlation of a child's cognitive development is consistent with a child's physical developmental stages. In order to understand Piaget's cognitive development theories, a child's social/emotional stages of development must be understood within the system's framework of how children grow and develop.

Moral development of children occurs within the context of daily role modeling and mentoring where children are exposed to real world applications of situations and events that provide them with opportunities to apply contextual meaning. It is within the structure of social engagement that children are able to develop into morally responsible and accountable citizens. Adult role models provide responsive teaching and monitoring of children's perceptions when dealing with situations that provide opportunities to teach children proactive moral behavior.

The social and emotional development of both students and staff occur through the interchanging of ideas and activities in a school community. As adults understand the importance of providing students with effective role modeling and tools to further personal and professional development, both parties create a synergy of collaboration that furthers the objectives and goals of the school community. Schools are social environments that either promote emotional development or impede development of the cognitive balancing of thoughts and academic success of future leaders

**Skill 7.4** **Identify strategies for collaborating with counseling staff, teaching staff, and community agencies to address student needs and ensure student access to adequate counseling, guidance, and other services.**

School leaders must recognize the fact that creating schools that promote student success and academic acquisition is the ultimate responsibility of the adult staff in learning communities. Dealing with students' social and emotional needs are a collective responsibility and accountability of the school staff. The power of adult influence is evident in effective school communities that work for students and staff. Recent studies suggest a positive correlation between providing support and resources for school related social issues that impact students and enhanced students' social and emotional needs.

School communities are microcosms of communication and exchange of ideas, opinions, conflicts, and directives between adults and students. In classrooms, curriculum designs are encrypted with today's social issues that engage students and teachers in emotional debates and exchanges of feedback that may or may not polarize the speaker on the subject matter. Given the multitude of curriculum offerings from basic math to AP (Advanced Placement) calculus, the intellectual capacity in the school community can become energized with emotive feedback and instruction.

If school related social issues are rooted in the three Rs of rigor, relevance, and relationships, students' social and emotional needs can become measurable and productive. In rigor, school communities expect and communicate high academic expectations that are embraced by all stakeholders in the learning environment. With rigorous designed curriculum that meets district and state essential learning requirements, high standards become the norm and not the goal. Rigor incorporated in assessments and student mastery of subject content areas can meet the needs of the myriad of learners.

Given that students' emotional and social needs are based in the accessibility of academic content area, developing high learning standards in school communities can create opportunities for students to learn at their own level and demonstrate proficiency once they have mastered the required material. Students become collaborative in the process of learning and not reactive in the process of failure.

Relevancy of curriculum to a students' culture, daily life, and both current and future interests can enhance the curriculum and create its own entry into academic accessibility for struggling students and students needing additional challenge. When students are provided with opportunities to personalize their learning communities, they grow both socially and emotionally.

Relationships create leadership opportunities for students and staff to adapt to school community change and innovation. In creating arenas where mutual learning, trust, and supportive communication create foundations for adult and student mentoring opportunities, relationships thrive and partnerships grow for all stakeholders.

Meaningful school communities effectively identify and meet the social and emotional needs of its valued students. With the current mandates and expectations that govern today's learning environments, providing students with personalized learning and effective leadership will enrich the learning and teaching experience for all members in school communities.

## Skill 7.5 Evaluate the implications of various behavior management practices.

Every student in school will not react to or need the same type of counseling. For some, it may be a simple conversation about their inappropriate behavior, while for others more intensive investigations will be needed. In all counseling situations, the administrator should keep the following steps in mind:

- Assess the situation. Begin at the student's level of understanding and help the student to develop goals and targets.
- Advise. If there are multiple problems, do not try to target too many at once. It is best to take on only one or two problems or issues and work to solve these. These targets need to be concrete and measurable, so that the student can experience success.
- Agree. There should be some plan in place with which the administrator, the teacher, the student and the parents agree with. This plan of action will have measurable goals that will be achieved in a specific time frame.
- Assist. During the plan of action, the administrator will ensure that all stakeholders are getting the assistance they need to carry it out.
- Arrange. Arrange for monitoring of the situation and if necessary make a new plan to address further problems or ones that were not included in the first plan.

## Skill 7.6 Examine strategies for promoting successful learning experiences for students with disabilities and ensuring that these students have access to appropriate resources.

One of the first things that a teacher learns is how to obtain resources and help for his/her students. All schools have guidelines for receiving this assistance especially since the implementation of the Americans with Disabilities Act. The first step in securing help is for the teacher to approach the school's administration or exceptional education department for direction in attaining special services or resources for qualifying students. Many schools have a committee designated for addressing these needs such as a Child Study Team or Core Team. These teams are made up of both regular and exceptional education teachers, school psychologists, guidance counselors, and administrators. The particular student's classroom teacher usually has to complete some initial paper work and will need to do some behavioral observations.

The teacher will take this information to the appropriate committee for discussion and consideration. The committee will recommend the next step to be taken. Often subsequent steps include a complete psychological evaluation along with certain physical examinations such as vision and hearing screening and a complete medical examination by a doctor.

The referral of students for this process is usually relatively simple for the classroom teacher and requires little more than some initial paper work and discussion. The services and resources the student receives as a result of the process typically prove to be invaluable to the student with behavioral disorders.

At times, the teacher must go beyond the school system to meet the needs of some students. An awareness of special services and resources and how to obtain them is essential to all teachers and their students. When the school system is unable to address the needs of a student, the teacher often must take the initiative and contact agencies within the community. Frequently there is no special policy for finding resources. It is simply up to the individual teacher to be creative and resourceful and to find whatever help the student needs. Meeting the needs of all students is certainly a team effort that is most often spearheaded by the classroom teacher.

*Family involvement*

Under the IDEA, parent/guardian involvement in the development of the student's IEP is required and absolutely essential for the advocacy of the disabled student's educational needs. IEPs must be tailored to meet the student's needs, and no one knows those needs better than the parent/guardian and other significant family members. Optimal conditions for a disabled student's education exist when teachers, school administrators, special education professionals and parents/guardians work together to design and execute the IEP.

*Due process*

Under the IDEA, Congress provides safeguards for students against schools' actions, including the right to sue in court, and encourages states to develop hearing and mediation systems to resolve disputes. No student or their parents/guardians can be denied due process because of disability.

*Inclusion, mainstreaming, and least restrictive environment*

Inclusion, mainstreaming and least restrictive environment are interrelated policies under the IDEA, with varying degrees of statutory imperatives.
- Inclusion is the right of students with disabilities to be placed in the regular classroom.
- Least restrictive environment is the mandate that children be educated to the maximum extent appropriate with their non-disabled peers.
- Mainstreaming is a policy where disabled students can be placed in the regular classroom, as long as such placement does not interfere with the student's educational plan.

**Skill 7.7** **Recognize the role of various types of activity programs in meeting all students' developmental, social, cultural, athletic, leadership, and academic needs.**

School is not just a place where students sit in seats and receive instruction in reading, writing, Math, Social Studies and Science. There is much more to helping all students develop to the best of their abilities that concentrating on academics. School should also be a place where students learn about themselves and learn how to develop their talents as well as learn about the great masters in art and music. Students need to be active and enjoy moving about as they develop in sports and physical activity. Through these activities, leaders will emerge and this needs to be fostered and developed to the fullest.

*Developmental*

Through teaching the fundamental skills students need in reading and writing, teachers can also include activities that help them develop physically, mentally and emotionally. Choose reading materials that discuss a variety of topics, such as ethnicity, cultural awareness and emotional issues.

Physical
- Teach children about good nutrition, dental and personal hygiene
- Give children opportunity to move about the classroom
- Include activities that involve play in the classroom
- Practice large motor skills through such activities as jumping, balancing, running, etc.
- Practice small motor skills through such activities as cutting, printing, drawing, etc.
- Include games and activities that involve active listening

Mental
- Ask open –ended questions that will make the children think rather than just recite answers from books
- Provide the students with choices about which activities they can complete to show they have achieved an objective
- Encourage creativity in completion of activities, such as through art, music or dance
- Use a variety of activities to help build language skills
- Provide opportunities for hands-on experiences, such as in Science experiments
- Take walks and field trips in the neighborhood
- Use charts in the classroom for children to make predictions
- Daily reading provides exposure to a variety of literature

Social
- Learning centers where children work together in groups encourages social interactions in the classroom
- Accept and praise all efforts
- Assign jobs and responsibilities in the classroom. Most early childhood classrooms have student helpers who are selected daily.
- Teach students how to clean up their workspace at the end of the activity
- Encourage sharing and help in the classroom
- Model being trustworthy and honest for the students
- Plan a structured day so students feel comfortable and safe in the classroom

Emotional
- Set a positive example for students to be able to control their own behavior
- Allow the students input into setting the classroom rules
- Teach children how to take turns and wait for others
- Allow children to express their feelings in appropriate ways
- Show respect to the students to help them learn to respect others
- Accept the children as they are
- Teach problem solving in real life situations

*Social*

There are many opportunities for students to learn social skills within the school. At recess and while playing on the playground, they should be encouraged to play with the other students and to respect each other. A "Hands-off" policy will help deter any fighting and if arguments occur, teachers can help students discuss the situation to reach an amicable solution.

Parties for various occasions and invitations for parents to come into the class to join in celebrations are also occasions to teach students how to socialize and behave properly.

For older students, giving them time to socialize at parties or dances where they can invite friends from other schools is important, although it means extra supervision for the teachers. Field trips can also be planned in cooperation with other schools so that students get a chance to meet and talk with other students and to make new friends.

*Cultural*

Depending on the location of the school, there may be children from many ethnic cultures in a classroom. These children should be encouraged to talk about their culture and to share stories. Whether or not there are any children from other cultures in the classroom, there should be a variety of books about other cultures that the teacher reads to the students and that they can select for independent reading.

Invite parents, grandparents, or others from the community to come into the class to meet and talk with the students. Some of these may be willing to give presentations to the class on various aspects of culture and history. When students hear the information and see artifacts from other people, they are more likely to realize that this is related to life outside of school.

Allow children to bring cultural items from home for Show and Tell or possible have a cultural fair in the school where all the students participate. If there are any museums or cultural locations in the community, this offers an opportunity for a field trip for the students.

*Athletic*

Each school should have a Physical Education program as part of the curriculum. Whether or not there is a dedicated Physical Education teacher depends on the staffing and budget of the school. If not, each teacher should be responsible for planning a Physical Education class, which can be in the gym or outside. In these classes students learn how to play sports appropriate for their age and how to use specific equipment. To develop a healthy lifestyle, it is ideal if schools can provide 30 minutes of daily physical activity for students. They can go for a walk, play in the gym, dance or any other activity that gets them moving.

The sports program is an important part of school life for elementary, junior high and high school students. This often takes the form of extra-curricular activities after school and on weekends. Through sports, the principal and the staff can also foster school spirit as the rest of the students rally around the teams. Students will feel proud of being on a team and learn how to act as a team member. In many schools, being part of a particular school team is tied to academics, where students so have to achieve a certain average in their subjects. Not only does the athletic program at a school help students develop physically, but it also helps them emotionally with self-confidence and self-esteem.

*Leadership*

As teachers get to know their students, natural leaders will develop in the classroom. These students need to be encouraged in their leadership skills, but opportunities should also be provided for those students who do not automatically volunteer to be leader. This could be something simple as asking a shy student to help another student or to take a turn at being the class helper in the early grades.

A school newspaper is one activity where students can show their leadership skills and talents as they take on specific jobs. Leadership classes as an option is also a good idea where the students help plan activities for the school and go into classes to help students. Peer tutoring gives students an opportunity to help their classmates and gain self-confidence at the same time.

The student council is one area where leaders truly develop within a school. Even the youngest students can learn how to be a class representative and take part in activities in the class and school.

*Academic*

The main focus of a school is on the academic needs of the students, to prepare them for life after they graduate and go on to their chosen careers. It is the duty of the principal to ensure that the mandated curriculum is followed and that the classrooms are equipped with all the textbooks students need. IPP meetings and Parent-Teacher conferences are necessary to ensure students can succeed. Supervision of the teaching staff is also essential to ensure that instruction is as it should be for the curriculum.

The principal should be cognizant of how students are doing, although it is impossible to know how all students are doing all of the time. When signing report cards, the principal should read each report carefully and discuss plans for students at risk with the teachers involved. There may be times when the principal needs to meet with students and parents to discuss the academic situation. Along with ensuring that programs are in place for students at risk, the principal should also ensure that there are programs for students excelling in all or some of their courses. These students need to be challenged so that they are working to the best of their abilities.

## COMPETENCY 8.0 UNDERSTAND HOW TO APPLY PRINCIPLES OF CURRICULUM PLANNING, DEVELOPMENT, AND EVALUATION TO PROMOTE THE SUCCESS OF ALL STUDENTS

### Skill 8.1 Identify basic principles of curriculum design and recognize relationships between child/adolescent/adult development and the curriculum.

The school curriculum is an action plan to educate children. The aims and goals that shape education are generated from nationwide commissions and task forces comprised of educators, and other influential citizens, including politicians. One example is the efforts to affect change by the 1938 Nation-At-Risk Report in which the Commission on Excellent in Education reported its findings on the quality of education in America and made specific recommendations. Another example is the effort made between President Bush and the governors of the states with the Goals 2000 effort, which emerged in 1990.

At the local level, task forces of parents, educators, and community groups impact school curriculum changes in similar ways as do nationwide groups. Data sources to affect change at the local level sometimes include attitudinal surveys of the students, groups, teachers, and other community groups. Other data sources for curriculum selection include direct student information, such as interviews and conferences which yield information related to disposition for learning, likes and dislikes, as well as difficulties experienced by students, because of the design of the curriculum or other related situations. Additionally, anecdotal records held by teachers and the contents of the cumulative folder, such as testing results and report cards, may contribute to the development of profiles of students to aide in the decision-making process regarding curriculum selection. Furthermore, today, curriculum selection is a result of national concerns about reading comprehension, math achievement, and science achievement, all in the name of economic competition with other countries.

Research findings about curriculum principles and design, as well as content organization, are also valuable information for decision-making. Sources for curriculum selection reflect the expectations of society and they directly impact the objectives for learning. For example, Goal Four (4) of Goals 2000 states "By the year 2000, U.S. students will be first in the world in science and mathematics achievement." The expectations of this societal goal affected the curriculum in every state, district, and school. Even if this goal is lofty and may not be fully attained, it has affected the selection and content of the local curriculum. The Commission for Goals 2000 uncovered the deplorable state of our students in math and science and by disclosing these conditions, parent, teachers, and community groups endorsed these goals as a way of improving education. As a result, they influenced a chain of reaction so that objectives would be identified at the lowest levels to change the outcomes in these subject areas. As a result, goals of the discipline were clearly written and became the driving force of curriculum change. Society is also concerned with producing citizens who are prepared to transmit the ideals of a democratic society. Therefore, the school as a societal institution must include in its teaching and learning process objectives that will produce desirable learner outcomes.

The design of the curriculum accounts for the manner in which the elements of the curriculum are organized. The design must account for the nature and organization of the aims, goals, and objectives, as well as the subject matter, learning activities, and the evaluation. Curriculum design precedes instructional design. It is the phase concerned with the nature of the component parts, which is influenced by various philosophies, theories, and practical issues The designer must specify the nature of each of the elements included in the design to develop a blueprint before initiating the process of implementation. The goals and objectives should be specific so that all those involved will clearly understand what will be done and what behaviors are expected of the learner. The next step is to identify the resources needed to attain the preset goals and objectives for the curriculum. All material and human resources deemed necessary must be identified and secured. Materials include textbooks, charts, maps, and other technology and equipment, such as projectors, computers, calculators, sport equipment, and microscopes. Human resources include administrators, teachers, volunteers, support staff, and others. Facilities are classrooms, gym, athletic fields, cafeteria, auditorium, and others. The subject matter, methods of organization, and activities, as well as the methods and instruments to evaluate the program, must be determined.

The conceptual framework or the organization of the components of the curriculum consists of two distinct organizational dimensions, which include horizontal and vertical organization. *Horizontal organization* is a typical side-by side course arrangement where the content of one subject is made relative to the concepts of another related subject. *Vertical organization* is concerned with longitudinal treatment of concepts within a subject across grade levels. The success of the horizontal organization depends heavily on the collaboration of teachers of various disciplines at the grade level, while the vertical organization depends heavily on collaboration and planning among teachers of various grade levels.

The dimensions within the curriculum content are also of important consideration in curriculum design. Therefore, attention should be given to curriculum scope, sequence, integration, continuity, articulation and balance. *Curriculum scope* refers to the breadth and depth of the curriculum content at any grade level in terms of the content, learning activities and experiences, and topics. *Curriculum sequence* refers to the order of topics to be studied over time in a vertical dimension. The sequencing of the curriculum is usually organized from simple to complex learning, but it can also emphasize chronological learning, whole to part learning, or prerequisite learning. *Curriculum integration* refers to the linking of the concepts, skills, and experiences in the subjects taught. *Curriculum continuity* deals with the spiral or vertical smoothness of knowledge repetition from one grade level to another in specific subjects or areas of study. *Curriculum articulation* refers to the interrelationship within and among subjects both vertically and horizontally. *Curriculum balance* refers to the opportunities offered for the learners to master knowledge and apply it in their personal, social, and intellectual life pursuits.

Curriculum content can be based on a number of different design principles. For example, *subject-centered* designs reflect the mental discipline approach to learning. The curriculum is organized according to essential knowledge that must be learned in the different subject matters.

The *discipline* design is based on the organization of content, which allows for in-depth understanding of the content and the application of meaning. It is used primarily in secondary schools to emphasize the organizational content inherent to the academic discipline such as science, math, English, etc. so that the students in science, for example, would approach science as a scientist would. Therefore, the emphasis becomes experiencing the discipline as learning takes place. In the *broad fields design*, unlike the subject field where a subject is studied separately from other subjects that are related, related subjects are broadened into categories, such as social studies encompassing history, geography, and civics or physical science encompassing physics and chemistry. The intent of the broad field design is to integrate the traditional subjects so that the learner develops a broader understanding of the areas included.

The *process centered* design addresses how students learn and apply the process to the subject matter. This design focuses on the student thinking process and incorporates procedures and processes for children to advance knowledge.

Curriculum selection must also take into account the contribution from the field of psychology, which is responsible for the major theories of learning. Learning theories serve as the foundation for methods of teaching, materials for learning, and activities that are age and developmentally appropriate for learning while providing the impetus for curriculum selection. Major theories of learning include the behaviorism, cognitive development and phenomenology or humanistic psychology.

*Behaviorism* represents traditional psychology that emphasizes conditioning the behavior of the learner and altering the environment to obtain specific responses. As the oldest theories of learning, behaviorism focuses specifically on stimulus response and reinforcement for learning. The work experiments of Thorndike led to the development of connectionism theories from which came the laws of learning:

> *Law of Readiness: when the conduction is ready to conduct, satisfaction is obtained and, if readiness is not present, it results in dissatisfaction.*
>
> *Law of Exercise: a connection is strengthened based on the proportion to the number of times it occurs, its duration and intensity.*
>
> *Law of Effect: responses accompanied by satisfaction strengthens the connection while responses accompanied by dissatisfaction weakens the connection.*

These laws also influenced the curriculum contributions of Ralph Tyler, Hilda Taba, and Jerome Brunner who discarded the view of specific stimuli and responses to endorse broader views of learning. For example, Taba recognized that practice alone does not transfer learning; therefore, rote learning and memorization should not be emphasized.

Jerome Bruner, on the other hand, contributed the notion that learning the structure provides a better basis for transferring learning than rote memorization. *Classical conditioning* theories of learning emphasized the elicit response aspect of learning through adequate stimuli. The experiments of Pavlov and Watson (the dog learned to salivate at the sound of the bell at which time food was presented simultaneously as a stimulus) gave the notion that the learner could be conditioned for learning and thus be trained to become educated in any profession. *Operant conditioning* theories or behavioral theories promoted by B. Frederick Skinner which emphasizes positive and negative reinforcers to operant behaviors *(operant: no stimuli explains the response)* by either providing or withdrawing the stimuli or providing new operants. *Behavioral theories* gave birth to behavior modification approaches to discipline and learning. Albert Bandura's theory of Observational Learning and Modeling focuses on children learning through modeling the behaviors of others. This theory contributed the notion that children's behaviors are shaped through observation of the behaviors of others which are interned modeled by the observer. *Hierarchical Learning Theories* represented by Robert Gagne organize types of learning in a classical model of hierarchy encompassing intellectual skills, information, cognitive strategies, motor skills, and attitudes learned through positive experiences.

*Cognitive development theories* focus on human growth and development in terms of cognitive, social, psychological, and physical development even though learning in school settings is cognitive in nature. The *Developmental Theories* of Jean Piaget is based on the supposition that growth and development take place in stages. Piaget identified four stages of development including the sensory stage (birth to age two) in which the child manipulates the physical surroundings; the pre-operational stage (ages 2-7) in which complex learning takes place through experiences; concrete operation stage (age 7-11) in which the child organizes information in logical forms using concrete objects; and the formal operation stage (age 11 and above) in which the child can perform formal and abstract operations.

*Phenomenology or Humanistic psychology*, while not widely recognized as a school of psychology, is recognized by many observers as a third grouping because it emphasizes the total organism of a person during the learning process rather than separating learning into the domains of behavior and cognition. Psychology rejects this school because of the belief that psychology in-and-of-itself is humanistic in nature. Therefore, there is no need for such school. The *Gestalt psychology* is representative of phenomenology and humanistic psychology. It represents wholeness as recognized in Maslow's Hierarchy of needs in which the end-product is a wholesome, happy and healthy child/person who has self-actualized and is fulfilled.

The school curriculum should satisfy societal needs and specific goals to produce an individual who has the social, intellectual, moral, emotional and civic development to function as an integral part of our democratic society. However, selecting the best curriculum to meet all of these needs is not an easy task. It should be a collaborative effort. A response to why program changes are necessary should be given through a clear rationale that examines the existing district and school goals. Clarification is needed pertaining to subject structure and content, and also the needs of the students regarding ability, performance, level of success and needed strategies. Consider the motivation of students and instructional staff, feasibility of time and resources, curriculum balance in terms of concepts, skills, and application.

Successful curriculum implementation is highly dependent on careful planning. Yet communication during the implementation process is pivotal, especially when the new curriculum will upset the status quo. The channels of communication must always be open so that frequent discussions and exchange is ongoing at all levels and across groups. Effective communication requires high quality exchange through two-way channels within a defined network. While the formal network remains the official way of communicating in organizations, the informal network should not be ignored or discouraged because it can be shaped into a very healthy system of communication between members of the organization.

School restructuring calls for communication models other than the traditional top-down model. Curriculum implementation requires that administrators and support personnel not only understand the curriculum but provide support to the classroom so that needs can be met. Therefore, the communication model must be responsive to the needs of all involved. Effective lateral communication allows information flow among all participants at varying levels of involvement in the curriculum while valuing their contribution and promoting involvement through the process of networking. Lateral communication is usually formal within the organization, yet the informal channels tend to be lateral as well. Informal lateral communication might be a small group of teachers deciding amongst themselves to get together and share ideas from an article that could be useful with certain children in their classroom or it could be the development of a simulation project for the grade level. Formal lateral communication messages may be written and disseminated in a systematic mode through newsletters, bulletin, memos, reports, and the like.

Formal lateral communication may also be verbal and communicated through speeches, lectures, oral reports where body language, tone of voice and other physical expressions can enhance the message being communicated.

The mode of communication should be adjusted to meet the needs of the audience. Workshops, bulletins, lectures, and other written and oral reports are all appropriate formats for disseminating program information, but while each approach serves a definite purpose they must be adjusted to meet the needs of their intended audiences. The approach used with teachers may generally be in-service training on procedures and methodology for curriculum implementation where well defined educational terms are used and specific strategies are developed or practiced. Conversely, a presentation for parents, community groups and other lay individuals should be free of educational jargon and adjusted to their educational levels and school experiences. Whatever the mode or approaches to communication, a steady flow of information exchange at every stage of program implementation is necessary.

A needs assessment is always the initial step in program planning. It provides the opportunity to survey and identify the context in which the program will be developed. The needs assessment survey should focus primarily on the needs of the students so that the achievement problems can be identified and goals can be written for the initial planning stage and specific objectives instruction can be formulated.

Identifying the educational goals and setting priorities before developing the curriculum are essential aspects of planning. Additionally, setting and prioritizing the goals must be carefully linked to the performance of the learner. The design of the curriculum follows with the careful selection and recommendation of instructional materials and equipment, as well as methods to attain the pre-established goals and objectives. The steps following include the actual organization of the personnel involved, the implementation of a plan to supervise and give direction and focus to the project. Finally, the product planning and implementation at the classroom level are followed by the evaluation process, which determines the effectiveness and attainment of the goals and objectives of the curriculum.

Data gathering in any assessment process is pivotal to give meaning to what is being measured. Ornstein and Huskins (1993) identify five distinct phases for gathering data to assess program effectiveness. These include the curriculum phenomena to be evaluated, the stage of collecting information, the stage of organizing the information, which is followed by analyzing the information, and finally the state of reporting and recycling the information. The curriculum phenomena to be evaluated is the phase in which the evaluator determines the design of the evaluation which includes exactly what will be evaluated. The evaluators will determine if the entire school will be included or just selected grade levels or subject areas. Whatever is decided at this stage must include a clear delineation of the relationship between the variables. This includes establishing a clear relationship between the objectives, the constraints of the learning activities and the expected outcomes.

Collecting information is the phase where the evaluator must identify the sources of the information to be collected which is based on the designed established in the previous phase. At this juncture, the evaluator must develop a plan to actually collect hard data from various sources including parents, teachers, staff, students, and other members of the school community. Organizing the information leads the evaluator to arrange the data so that it is usable. This includes coding and storing the data into a system where it can be retrieved for analyzes. The phase of analyzing the information leads to the use of selected techniques based on the design of the evaluative process. From the onset of the process, beginning with the identification of the curriculum phenomena, the evaluator identifies the specific data analyzes or statistical approaches that are suitable for the information collected. Reporting the information leads the evaluator to a number of important decisions related to the level of formality of reporting to meet the needs of the various audiences. While it does not negate the use of statistical analysis, it does call for making a judgment on how to best convey appropriate meaning and make recommendations for use. Finally, recycling the information obtained gives meaning to the notion that evaluation is a continuous process. The implication is that the information received from this process will provide feedback for program modification and adjustment which will leads to continuous change in an organization that is continuously changing.

The implementation process must be strategically planned with benchmarks to determine specific levels of program goal attainment leading to the reexamination of the strategies being used for specific learning outcomes. When placed on a time line, the benchmarks may also serve as pointers for communicating with the various audiences. Feedback from the various audiences must be used to determine the extent to which the curriculum goals and expected outcomes, content and implementation strategies, as well as outcome measures, are clearly understood. The plan will supply the agenda items which will be acted upon in a timely manner and hence drive the implementation process as well as the dissemination process.

In the process of educational program evaluation or classroom instructional evaluation, outcomes are reflected in terms of aims, goals, and objectives. Aims are general statements that reflect value judgments that give overall direction of the curriculum. They guide the educational process to achieve future behavioral outcomes. Aims are the results of societal concerns, which usually are expressed through national commissions and task forces. Goals are more specific than aims.

Even though goals may be written in a general manner similar to aims, aims become goals when the statement of purpose reflects specificity to particular areas of the curriculum. Objectives are the most specific statements of expected learner outcomes. Examples of goals are expressed in the 1990 national Goals 2000. Goal one states "By the year 2000 all children in America will start school ready to learn. Goal two states "By the year 2000 the high school graduation rate will increase."

As observed, these goal statements are very general and they do not include specific behaviors or terms for the behavior. Objectives are generally expressed in behavioral terms, which are measurable. Non-behavioral objectives, on the other hand, are generally used to express higher order learning suggesting non-quantifiable measurement, such as appreciation, understanding, and the like. In most schools, behavioral objectives are preferred to non-behavioral objectives. Behavioral objectives state what is expected of the student at the conclusion of the unit or lesson. They state the terms for the behavior and the minimum expectancy. An example of a well-written behavioral objective follows: after completing the unit on telling time, the students will be able to complete 25 problems with 80% accuracy within a thirty minute time span.

From the onset of the program, the goals and objectives are vital. It is through the goals and objectives that the identified problems are addressed. Goals and objectives should be clearly written and examined to make sure that they represent what is expected to be attained. This must be a process that involves not only faculty, but also parents, students, staff, and other members of the school community to provide buy-in and obtain ownership in the attainment of the goals and objectives set by the team. Objectives should be written in measurable terms. With objectives being more specific, special attention must be given to the behavior to be measured and the situation in which the performance will take place and the criterion for the performance. For example, students will be able to solve multiplication word problems (behavior) at the rate of one problem per minute (situation) with 80% accuracy (condition). Objectives can be written to give directions at various program levels including grade levels or subject levels.

## Domains of Curriculum Planning

In the *Domain of Planning*, a course of action for teaching is formulated. The teacher organizes the subject matter to be taught, the materials to be used for instruction, the activities that will be implemented, and the method of assessing the learning outcome. Specific concepts included in this domain are content coverage, utilization of instructional materials, activity structure, goal focusing, and diagnosis. Effective indicators of planning included on the school district's formative assessment instrument may vary, but they will generally correlate with the selected concepts for the domain. For example, *"assesses students' needs before instruction"* might be used as an indicator of diagnosis, while *"presets goals for teaching"* might be used as an indicator of the concept of goal focusing. The domain of *Management of Student Conduct* is inclusive of teacher behavior that reduces probable student misconduct, ways of halting disruptive student behaviors once they occur, and ways of dealing with serious misconduct. The effective teacher knows that the misconduct of a student affects the behavior and learning of other students in the classroom. It is expected that the teacher will use appropriate techniques to stop a deviancy with minimal disruption to other children while using effective response to the misconduct. The effective teacher is aware that teacher behavior may also increase or decrease negative responses from students. The teacher is also aware of the need for appropriate teacher-student interaction. Specific concepts included in this domain are rule explication and monitoring, teacher with-it-ness, overlapping, quality of desists, group alert, movement smoothness, movement slowdown, and praise. Effective indicators of planning included on the school district's formative assessment instrument may vary, but they will generally correlate with the selected concepts for the domain. For example, *"stops misconduct while maintaining instructional momentum"* might be used as an indicator of movement smoothness.

The *domain of Instructional Organization and Development* includes the specific concepts such as efficient use of time, review of subject matter, lesson development, teacher treatment of student talk, teacher academic feedback, and management of seatwork/homework. A formative assessment instrument for teacher performance may use an indicator such as *"circulates and assists students"* to assess the concept of management of seatwork or *"recognizes responses, amplifies and gives corrective feedback"* to assess treatment of student talk.

The *domain of Presentation of Subject* focuses on the interaction with students as well as the treatment of the subject matter. Specific concepts included in this domain are presentation of interpretive (conceptual) knowledge, presentation of explanatory (law or law-like) knowledge, presentation of academic rule knowledge, and presentation of value knowledge which refers to statements about the worth of things. A formative assessment instrument for teacher performance may use an indicator such as *"develops concept, gives definition, attributes, examples and non-examples"* to assess the concept of presentation of interpretive or conceptual knowledge.

The *domain of Communications* (verbal and nonverbal) focuses on verbal and nonverbal skills to express information and establish personal relationships. Communication is based on the notions that while verbal interaction is important to successful teaching, body language and other nonverbal expressions are also crucial in establishing relationships and engaging students in meaningful learning. This domain includes the concepts of control of discourse, emphasis, task attraction, and challenge, speech, and body language. A formative assessment instrument for teacher performance may use an indicator to assess body language such as *"uses nonverbal expressions that show interest, such as smiles, gestures, etc."*

The *domain of Testing* (student preparation, administration, and feedback) addresses the environment in which students are tested, as well as the feedback they receive about their test performance. Administrators are seldom present during direct student assessment periods, which makes observation of classroom testing infrequent. Indicators for teacher testing competencies are usually initiated through the development of a school-wide plan for testing, but are individually assessed through conferences with teachers and feedback from parents and students.

### Skill 8.2 Demonstrate knowledge of strategies for designing and implementing curricula that fully accommodate learners' diverse needs.

In this age of school accountability, principals are indeed instructional leaders. They must be responsible for the quality of instruction on their campuses. While they cannot be fully responsible, as schools are made up of many professionals, they do have great influence on the instruction in each classroom.

In terms of curriculum, decisions are often made at the district level or within departments or committees. School leaders generally defer to the expertise of teachers or curriculum specialists, however, they can have a strong impact on procedures, standards, and outcomes. By being present, informed, and collaborative, they can help to create high level curriculum for all classrooms.

Where does curriculum come from? First, it originates in the purposes of education that the community, board, state, or region hold dear. In other words, when local stakeholders, for example, believe that all students should have strong knowledge of civic foundations, developing a curriculum is the most pertinent next step. Schools are not likely to develop curriculum for academic areas that are not important to any stakeholder group. When appropriate topics are decided upon, curriculum is developed in order to organize the content into a manageable and logical progression. Curriculum usually is organized by topic areas; added to those topics are texts, outside resources, assessments, projects, and activities. Additionally, specific instructional techniques are recommended.

Usually, in most schools, curricula are already developed for most subjects. Why is curriculum still an issue, then? Primarily because all curriculum can be improved. Most schools take it upon themselves to modify curriculum on a regular basis as they draw from previous experience on what worked and what didn't work. Or, when new priorities are handed down to schools in the form of legislation, for example, schools want to create a curriculum that will reflect their own individual needs, even though the basic structures may be place already. In such cases, pieces of the curriculum are adapted. Sources, such as conferences, books, programs, and formal interventions are helpful in creating curricula.

Instructional objectives are met, most basically, though trial, feedback, improvement, and new knowledge. Teachers cannot teach better without new ideas, practice, and advice. Principals, and other teacher-leaders, instructional coaches, and mentors, can provide valuable assistance to teachers as they seek to improve their practice. This brings up an important point. Effective resources for teachers include sources of new knowledge (such as conferences, books, training seminars, etc.); however, one-on-one coaching or mentoring is particularly effective in helping teachers to improve. Although principals can be effective at this, teachers may trust non-evaluative staff more with questions, concerns, or problems that they need addressed.

A clear relationship between goals, activities and students' assessment is established. Collaborative curriculum planning and decision making is the typical way of work. Curriculum continuity is built across grade levels, programs, and courses. Curriculum alignment is periodic, and staff, students, and parents know the priorities of the scope of the curriculum. The content of the curriculum is free from biases including gender, ethnic and racial biases.

The school curriculum is in reality a plan of action to educate children. The plan includes goals and objectives, activities for learning and materials to support learning and the evaluation process to determine the attainment of the goals and objectives. This plan is placed into a design that is under-girded by the selected approach and philosophy of learning. There are many different approaches to curriculum. These approaches are a reflection of educational philosophies, psychological foundations and social and developmental theories. Approaches to curriculum also include viewpoints about curriculum design; the roles of the learner, teachers, specialists, goals and objectives; and other important content to be examined.

Curriculum approaches can be technical scientific or non-technical/non-scientific. Among the technical scientific approaches are specific behavioral approaches, the managerial approach and the systems approach. Among the non-technical/nonscientific approaches to curriculum are the academic approaches and the humanistic approaches.

*The Behavioral Approach* pioneered by Ralph Tyler, Franklin Babbit, Hilda Tabba and others is a very efficient model to run schools. It is a blueprint that is inclusive of goals and objectives, step-by-step sequencing of content, activities, and learning outcome. Their legacy is still observed in teacher lesson plans and units. This approach is rooted in the scientific management theory of Frederick Taylor, which emphasized efficiency and productivity.

*The managerial approach* considers the school as a social system in which students, teachers, administrators, and other members of the school community interact based on certain social norms. In this setting, space, schedules, and programs are important factors. While logical and sequential steps are expected, the focus is on the organizational aspect of curriculum rather than the implementation. This approach brought about innovations, such as non-graded schools, departmentalization, the homeroom concept, and others. Its main goal is to organize the curriculum into a system.

*The system approach* views units and sub-units of organization as integral parts of the whole. Diagrams and flow charts are important to view the curriculum as a whole system that can be monitored. It is viewed as curriculum engineering. With this approach, particular issues are related to the whole system in terms of the relationship of the entire program.

*The academic approach* is among the nonscientific/non-technical approaches to curriculum. It is philosophical and theoretical and especially concerned with broad aspects of schooling, background information, and overview of events and people which makes it rigid and non-practical for the classroom and schools. Nonetheless, it does reflect useful educational views for curriculum developers and theorists.

*The humanistic approach* is another non-scientific/non-technical approach rooted in the child-centered movement, which gained recognition with the growth of child psychology and humanistic psychology in the 1940s and 1950s. This approach is concerned with the social, artistic, physical, and cultural aspects of curriculum. Additionally, it is concerned with the need for self-reflection and self-actualization of the learner along with the social and psychological environmental dynamics of the classroom.

Educational philosophies provide the primary foundation on which educators build the curriculum. Philosophies reflect a particular school of thought, which also provide the impetus for the aims, goals, and content as well as the organization of the curriculum. Educational Philosophies provides educators with a basis for school and classroom organization. They provide information related to methodology to be used, materials for instruction, what content should be taught, what experiences to prefer, and other structural issues related to the teaching and learning process.

In the United States, four major philosophies influenced education: Idealism, Realism, Pragmatism, and Existentialism. Idealism and realism are considered traditional philosophies while pragmatism and realism are considered contemporary philosophies (Pulliam and Patten, 1995). *Idealism* places emphasis on moral and spiritual concepts to explain the reality of the world truth and other values as timeless, universal and permanent, and unalterable. Idealism is the philosophy of early philosophers such as Plato and others. Based on this philosophy, learning involves conceptualization and recall. The curriculum is hierarchical and should include and prefer abstract thoughts such as philosophy and theology, which are at the highest level of the hierarchy. Next mathematics which is absolute, history and literature which provide moral and cultural values, and language which fosters communication to support the concepts and thoughts that are central to this philosophy.

*Realism* views the world in terms of objects and matter that are real and perceived through sensing and reasoning. This school of thought is represented by great philosophers such as Aristotle and Pestalozzy. The notion that all things are derived from nature and are governed by the laws of nature, including human behavior, is prevalent in this school of thought. The type of curriculum stressed is one that is organized and separated into subject matter consistent of specific knowledge. Therefore, content and subjects that can be classified should be included into the curriculum. Basic skills such as reading, writing and mathematics would have priority.

*Pragmatism* is mainly an American philosophy as opposed to the previous philosophies, which originated in Europe. Pragmatism is based on change and experimentation. It views knowledge as a process in which change is constant. In this school of thought, learning occurs through problem solving, which is transferable to a variety of situations. Scientific development of the turn of the century influenced the development of this school of thought as well as the work of John Dewey and the child study movement. Pragmatists see learning through the scientific process where learning takes place through discovery and problem solving in response to the stimulus from the world that surrounds the learner.

*Existentialism* emerged as a response to previous philosophies. It stresses individualism and personal self-fulfillment. It is subjective to values chosen on the basis on the individuals' own perceptions. In this school of thought, the teacher's role is to cultivate the student's personal choice and help the individual to self-define. The curriculum endorsed by this school of thought is one that is void of structured discipline where students select their learning situations. Also favored by this philosophy are literature, drama, art and other areas that foster choice making and self-expressive activities, dialogue between the teacher and students, and discussions for new choices.

### Skill 8.3  Identify appropriate criteria for use in evaluating, modifying, and integrating curricula.

It is extremely naïve to think that the introduction of yet another program or textbook or the addition of a new instructional technique will improve teaching and learning. Schools are very complex places, and all changes that get introduced are susceptible to failure or success, mainly based on how those changes are received by stakeholders (including teachers, students, and parents). In a nutshell, the change process at schools is very slow, and principals who come into schools seeking to immediately change them may find themselves in a very precarious position. Teachers are professionals with significant histories, cultures, and traditions. Many have been doing the same things for years (and some have great success at it). Others have tried new ideas, failed, and are fearful of doing anything new again. Therefore, principals who seek to change schools, introduce new curricula, or simply improve instructional quality must do so carefully and honestly.

The change process in schools is particularly slow as schools are typically thought of as highly bureaucratic. It is difficult for changes to occur, primarily because teachers are alone with students each day, rarely able to work with colleagues on problems and solutions. By being alone all that time, it is easy for teachers to cement ideas about what entails good and bad instruction. Their ideas are further shaped by the responses of students and parents. When new changes are introduced, often teachers assess the change prospect based on their level of comfort or fear with the new idea. If they believe the new idea will meld in with their current beliefs or practices, they are more likely to adopt that change (Coburn, 2004).

Lately, school change has been less an issue of "hoping" that teachers will adopt new ideas and more of an issue of forcing new ideas on teachers and schools. Even in this case, research shows that teachers may not fully adopt ideas they do not like. Therefore, whether change is imposed from above or simply encouraged from peers or leaders, attention must be given to increase motivation. Again, getting teachers involved in the planning and development process is critical to success.

As already stated, one primary reason teachers are less willing to adopt new ideas is fear of failure. Instructional motivation, therefore, seeks to minimize the fears associated with adopting new instructional innovations. Possible ways to do this include professional learning communities (where teachers can come together to discuss instructional problems and solutions), lesson study (deliberate analysis of specific lessons in small groups of teachers), instructional coaches, and classroom observations (where teachers are given time to watch other teachers teach).

**Skill 8.4** Apply knowledge of procedures for involving and leading stakeholders in curriculum development, implementation, and evaluation.

The principal's key role in the school community is to be an instructional leader and lead others in curriculum decisions and planning, in order to achieve the desired goals and learning outcomes.

In order to be an effective educational leader, and in order to hold others accountable for their performance, the principal needs to follow some guidelines in curriculum planning:

- Teachers and other community members need to understand and accept the educational philosophy of the school, because all other educational activities will fit in with that philosophy.
- Teachers need to be included in the needs assessment, as they have valuable input about student needs.
- Teachers must be involved in the process of developing goals and objectives.
- Instructional goals need to be regularly assessed and revised to fit changing needs, in order for the learning outcomes to be realistic.
- Teachers have input in their schedule requirements, teaching duties and other tasks required of them.
- Teachers have adequate resources to support their teaching.
- Teachers have a choice of teaching materials and other instructional resources that they feel comfortable using.
- Teachers understand the process of curriculum planning, implementation and evaluation.
- Student and parent input is consistently sought in the process of curriculum planning.
- New ideas and changes are introduced in a non-threatening manner, and all people affected by the changes are trained and have adequate support to implement those changes.
- There is effective two-way communication among all parties involved in the process of curriculum planning.
- Teachers, parents and community members feel they are a valuable part of the instructional program, and that their voices and input are heard.

The process of curriculum planning will find more success when the principal sees that all community members are appropriately involved and feel that their needs are being met.

Reference:
Stoops, E. et al. Handbook of Educational Administration. Allyn and Bacon Inc., Boston, 1981.

# TEACHER CERTIFICATION STUDY GUIDE

**Skill 8.5  Demonstrate knowledge of the relationships between Oklahoma's Priority Academic Student Skills and local curricula.**

Oklahoma's Priority Academic Student Skills (PASS) outlines the life learning skills that all students in Oklahoma schools should achieve. These skills are overarching goals that shape the local curriculum and include all subject areas. They are set out in sections for Kindergarten, Elementary, Junior High and Senior High grades.

Within the field of Social Studies there are ten major themes that all curricula need to encompass. These themes are designed to strengthen student learning by building connections between the students' present lives and the past history and demonstrate how each of the themes affect the students' lives. They are also intended to provide a flow of the story of human development throughout history.

The outcomes presented in PASS are very general, but provide direction for the local curricula. In Health, for example, the first goal for Grades 1 –4 states "The student will comprehend concepts related to health promotion, disease prevention, and safety practices". This goal allows local curriculum planners the freedom they need to plan the various stages students need to achieve this objective as they progress through the grade levels, with each grade including more information, skills and concepts that are age appropriate.

There are lesson plans for these priority skills that teachers can incorporate into the local curricula to ensure that all students achieve the mandated outcomes. These lesson plans can also be cross-curricular in that teachers can choose to combine subject areas with similar objectives or teach the lessons in conjunction with other classes.

Locally developed curricula should encompass the standards set out in PASS. This ensures that all students develop the skills they need to graduate from school and go on to a career or post-secondary education. The standards are intended to ensure that all students in Oklahoma schools are literate in all subjects and can read, write, speak, and listen effectively along with having knowledge in core subjects of Math, Social Studies, Science and Health.

**Skill 8.6** **Analyze issues and procedures related to the development of curricula to meet the needs of all students.**

Working with curricula is an opportunity to enhance both student and teacher learning. In order to ensure that students are receiving a high-quality education, instructional leaders must now more than ever take up the challenge to redesign professional development into a bold, useful use of time. Curriculum mapping is one powerful way to sharpen teachers' curriculum-design and teaching skills while promoting collaboration across subjects and grade levels.

Mapping is a system of curriculum analysis and alignment and has often been cited as a valuable component of curriculum renewal and staff development. Primarily, curriculum mapping offers the much-needed flexibility to address the changing curricular needs of school districts. Its dependence on a wide range of instructor participation also strengthens the efforts to restructure the curriculum of a school or district.

The development of a school's entire curriculum allows every one to have an overview of what is being taught, so that every person involved: students, parents, teachers, administrators, in the educational process can view where their own curriculum might coordinate with other department's objectives. For example, it allows English teachers to see when they might help a History teacher who has assigned a research paper.

To ensure success for all students, schools should be committed to regular planning of and also reflection upon what is taught. A formatted lesson plan includes the following:

- Content and skills to be covered.
- Assessment strategies.
- Essential questions, which serve as the scope and sequence of a unit.
- State subject area and learning standards to be mastered.

Using the formatted lesson plan as an overview, instructors can create their daily lesson plans. At the end of each lesson, instructors can reflect upon the objectives they outlined in the formatted lesson plan and ultimately create a curriculum map of what material they had actually taught the students.
Just as formatted lesson plans represent an goal of what is to be taught, maps are the reality of what an instructor had actually taught Once the formatted lesson plans are created, the directed instruction has taken place, and each teacher has completed a chart of what they had actually taught, the faculty can then compare the curriculum in various ways: within a subject area or department, across all disciplines, or across grade levels.

It is essential that all teachers be involved in this official process of curriculum repositioning and verbalization. Teachers' collaboration with their peers promotes a commitment to adhering to specific state and organizational curriculum frameworks and also incorporates a team approach to teaching all students in all disciplines and subject areas.

An effective curriculum supports the practice of constant reflection and awareness to meet the needs of all students. Activities associated with curriculum development, such as making inquiries, creating strategies, and sharing various components of professional development provides both direct relevance to teachers' classroom practices and sustained opportunities for reflection and growth.

Ultimately, developing high-quality curriculum enables teachers to use new and traditional curricular materials in ways to better instruct their students.

**Skill 8.7     Demonstrate knowledge of strategies for infusing diversity awareness into the curriculum.**

When diversity is promoted in learning environments and curriculum, both students and teachers are the beneficiaries of increased academic success. Using classrooms as vital resources for cultural and ethnic inclusion can assist students in contributing cultural norms and artifacts to the acquisition of learning. Teachers are able to create global thinkers by helping students identify cultural assumptions and biases that may direct the type of social and academic groupings that occur in the classroom and influence the type of thinking and construction of learning that happens within a classroom. For example, if a student is struggling in math, a teacher can examine the cultural aspect of learning math. For some students, math is insignificant when socioeconomic issues of poverty and survival are the daily reality of existence. When students see parents juggling finances, the only math that becomes important for them is that less is never enough to keep the lights on and mortgage paid.

When there is equity pedagogy, teachers can use a variety of instructional styles to facilitate diversity in cooperative learning and individualized instruction that will provide more opportunities for positive student experiences and academic success. Empowering the school culture and climate by establishing an anti-bias learning environment and promoting multicultural learning inclusion will discourage disproportionality and unfair labeling of certain students.

Teachers can use various toolkits of assessing integration and incorporation of ethnic and cultural inclusion in classroom. Effective promotion should translate into increased academic success and opportunities for all students. Looking at diverse or homogenous groupings in the classroom can provide teachers with opportunities to restructure cooperative learning groupings and increase diverse student interactions, which can provide increased improvements for school communities.

*Working with Diverse Groups*

A classroom is a community of learning, and when students learn to respect themselves and the members around them, learning is maximized. A positive environment, where open, discussion-oriented, non-threatening communication among all students can occur, is a critical factor in creating an effective learning culture. The teacher must take the lead and model appropriate actions and speech, and intervene quickly when a student makes a misstep and offends (often inadvertently) another.

Communication issues that the teacher in a diverse classroom should be aware of include:

- Be sensitive to terminology and language patterns that may exclude or demean students. Regularly switch between the use of "he" and "she" in speech and writing. Know and use the current terms that ethnic and cultural groups use to identify themselves (e.g., "Latinos" (favored) vs. "Hispanics").
- Be aware of body language that is intimidating or offensive to some cultures, such as direct eye contact, and adjust accordingly.
- Monitor your own reactions to students to ensure equal responses to males and females, as well as differently-performing students.
- Don't "protect" students from criticism because of their ethnicity or gender. Likewise, acknowledge and praise all meritorious work without singling out any one student. Both actions can make all students hyper-aware of ethnic and gender differences and cause anxiety or resentment throughout the class.
- Emphasize the importance of discussing and considering different viewpoints and opinions. Demonstrate and express value for all opinions and comments and lead students to do the same.

When teaching in diverse classrooms, teachers must also expect to be working and communicating with all kinds of students. The first obvious difference among students is gender. Interactions with male students are often different than those with female students. Depending on the lesson, female students are more likely to be interested in working with partners or perhaps even individually. On the other hand, male students may enjoy a more collaborative or hands-on activity. The gender of the teacher will also come into play when working with male and female students. Of course, every student is different and may not fit into a stereotypical role, and getting to know their students' preferences for learning will help teachers to truly enhance learning in the classroom.

Most class rosters will consist of students from a variety of cultures, as well. Teachers should get to know their students (of all cultures) so that they may incorporate elements of their cultures into classroom activities and planning. Also, getting to know about a student's background/cultural traditions helps to build a rapport with each student, as well as further educate the teacher about the world in which he or she teaches.

For students still learning English, teachers must make every attempt to communicate with that student daily. Whether it's with another student who speaks the same language, word cards, computer programs, drawings or other methods, teachers must find ways to encourage each student's participation. Of course, the teacher must also be sure the appropriate language services begin for the student in a timely manner, as well.

Teachers must also consider students from various socioeconomic backgrounds. These students are just as likely as anyone else to work well in a classroom; unfortunately, sometimes difficulties occur with these children when it comes to completing homework consistently. These students may need help deriving a homework system or perhaps need more attention on study or test-taking skills. Teachers should encourage these students as much as possible and offer positive reinforcements when they meet or exceed classroom expectations. Teachers should also watch these students carefully for signs of malnutrition, fatigue and possibly learning disorders.

Teachers should create a classroom climate that encourages extensive participation from the students. Collaborations and discussions are enhanced when students like and respect each other, and therefore, each student's learning can benefit. This is even more true when students engage in full participation. When everyone's thoughts and perspectives and ideas are offered, the class can consider each idea carefully in their discussion. The more students' participate, the more learning is gained through a more thorough examination of the topic.

To create this environment, teachers must first model how to welcome and consider all points of view for the students. The teacher should then positively affirm and reinforce students for offering their ideas in front of the other students. Even if somewhat amiss, the teacher should receive the idea while perhaps offering a modification or corrected statement (for more factual pieces of information). The idea is for students to feel confident and safe in being able to express their thoughts or ideas. Only then will students be able to engage in independent discussions that consider and respect everyone's statements.

### *Students Acquiring English*

There are many factors that impact someone's ability to pick up a second or third language. Age is one common factor. It is said that after a certain age (usually seven), learning a second language becomes dramatically harder. But there are also many social factors, such as anxiety, that influence language learning. Often, informal, social settings are more conducive to second language learning. Motivation is another factor, obviously. A final important factor, particularly for teachers, is the strategies one uses to learn a language. For example, memorizing words out of context is not as effective as using words strategically for a real-life purpose.

NOTE: See www.everythingesl.net or http://www.nwrel.org/request/2003may/overview.html for more information.

### *Culture in the Classroom*

In personalized learning communities, relationships and connections between students, staff, parents and community members promote lifelong learning for all students. School communities that promote an inclusion of diversity in the classroom, community, curriculum and connections enable students to maximize their academic capabilities and educational opportunities. Setting school climates that are inclusive of the multicultural demographic student population create positive and proactive mission and vision themes that align student and staff expectations.

The following factors enable students and staff to emphasize and integrate diversity in student learning:
- Inclusion of multicultural themes in curriculum and assessments
- Creation of a learning environment that promotes multicultural research, learning, collaboration, and social construction of knowledge and application.
- Providing learning tasks that emphasize student cognitive, critical thinking and problem-solving skills.
- Learning tasks that personalize the cultural aspects of diversity and celebrate diversity in the subject matter and student projects.
- Promotion of intercultural positive social peer interrelationships and connections.

Teachers communicate diversity in instructional practices and experiential learning activities that create curiosity in students who want to understand the interrelationship of cultural experiences. Students become self-directed in discovering the global world in and outside the classroom. Teachers understand that when diversity becomes an integral part of the classroom environment, students become global thinkers and doers.

In the intercultural communication model, students are able to learn how different cultures engage in both verbal and nonverbal modes of communicating meaning. Students who become multilingual in understanding the stereotypes that have defined other cultures are able to create new bonding experiences that will typify a more integrated global culture. Students who understand how to effectively communicate with diverse cultural groups are able to maximize their own learning experiences by being able to transmit both verbally and non-verbally cues and expectations in project collaborations and in performance based activities.

The learning curve for teachers in intercultural understanding is exponential in that they are able to engage all learners in the academic process and learning engagement. Teaching students how to incorporate learning techniques from a cultural aspect enriches the cognitive expansion experience since students are able to expand their cultural knowledge bases.

**Skill 8.8   Apply knowledge of current research in curriculum development and strategies for developing an inclusive curriculum that reflects the diversity of the classroom, the community, the nation, and the world.**

Curriculum in today's schools must develop and optimize strategies that enable students and teachers alike to about themselves, their communities, and their cultures—and how these connect to other people, communities, and cultures around the world. Discovering these connections is important, because the events that occur in the United States affect other parts of the world, and events in other countries also have an important impact on the United States. Education needs to teach what reality is, and respond to whatever conditions exist, and also the fact that the world is becoming more global. People travel abroad, move to various parts of the world, communication through e-mail is a common every day occurrence, movies and sports are apart of the international markets.

Curriculum should be implemented that focuses on a global education for all students. Global instruction organizes teachers so they can prepare their students to live in a global society. A global education should be an approach to teaching, rather than an addition to the curriculum.

As a result, teachers can approach global education from different perspectives:

- emphasizing multiple perspectives
- relating global interdependence
- teaching social justice
- cross-cultural understanding

An effective curriculum should teach students not only need to learn about the world, but to explore their role in it. Instructors should show that global education relates to understanding the interconnections of global systems while gaining an appreciation of different perspectives. Teachers may begin by starting with a focus on the students and their community, and then making connections to the rest of the world by bringing in various newspaper articles about events in another country or culture.

*Strategies*

- The teacher can bring in various newspaper articles about events in Africa, for example. . A classroom discussion can be centered on Africa by informing the students the fact that, although we tend to think of all people from that continent as Africans, there is a lot of variety. For example, a person from Ghana speaks a different language than someone from South Africa. During the Africa unit, the class can study other differences and similarities in the geography, history, music, and languages of Africa and the United States. The most important aspect of the assignment would be to show the students how this story affects people in the United States and how the similarities between their world and ours. Activities such as these help young people recognize that there are multiple perspectives. Teaching students that a person's perspective influences his or her actions can be an important tool to understanding how the world works.
- Students can also be assigned a generic geography and climate, such as a rain forest, pine forest, or desert. Students research the plants, animals, geographies, and cultures of areas with similar features around the world. In another activity, students can study that culture's writing system.
- A teacher can emphasis experience by enabling students to gain an understanding of other countries by providing opportunities for students to meet people from other countries or cultures. Exposure to people that have traveled worldwide and people from other cultures is essential to preparing today's students to work in a global economy. Teachers can also invite international people to speak to their classrooms. By sharing their personal cultures with the students this allows the students to compare countries, cities, schools and family life.

Effective teachers need quality content knowledge and as much international experience as possible in order to provide an effective curriculum which is compelled to explore emerging global issues because as the world changes, the content of global education continually changes also.

## COMPETENCY 9.0 UNDERSTAND HOW TO APPLY PRINCIPLES OF INSTRUCTION AND INSTRUCTIONAL LEADERSHIP TO PROMOTE THE SUCCESS OF ALL STUDENTS

### Skill 9.1 Apply knowledge of strategies for helping school personnel apply best practices and sound educational research to improve instructional programs.

Teachers need to use a variety of instructional methods and techniques in the classroom and no two teachers will approach the teaching of the same objectives in the same way. In traditional classrooms, direct teaching with the students in rows and the teacher at the front of the classroom was the norm. Direct teaching is still used in classrooms but it varies from whole class to small group instruction. Guided reading, for example, is a method of direct instruction to a small group of students who are all at the same level of reading and need instruction in the same strategy.

Team teaching can involve two teachers in the same classroom at the same time, both teaching the same subject. They can each be teaching small groups or one teacher can be instructing a group while the other is helping individual students. Team teaching can also mean teachers of different subjects who integrate the learning outcomes so that they are each reinforcing what the others are doing in their classrooms. This type of instruction needs a lot of planning outside the regular school day. Administrators in schools where team teaching takes place usually schedule the day so that the teachers have their prep periods at the same time to facilitate planning.

Group instruction can be for the whole class. This is usually to give directions or to introduce a unit. For the most part, group instruction in today's classrooms takes the form of the teacher working with small groups of students. The other students in the class have work to do, through learning centers where they are also doing activities related to the instructional objectives.

A learning contract is a way of individualizing instruction and making the student responsible for his/her own learning. In the contract method, the student can progress at his/her own pace and learn at the rate they need in order to achieve the learning outcomes of the subject. When working with learning contracts, the teacher can structure the activities that best suit the student's learning style and use the appropriate resources so that the student can experience success. Learning contracts can also be used with small groups of students whom the teacher feels need to learn to work more independently.

Interdisciplinary instruction enables teachers to teach objectives from several different courses at the same time. This approach is best suited to teachers who teach all subjects in a classroom. They can take the outcomes from Social Studies, for example, and teach them along with Language Arts outcomes. This instructional technique allows teachers more time to teach the basic language outcomes while still covering the content from other subject areas.

## Skill 9.2 Demonstrate knowledge of principles and techniques associated with various instructional methods, including technology-based methods.

School administrators must implement appropriate assessments to measure individual student growth during the school year, and from year to year, rather than measuring student achievement at a single point in time. Implementing a system like this assures that teachers and administrators can understand and influence growth for all students, regardless of achievement status, age and class groupings. Analyzing these growth measures over time will also help to determine how student achievement is aligned with district or state standards. Teachers should also be able to determine if classroom instruction is challenging individual students appropriately.

Teachers must be encouraged to shift from assessment of learning to assessment for learning. Assessment for learning is the process of seeking and interpreting evidence for use by learners and their teachers to decide where the learners are in their learning, where they need to go and how best to get there (http://www.aaia.org.uk/pdf/AFL_10principlesARG.pdf). Assessment for learning is an on-going process whereas assessment of learning is done at a point in time for the purpose of summarizing the current status of student achievement.

Additionally, research shows that assessment is most effective when it includes the following characteristics:

- student centered
- congruent with instructional objectives
- relevant
- comprehensive
- clear (in purpose, directions, expectations)
- objective and fair
- simulates "end" behavior/product/performance
- incites active responses
- shows progress/development over time

Data driven instruction is based on assessment data from various sources. Teachers should analyze state achievement scores, district and school benchmark scores, as well as formal and informal classroom assessments. This data provides valuable information about the current understanding and learning that is taking place. Teachers should use this data to determine if they are meeting established objectives, and re-plan and re-teach as necessary.

Using technology to support student learning is not a new concept in education. Technology in various forms has been introduced into the educational environment over the decades. Technology can be seen in the form of books, radio, television, and duplicating machines. The advent of the computer, however, affords perhaps the greatest opportunity for students to engage in learning through an interactive medium. Computer technology provides and interactive environment in which students can respond and receive feedback.

Computer Assisted Instruction (CAI) describes a way in which the computer can be used as a tool to instruct students. The software used in CAI is categorized into five categories. Those categories are tutorials, simulations, drill-and-practice, educational games, and exploratory environments (Grabe & Grabe, 1996). Each of these provides meaningful learning experiences in the classroom and address specific teaching objectives.

Educators must consider the kinds of learning outcomes to be derived from instructional experiences. Matching the appropriate technologies to the desired behavioral objectives requires an understanding of the characteristics of the given technologies. Bringing to bear the capabilities of technology to the needs of the learners and tailoring the advantages of that technology to objectives are important in taking advantage of technology. Understanding what is being asked of students and then identifying the best technology available to deliver a solution is important in the educational environment.

Technology, especially computer technology is viewed by many as an advantage in achieving a school's stated learning objectives. The use of technology in achieving the learning objectives is not as widespread as should be. Few of America's 2.8 million teachers are using technology in their teaching (Hancock, 1993; Office of Technology, 1995). What accounts for slow pace of technology's diffusion and integration into teachers' practice? Kearsley and Lynch (1994) concluded that teachers and administrators are not prepared to advance and manage technology in schools.

One can attribute the lack of adoption of technology in the teaching and learning environment to a number of causes. These causes can be characterized under the headings of organizational factors and individual factors (Hope, 1997). Organizationally, integration of technology is hampered by a lack of specific plans. Incorporating technology into the teaching and learning process requires access to the technology that is to be used in the teaching environment. Because technology is expensive, teachers often do not have access to the technology. As well, teachers need training in the use of technology. The lack of effective training opportunities for teachers to visualize the capabilities of technology impedes its use in classrooms.

Leadership is an important ingredient in adopting technology and using it in the teaching and learning process. Without leadership from principals, teachers are often reluctant to introduce new methodology into the learning process. Because teachers are familiar with the processes and methodologies of earlier generations of teaching, and technology is a recent phenomenon, many do not have the background for using technology in the classroom. Teachers resist integrating technology into the teaching and learning process when they have not been exposed to the advantages technology affords beyond the methodologies they presently use.

The thrust to use technology in the learning environment is not likely to abate in the near future. So, for school administrators, it is important to recognize the capabilities of technology and the advantages it brings to the classroom, as well as becoming an advocate for using technology. A major responsibility falls on the school leader to model technology use and to also provide access and training for teachers to use technology.

The use of technology in schools by teachers and students is contingent upon an understanding of the capabilities of various technology and an ability to integrate these capabilities into the curriculum framework of a school. The application of technology to curriculum goals and objectives is an important function of school leadership. Involving students in learning sequences that utilize technology provides a new and motivating context to learning. Proponents of technology assert a significant role for technology in the teaching and learning process. They view technology as an ingredient with potential to transform the relationship between students and teachers and the dynamics that take place in the classroom. Computer technology offers teachers and students a constructivist learning environment. That is, opportunity exists for students to engage in hands-on learning.

The placement of computers in individual teacher's classrooms offers the most benefit. This placement maximizes both teacher and student access to technology. Computers can be used in schools for achieving a number of instructional objectives. They can be used for remediation, drill and practice, and to simulate real world activities. Effective teaching utilizing technology is available. Understanding the appropriate application of technology to specific curriculum and learning objects is a key administrative skill. Knowing which applications of technology advance student learning is necessary.

Educational technology evidences itself in many forms in schools. By far, however, the computer and various software applications predominate as the technology of choice in the teaching and learning environment. In an era of constructivist thinking in classrooms, where students take charge of their own learning, computer technology is perceived as an advantage to students' working independently, learning to think critically, and using computer technology as a productivity tool.

Technology should support the curriculum of a school. It should be utilized to obtain the objectives and outcomes desired by school leaders, the community, and ultimately the nation. Determining how best to incorporate computer technology into the curriculum should be a process that not a little time is spent on. In fact, the appropriate design and integration of computer technology into a schools curriculum is a major undertaking.

Integrating computers into school curriculum takes on the character of more than the aspect of fun. Computers can be significant in the teaching and learning process when the advantages and applications are carefully thought out and implemented. There are traditional uses of computers in classrooms like drill and practice, games, and remediation. However, the capabilities of computers and software applications make it a versatile teaching tool with potential beyond traditional computer use. Computer technology can be used to support students in analysis, creative thinking, and problem solving. Specifically, information management, writing, and mathematical concepts can all be taught to students using the computer.

Video has a powerful potential for education (Maurer & Davidson, 1998). Video formats have the potential for being the most creative educational applications developed thus far (Picciano, 1998). Moving images have an advantage over still visuals in the teaching and learning process. Video can be used in the learning environment for both affective and cognitive learning. Video technology comes in a variety of formats. These are DVD, videodisc, videocassette, (U-matic and VHS), videocassette (8 millimeter), and compact disc. DVD, videodisc and videotape are common media being used in the instructional process in schools today.

Each of these formats presents advantages and disadvantages in the instructional environment. Video technology can be used to analyze human interactions, mastery of skills through repeated observations, and the shaping of attitudes (Heinich, Molenda, Russell, & Smaldino, 1996). However, in the classroom, it can promote in-active learning. Teachers need to ensure that their use of video technology in the classroom is appropriated for deep learning, only.

**Skill 9.3    Examine the significance of student differences (e.g., in regard to learning styles, cultural background, home language, disabilities) for instructional planning and implementation.**

See Skill 7.2

**Skill 9.4    Describe methods of assessing student learning and achievement and examine the role of student assessment for instruction and program evaluation.**

Indicators of achievement determine the level students must achieve in order to prove that they have mastered the objectives. Indicators are used to measure the student performance and one objective can have multiple indicators. The indicators define the specific level of attitude, skills or knowledge the student needs to demonstrate for the objective.

The prescribed learning outcomes for each subject area are mandated by the standards set by the state. These are statements of what the students are expected to know or achieve in order to pass the course of study.

Each teacher should have a checklist of outcomes for each unit of study for each child. They can then check off the outcomes as the child achieves them. Each of the outcomes listed in the standards also carries with it a level of acceptable performance, such as in Language Arts – "all students will write in complete sentences". Students who are not achieving this indicator need to have extra instruction in order for them to meet the performance indicator.

Rubrics are used to test the Writing skills of students, whereas in the other areas of English Language Arts and the content subjects, there are right and wrong answers. The standardized tests at the end of the year are based on the objectives teachers are expected to teach in the classroom. When the tests are corrected there is a range in which the scores fall. Students are then given a grade as well as a comment such as Falls Below, Approaches, Meets or Exceeds.

At the beginning of each year, the administrator should go over and analyze the results of the previous year in order to plan for instruction for the students. Students who are exceeding need to be challenged and students who fall below need to have extra supports put in place in order for them to experience success.

**Skill 9.5** **Examine how various staffing patterns, student grouping arrangements, behavior management practices, class scheduling formats, school organizational structures, and facility designs affect teaching and learning.**

Many factors influence teaching and learning in schools. Often, it is hard for teachers to see the impact of various factors, as they are most familiar with what happens in their own classrooms once the close their doors. Yet, the entire structure of the school and school day sends many messages about values. Let us go through a variety of factors separately.

**Staffing Patterns:** It should come as no surprise that who we have teaching our students makes a significant difference in how students learn. Of course, with collective bargaining (union) regulating how teachers are hired and fired, many principals must learn to coexist with teachers who may not be very good. However, principals can find ways of minimizing the impact of poor teachers on the neediest students. Additionally, we all know that some teachers have specific strengths—and other teachers have entirely different strengths. It is useful to ensure that such teachers are spread out so that as many students can benefit from as many teachers' strengths as possible.

**Class Schedule Formats:** Particularly at the secondary level, formats of schedules are critical to successful student learning. Many schools now see the value of block scheduling, a format that allows classes to meet for much longer periods of time on an alternating day schedule. Other schools have combined Social Studies with Language Arts or Math with Science in order to encourage cross-disciplinary studies. Some schools have students clustered in "houses" where all teachers rotate the same group of students. The purpose of this format is to allow teachers to discuss specific student issues. At the elementary level, class scheduling might permit students, for specific subjects, to be grouped homogonously. This allows teachers, in those subjects, to work more closely with specific student issues. Conversely, at other times, students can be grouped heterogeneously in order to provide a diverse climate among students.

**School Organizational Structures:** Typically, in secondary schools, organizational structures refer to departments or grade-level configurations. In elementary schools, organizational structure is based on grade levels and non-core subjects. In both cases, organizational structures have a bearing on scheduling, physical location, and personnel. For example, secondary schools that have "houses" are typically better positioned to deal with student emotional issues. A student's teachers would have better access to one another—in a physical sense—to provide services and support. At the elementary level, an organizational structure that allows grade-level teachers to work in physical proximity to special needs' teachers is conducive to better collaboration on students learning requirements.

**Student Discipline Practices:** From a student motivation perspective—as well as a building climate perspective—the ways in which a school handles discipline directly impact teaching and learning. First, high expectations with reasonable consequences must be clear to all students and teachers. Second, fair procedures must be followed. Teachers need to know that if they send students out of their classrooms that they must follow procedures, as well. The attitude at a school is more productive, though, when the emphasis is taken off of rules and consequences and instead put on fairness, kindness, and other positive elements. When everyone sees that the school values equity more than it values rule-following, for example, people in the school will be more inclined to consider the value of the rules when they must be considered.

### Skill 9.6 Identify strategies for using resources within the community (e.g., school-business partnerships) to enhance education and promote achievement.

The student's capacity and potential for academic success within the overall educational experience are products of her or his total environment: classroom and school system; home and family; neighborhood and community in general. All of these segments are interrelated and can be supportive, one of the other, or divisive, one against the other. As a matter of course, the teacher will become familiar with all aspects of the system, the school and the classroom pertinent to the students' educational experience. This would include not only process and protocols but also the availability of resources provided to meet the academic, health and welfare needs of students. But it is incumbent upon the teacher to look beyond the boundaries of the school system to identify additional resources as well as issues and situations which will effect (directly or indirectly) a student's ability to succeed in the classroom.

**Examples of Resources**
- Libraries
- Museums
- Zoos
- Planetariums
- Businesses
- Clubs
- Societies and civic organizations
- Community outreach programs of private businesses and corporations and of government agencies
- Departments of social services operating within the local community

These can provide a variety of materials and media as well as possible speakers and presenters, and these can provide background and program information relevant to social issues which may be impacting individual students. And this can be a resource for classroom instruction regarding life skills, at-risk behaviors, etc.

Initial contacts for resources outside of the school system will usually come from within the system itself: from administration; teacher organizations; department heads; and other colleagues. Teachers can scrutinize the learning outcomes for the courses they teach to determine which outside agencies can provide extra resources for the school. Most of these agencies have literature that could be distributed in class or will come to the school to give presentations to groups of students. Some of them are also in a position to come into the school to teach classes, such as nurses who can teach aspects of the Health curriculum.

There may be a wealth of resources in the community that will provide information to add to the learning situations in the form of field trips for the students. When students can visit a location and become involved in hands-on activities, this enriches the learning experience and creates a lasting impression.

See also Skill 6.3

**Skill 9.7      Describe how to use technology and information systems to enrich the school's curriculum and instruction.**

One of the major impediments to establishing successful computer-based applications in schools is the lack of careful and extensive planning (Picciano, 1998). Kearsley (1995) wrote that the role of leadership in schools requires the ability to identify how computers can improve the efficiency of school operations. He continues, stating that a school leader must adjudicate computer use so that it serves the interests and needs of all school constituents. A specific list of competencies is associated with school leaders' ability to make policy and decisions governing the use of technological resources. A school leader must have knowledge of computer terminology, a knowledge of instructional and administrative applications, and an understanding of the impact of technology in the school environment.

An essential ingredient of good administration is planning. A school leader must plan for all aspects of integrating technology in a school. The determination of hardware and software are essentials in the process. The identification of goals and objectives for the introduction of technology is important. Missing components from a computer system that is expected to be implemented thwarts the ability of technology to be used to its potential. To ensure that computer implementation proceeds unhindered from problems, it is important to have policy statements and procedures governing technology.

The introduction of technology in a learning environment should not be based on technology for technology's sake, but rather on a calculated and planned agenda to which technology will be used to address identified needs. Will the introduction of technology address productivity, administrative functions, or will its introduction address student achievement? In each of the situations, a different set of resources, policies, and decisions regarding the implementation will need to occur. An administrator's depth of understanding regarding salient issues in each area is required to make informed decisions.

The classroom environment, in many instances, is characterized by teachers being at the center of attention, performing, and students acting as passive vessels, consuming knowledge and information. A learning environment characterized by technology, however, offers a much different scene, and, of course, a very different mode of instruction and interaction. When technology is a part of the learning process, a different model of teaching and learning unfolds. It is a student-centered, constructivist model, where students are challenged to engage in higher order thinking skills, interact with technology at their own level, and learn what interests them.

Jonassen (1996) discusses how computers in the classroom become powerful tools for learning when they are applied in the learning process. Specific applications, like databases and spreadsheets, become key elements of the learning process, allowing students to integrate and relate content ideas (Jonassen, 1996).

See also Skill 9.2

**COMPETENCY 10.0 UNDERSTAND STRATEGIES FOR PROMOTING PROFESSIONAL GROWTH AND DEVELOPMENT AND STRATEGIES FOR CREATING A POSITIVE SCHOOL CULTURE FOR LEARNING.**

**Skill 10.1** Demonstrate knowledge of research-based professional development that includes authentic problems and tasks, mentoring, coaching, conferencing, and other techniques for promoting adult learning and developing new knowledge and skills in the workplace.

In the research on schools as organizations over the past two decades, significant accomplishments have been made in characterizing teachers as professionals, schools as learning communities, and educational work as complex. What does all this amount to? The more we see teachers as professionals—who can make individualized decisions regarding their work in the classroom, even if they must follow prescribed curriculum—the more they are willing to demonstrate commitment to their work. This is important for many reasons.

First, considering that we are asking teachers, principals, and schools to utilize assessment data more frequently to make instructional decisions, we need to provide a climate and context in which to do so. Let's say, for example, that a teacher is told that he or she must use assessment data to make instructional decisions—but then is provided a curriculum to follow and told not to deviate from it. Is this teacher going to feel that his or her instructional decisions will be valued? What happens when this teacher noticed a problem that needs to be addressed—and the curriculum provides no assistance for that particular problem? Do the messages from the school indicate that the teacher's first priority is the curriculum? And if so, when problems arise, will the teacher be willing to expend energy to find solutions?

Second, if teachers feel supported in making decisions based on data, do they have the resources and tools in which to do so? Many critics argue that teachers who have entered school systems prior to the huge emphasis on data use will struggle more with making instructional decisions based on assessment results. Principals, staff developers, and teacher-leaders must be called on to provide assistance and motivation so that all faculty will feel supported in this very new and complex challenge.

Third, when teachers are committed to their work as professionals, they will see greater value in learning new instructional techniques and experimenting with assessment ideas. Learning new tricks for the trade of teaching takes significant time—and it also opens teachers up to a host of problems when something does not work right in the classroom. As professionals, teachers need to feel safe with experimenting with new approaches to teaching, and they need multiple avenues for feedback and assistance.

So, how do we create communities of professionals in our schools? How do we help teachers become more committed to their work in their classrooms? Many people would argue that schools have to encounter cultural shifts that allow professional discussions to not only take place—but to be demanded by teachers. Typically, professional discussion about student learning and teacher technique is said to take place in Professional Learning Communities (PLCs). PLCs take many different forms, but they all have one thing in common: Teachers—working as professionals—to problem solve, dialogue, and question all in regard to instruction. For example, some PLCs operate through reading groups. In reading groups, teachers select professional books to read and discuss on typically a monthly basis. A group of English teachers might select a new publication about student portfolios, read the book on their own, and then discuss both the content of the book and the possible applications of the book to the school and to each of their classrooms.

Another common format for PLCs is group scoring sessions. Let's say a group of 10th Grade Social Studies teachers assign their students a similar end-of-unit writing project. They utilize the same assignment, have the same standards, and assess the work according to the same rubric. As a group, the teachers can score these essays together, discussing similar problems they notice, seeking help from one another on making sense of quality, and brainstorming solutions so that they can better prepare students for the next assessment.

The list of options for PLCs goes on and on. Any type of format is possible, so long as it focuses teachers on student learning (i.e., it would be counter-productive to have teachers sit around and complain about certain "problem" students, for example). The trick of making PLCs work, though, is that teachers have to feel supported as professionals in all aspects of their work—not just in these PLC settings.

**Skill 10.2　Identify procedures for working collaboratively with school personnel to develop and implement comprehensive professional growth plans.**

Effective teachers plan for instructional delivery even if they have taught the same lessons before. They continue to improve upon the presentation by finding new or additional materials to bring new energy into the teaching and learning process. As part of teaching, planning is a deliberate act that can be long-range, short range, formal, and informal.

Long-range planning, such as units or semester plans, takes into account milestones, standards, and major goals over a period of time. It takes into account the nature of the content to be covered, the process in which the content will be covered, the approaches to take at varying stages, the activities to be used as well as resources needed. Short-term planning consists of daily lesson plans, weekly or even monthly plans or units for instruction. Daily and weekly lesson plans are usually more detailed and specific, while unit plans can be more general and serve as the source of the daily lesson plans. Daily, weekly or unit written plans, grouping of students, instructional materials selection, activities for specific experiences to attain specific goals, student assessment, and the like are all part of the planning process

The formal aspect of planning has greater breadth and scope, which includes long-term and short-term written plans. The informal aspect of planning is continuous and includes teachers ideas' that emerge (1) as resourceful teachers gather materials they believe will be useful for learning, (2) as teachers consider varying experiences that could be used for specific students, (3) as they share ideas with other professionals, (4) and as they toy with ideas on how to do things better. Whether long-term or short-term, effective planning begins with a goals and objectives specification for learning. Once the goals and objectives are specified, instructional strategies and materials should be selected, followed by the appropriate evaluation techniques to assess learning.

Instructional planning also involves organizing the students for learning. Whole group and small group instruction are beneficial in different ways. Whole group instruction is beneficial when the teacher is introducing new concepts and skills while small group instruction is recommended when teachers want to ensure that the student master the material or that thorough learning has taken place. Students may be placed in ability groups for short-term activities. Long-term ability grouping such as tracking should be avoided to allow children, who would have been place in regular track and higher college bound track, to benefit from each other by learning together.

Generally, teachers believe that ability groups save time and allow focusing on the specific collective needs of the students. However, it is recognized that approaches such as cooperative groups at all levels of schooling where students of mixed ability work together result in higher academic achievement. Other added benefits include improved time on task and increased interpersonal skills. Cooperative grouping as a dominant approach to instruction does not negate the need to use, on a short-term basis, homogeneous groupings to work with children within the classroom. The teacher must be careful that short-term ability groups remain as such and that the lower groups still receive high quality instruction.

Instruction should be clear and focused, beginning with an orientation to the lesson and instructional objectives presented to students in a language that they can easily understand. The relationship between the current lesson and previous lessons should be made. Key points should be emphasized, concepts defined with examples and non-examples, cause and effect relationships established, and careful attention given to learning styles through the use of appropriate materials and strategies for learning. Students should be provided ample time for guided and independent practice in the form of class work and homework, and strategies to develop higher level thinking skills are used.

Effective teacher expressions are key in the verbal aspect of instructional delivery. Enthusiasm and challenges that are clearly articulated are as important as the planned delivery of instruction of itself. Instruction, demonstrated through body language that expresses interest and caring, may also contribute to verbal effectiveness. The teacher should use good verbal skills for effective questioning to monitor understanding, to keep student focus, and to give feedback to reinforce learning progress.

See also Skill 10.1

**Skill 10.3  Recognize how to evaluate professional development programs to ensure that they advance the school's vision of learning.**

Professional development opportunities for teacher performance improvement or enhancement in instructional practices are essential for creating comprehensive learning communities. In order to promote the vision, mission and action plans of school communities, teachers must be given the toolkits to maximize instructional performances. The development of student-centered learning communities that foster the academic capacities and learning synthesis for all students should be the fundamental goal of professional development for teachers.

The level of professional development may include traditional district workshops that enhance instructional expectations for teachers or the more complicated multiple day workshops given by national and state educational organizations to enhance the federal accountability of skill and professional development for teachers. Most workshops on the national and state level provide clock hours that can be used to renew certifications for teachers every five years. Typically, 150 clock hours is the standard certification number needed to provide a five year certification renewal, so teachers must attend and complete paperwork for a diversity of workshops that range from 1-50 clock hours according to the timeframe of the workshops.

Most districts and schools provide in-service professional development opportunities for teachers during the school year dealing with district objectives/expectations and relevant workshops or classes that can enhance the teaching practices for teachers. Clock hours are provided with each class or workshop and the type of professional development being offered to teachers determines clock hours. Each year, schools are required to report the number of workshops, along with the participants attending the workshops to the Superintendent's office for filing. Teachers collecting clock hour forms are required to file the forms to maintain certification eligibility and job eligibility.

The research by the National Association of Secondary Principals,' "Breaking Ranks II: Strategies for Leading High School Reform" created the following multiple listing of educational practices needed for expanding the professional development opportunities for teachers:

- Interdisciplinary instruction between subject areas
- Identification of individual learning styles to maximize student academic performance
- Training teachers in understanding and applying multiple assessment formats and implementations in curriculum and instruction
- Looking at multiple methods of classroom management strategies
- Providing teachers with national, federal, state and district curriculum expectations and performance outcomes
- Identifying the school communities' action plan of student learning objectives and teacher instructional practices
- Helping teachers understand how to use data to impact student learning goals and objectives
- Teaching teachers on how to disaggregate student data in improving instruction and curriculum implementation for student academic equity and access
- Develop leadership opportunities for teachers to become school and district trainers to promote effective learning communities for student achievement and success

In promoting professional development opportunities for teachers that enhance student achievement, the bottom line is that teachers must be given the time to complete workshops at no or minimal costs. School and district budgets must include financial resources to support and encourage teachers to engage in mandatory and optional professional development opportunities that create a "win-win" learning experience for students.

Whether a teacher is using criterion-referenced, norm-referenced or performance-based data to inform and impact student learning and achievement, the more important objective is ensuring that teachers know how to effectively use the data to improve and reflect upon existing teaching instructions. The goal of identifying ways for teachers to use the school data is simple, "Is the teacher's instructional practice improving student learning goals and academic success?"

School data can include demographic profiling, cultural and ethic academic trends, state and/or national assessments, portfolios, academic subject pre-post assessment and weekly assessments, projects, and disciplinary reports. By looking at trends and discrepancies in school data, teachers can ascertain whether they are meeting the goals and objectives of the state, national, and federal mandates for school improvement reform and curriculum implementation.

Assessments can be used to motivate students to learn and shape the learning environment to provide learning stimulation that optimizes student access to learning. Butler and McMunn (2006) have shown that "factors that help motivate students to learn are 1) Involving students in their own assessment, 2) Matching assessment strategies to student learning, and 3) Consider thinking styles and using assessments to adjust the classroom environment in order to enhance student motivation to learn." Teachers can shape the way students learn by creating engaging learning opportunities that promote student achievement.

**Skill 10.4** Recognize the importance of encouraging reflective practice for one's self and staff, including reflection on the role that one's own attitudes, biases, and preconceptions play in interactions with students, colleagues, and others.

## *Reflection*

The very nature of the teaching profession—the yearly cycle of doing the same thing over and over again—creates the tendency to fossilize, to quit growing, to become complacent. The teachers who are truly successful are those who have built into their own approach to their jobs and to their lives safeguards against that. They see themselves as constant learners. They believe that learning never ends. They are careful never to teach their classes the same as they did the last time. They build in a tendency to reflect on what is happening to their students under their care or what happened this year as compared to last year. What worked the best? What didn't work so well? What can be changed to improve success rates? What about continuing education? Should they go for another degree or should they enroll in more classes?

There are several avenues a teacher might take in order to assess his or her own teaching strengths and weaknesses. Early indicators that a self-evaluation might be necessary include having several students that are not understanding a concept. In such a case, a teacher might want to go over his or her lesson plans to make sure the topic is being covered thoroughly and in a clear fashion. Brainstorming other ways to tackle the content might also help. Speaking to other teachers, asking how they teach a certain skill, might give new insight to one's own teaching tactics.

Any good teacher will understand that he or she needs to self-evaluate and adjust his or her lessons periodically. Signing up for professional courses or workshops can also help a teacher assess his or her abilities by opening one's eyes to new ways of teaching.

## *Observations*

It has often been said that "everyone is a critic," and this is certainly true when one is a teacher. Students, other teachers, supervisors, and parents will all have something to say about the way a teacher handles any given situation or subject. If you are hearing the same critiques from many different sources, then there is probably some truth behind what is being said. Take a step back and examine the criticism. Putting personal feelings aside is key; look at the mechanics of the problem. Work with your supervisor, your mentor, and/or your colleagues to restructure your lesson plans or your way of interacting with the students.

Even when a piece of feedback seems spurious, a fair response is to thank the person for their thoughts and say that you will take them into consideration. Always give the critic the benefit of the doubt; chances are they have your and your students' best interests at heart. If a discussion becomes heated, everyone will lose sight of the goal: to make your classes the best they can be so that your students meet the standards they need to meet in order to progress, learn, and grow.

In terms of utilizing feedback from observations and assessments for growth, it is important to understand how to turn feedback into specific advice for moving forward. When feedback comes from supervisors (principals, for example) or instructional coaches, it is important for teachers to ask specifically, "What do you recommend I do next time?" This way, teachers will get specific recommendations.

On a more personal level, teachers can turn feedback into progress by assessing the situations, evaluating their knowledge for impacting change, and seeking specific solutions to problems. Teachers simply cannot improve if they do not have the knowledge for improving. This is often the case, and it is very important for teachers to realize that they can—and should—seek new knowledge. Professional development is critical in every stage of a teachers' career, and seeking new methods should be seen as a sign of strength.

**Skill 10.5  Demonstrate knowledge of principles and procedures for effective personnel evaluation and developmental supervision.**

Career and staff development refers to the continual process of increasing the skills of professionals within the organization. In this day and age, the methods of staff development are extensive; however, the evidence of impact of most methods is sparse. It is important to understand what works and what doesn't work when finding new ways to improve the skills of school staff members.

Let us first differentiate between career and staff development. Career development is deliberate training and practice meant to move a person into another career stage. For example, teachers who feel the call to school leadership typically go back to school, earn a master's degree, and become certified to be a principal. Usually, this process takes place outside the schooling organization (at universities), however, some districts are experimenting with their own "in-house" training programs.

Staff development, the domain typically of school districts themselves, is meant to increase the skills of people already in current positions. So, while teachers may have been trained as teachers in certification programs, they will constantly need to be taught new strategies, skills, and techniques to use in their classrooms. Furthermore, good staff development helps to motivate teachers to improve their practice further.

The old model of staff development consisted of teaching discrete skills to teachers, often in impersonal large groups. Often, staff development topics were irrelevant to most teachers; typically, they had no follow-up for teachers to discuss or reflect new learning. Even though this is considered the "old" model of staff development, it is still used in many schools and districts across the country. Slowly but surely, schools and districts are learning that this model does not provide the impact needed to improve teacher practice and student learning.

The new model of staff development focuses on specific skills tailored to specific teacher needs. It includes significant follow-up time, sustained learning, and collaborative discussion. This model is specific in that it typically deals with individual subject areas or teacher techniques related to a particular grade level or subject. For example, instead of teaching all teachers in a high school about a particular technique, each department would learn things related to what they typically teach.

Additionally, the new model of staff development focuses a lot on sustaining learning. Instead of providing teachers with a single training session, the new model of staff development encourages that the topic is brought up a few times throughout a school year. This might, for example, allow teachers to learn the strategy at the beginning of the year so that they can try it out for a few months. Then, possibly half-way throughout the year, the topic can be brought up again in a staff development session so that teachers can learn new strategies to deal with some of the problems they have experienced with it in their "trial" period. Later in the year, teachers can get together and further reflect on the strategy and plan out how they will use it in upcoming years.

Staff needs and satisfaction should be surveyed on a regular basis. During the school improvement process, staff development needs should be identified and included in the plan to help acquire funding and other resources as necessary. Staff should be surveyed at least once per year to determine their interests, weaknesses, and preference for development. Many schools now have staff development committees that represent the entire staff and assist the administration in the planning of development. Each development session should also conclude with an evaluation to determine the usefulness of the session.

Professional development is a crucial component of successful school change. New standards and accountability systems demand so much more of teachers than ever before, and many teachers simply do not have the skills or knowledge to implement the many things they are not responsible for.

Significant research on professional development has concluded that among the worst ways of helping teachers learn new skills or knowledge is by putting them through a "one-shot" staff in-service. A staff in-service is a session that focuses on a particular strategy or technique for the classroom. Sometimes, these sessions are one to two hours. Other times, they are five to six hours. In either case, these sessions give teachers no reason utilize their new learning, nor do they take into account adult learning theory. Adult learning theory suggests that adults learn best when they have an immediate application to their learning. Since most staff in-services have no follow-up (i.e., discussion about how the strategy worked, one-on-one coaching, etc.), most teachers will not try the new strategies. After all, they feel safe and comfortable with their current strategies.

Effective professional development consists of deep learning across time with significant opportunities for follow-up, discussion, assistance, and reflection. Often, when professional development sessions, on one topic, are spread out over a whole year (perhaps, one three hour session per month), teachers have more reason to follow through with trying new ideas in the classroom. When schools add components of Professional Learning Communities—group configurations that allow for discussion of new learning—then teachers have more opportunity to reflect, discuss, and question the new ideas. This allows teachers to work through personal concerns and problems they might be facing in their classrooms.

Consistently, teachers report in surveys that they never have enough time to learn new strategies. Therefore, it is crucial that professional development not be limited to just a couple hours per year. Schools must provide teachers with multiple opportunities, often by re-arranging the school day, so that teachers can interact with each other and with new teaching ideas on a more regular basis.

Funds for professional development are critical, as well. While grants are often available, principals must get creative about providing teachers with the resources they need to be effective teachers. If teachers do not get these professional development resources, it directly impacts student learning. As such, principals must view allocation for professional development as a necessity—not as a financial burden.

In most schools staff members are required to attend monthly or bi-weekly career and staff development meetings in order to engage in professional development opportunities of theory and practice of effective instructional practices. With school budgets allowing only minimal expenditures for staff professional development, the selection of how to construct selection processes that are beneficial to a 100% of staff is a precarious slop for the Administrator to climb.

Most school communities have career coordinators for directing student learners towards higher education careers. The job of the Administrative leader is to develop career coordinators and pathways to provide staff professional development opportunities. It is also with the role of Administration to provide leadership opportunities for staff to practice professional theory during staff meetings or in organized leadership seminars. In some school communities, entire departments create for the entire staff, effective instructional strategies that are commonly and consistently used to promote student learning and achievement in their departments.

Having an understanding of the diversity of career and staff development practices that are incorporated into highly effective school communities is another role of the Administrator. As each Administrator in a school community assumes the role in designing and participating in educational seminars or leadership experiences that instruct staff, it is within this role modeling that future leaders and Administrators are professionally grown.

Administrators who engage in scholastic writing of educational strategies that move communities forward are coveted in school Districts. The ability to present new paradigms and theoretical constructs of leadership and professional designs demonstrates an Administrators ability to engage in scholarly professional leadership that is proactive for everyone in the school community.

Career and professional development connections must provide additional tools for the toolkits of staff and students to provide collaborative and participatory experiences that define and exemplify the goals and mission of the school. When Administrators provided professional development that is inclusive of cultural identity and ethnic diversity, everyone wins in being presented with a global opportunity in understanding our common humanity.

All career and professional development opportunities that Administrators can provide for staff will contribute to their educational portfolios of 150 hours that must be submitted for teaching certificate renewal with a specified timeframe by the Superintendent's office. Professional development grows the leadership component of all stakeholders in the school community, so for Administrators, creating that development is both reflective and proactive.

**Skill 10.6 Describe how to create a personal development plan that reflects commitment to life-long learning and best practices and that takes advantage of varied resources for continuing professional development.**

A personal development plan can show the reflection and demonstrated performance in order to enable teachers to focus their efforts on critical issues. The personal development plan can enhance this process. By creating their own personal development plan educators can show their supervisors the growth of their teaching expertise Included in the portfolio can be audio clips of students' oral assignments, video demonstrations of how the physically arrangement the classroom to encourage learning, and also PowerPoint slides from lessons. Educators can also add newsletters, examples of how students had met standards on given assignments, and links to web resources.

The teachers' personal development plan can help schools and districts plan better professional development opportunities. For example; by recording their attempts to employ new teaching strategies such as guided reading and interactive writing., other faculty members could judge the successfulness of the teaching strategy and implement it in their classrooms. Just as student portfolios show how a student is progressing toward meeting academic standards, a developmental plan can also show how a school as a whole, is progressing towards its learning goals. The developmental plan is centered around the goals of the school that are to be met. For example, if a school's goal is to "achieve global awareness," each teacher should carefully record and reflect on activities they have met to achieve this goal.

The personal development plan should support two important levels of reflection. First, the school as a community is aware of what is being accomplished to meet the goal, so the faculty can reflect on what other steps they may need to address the goal. Second, the faculty is aware of how it is progressing by considering the individual reflections of the teachers and by observing the results as a whole. Faculty can decide what measures need to be implemented to meet their goals.

**Skill 10.7    Analyze strategies for creating and maintaining a positive school culture that draws on the diversity of the school community and fosters the belief that all children can learn and succeed.**

The dynamics of classroom management generally correspond to the leadership styles of individual teachers. An autocratic leadership style yields a punitive, harsh, and critical classroom environment. A laissez-faire leadership style, on the other hand, yields a permissive classroom environment where disorder and anarchy dominate. The democratic leadership style is more characteristic of today's school reform in which a participatory classroom is expected. The democratic leadership style yields a classroom that is firm but friendly, encouraging and stimulating, caring and guiding, and most of all fairness prevails as a way of resolving conflicts (Moore, 1995).

Regardless of the discipline model endorsed by the school, the effectively managed classroom follows basic principles generated by research. Discipline models such as the Behavior Modification, Glasser Model, Lee Canter Assertive Discipline Model, and other models dealing with prevention and correction of misbehavior may produce good results based on the teacher's leadership/management style and philosophy. Yet, a general focus on procedures to manage and prevent behavioral problems may prove much more effective than many of the leading models. Current educational research supporting effective school concepts, such as beginning class on time, setting up classroom procedures and routines, and keeping desk and storage spaces clean and organized from the very beginning of the school year, seems to set the initial expectation of order.

Making smooth transitions from one activity to another, or from one class to another in a quick and orderly manner cuts down on idle time that generally encourages misbehavior. Making eye contact with students, being polite to the students and reinforcing positive interaction with and among the students all provides a healthy learning atmosphere. Having a general sense of what is going on in the classroom at all times, giving verbal and nonverbal encouragement, and stopping misbehavior in a firm and consistent manner as soon as they occur, without the use of threats, conveys constancy of purpose and expectations. Careful instructional planning and pace of teaching may also reduce opportunities for problems in the classroom. Additionally, involving the parents as partners in the education of their children serves as a prevention to discipline problems and as a support to continuous involvement in the solutions of problems as they occur.

## COMPETENCY 11.0 UNDERSTAND PRINCIPLES OF ORGANIZATIONAL MANAGEMENT, BUDGETING, RESOURCE UTILIZATION, FINANCIAL MANAGEMENT, AND TECHNOLOGY USE.

### Skill 11.1 Examine ways to apply knowledge of organizational development and data management to optimize learning for all students.

Educators and other school staff can use individual data management to demonstrate their work over time. Likewise, teachers and administrators can collaborate to create a digital school portfolio, where they can see and learn from each other's organizational developmental work. In both cases, the school's work can be represented with rich, varied, and concrete examples, rather than with scores on a school report card. Thus, schools can use data management as a tool for collecting the data that can enhance school improvement.
Data can be used in the following methods

1. **Change the curriculum.** Close analysis of exam questions can reveal that some students are weak in a particular subject. If state test scores also mirror those same results, changes need to be implemented.
2. **Improve instruction.** Item study by objectives can also reveal the strengths and weaknesses of individual teachers. Data can provide a resource for improving instruction, thereby prompting teachers to examine teaching strategies and materials.
3. **Address individual student weaknesses**. Collect data regarding the individual strengths and weaknesses of our students. This information can be used to increase individual achievement by placing students in the most appropriate courses.

By using these methods educators will be able to increase student achievement. The data from the common assessments allow teachers to see the individual strengths and weaknesses of their students. Effective data management should focus on student growth and the growth of the school. Successful data should be:

- In a format that makes sense to those who need to use it to improve.
- Readily accessible.
- A reflection equal in importance to the performance or measure.

Data collection can help a school determine what changes have helped it to succeed.. As part of the process, educators can used their own tests as the foundation for creating common assessments and an indicator to new common course objectives.

Today, almost every school administrator is using data as a guiding force. Daily decisions about curriculum, student grouping, and almost any other facet of school life have data at their foundation. Data is used to determine everything from curricular issues to dances and the number of pep assemblies. Even a school's code of conduct is adjusted according to the data that can be collected about student infractions during the course of the school year.

**Skill 11.2　Analyze ways to apply long-range planning procedures and problem-solving skills to promote effective and equitable resource allocation that focuses on teaching and learning.**

Many principals do not have control over entire personnel budgets (e.g., usually, district human resource offices control personnel issues at school sites), but schools often do have discretion over many resources, including materials, additional funding, and support services. In an age of accountability for student achievement, accountability must also be in place for the use of funds.
For a principal to make sense of the instructional needs at a school, various analyses must be done. First, by looking at student achievement, principals can see which groups of students require more resources. When referring to resources, the term equity is often used. This term may imply that all students should get the same resources—or same level of monetary allocations. The current thinking, though, is that in order to reach certain standards, different students will require different resources. Therefore, when leaders think about allocating resources effectively and equitably, it is helpful to consider the term adequacy. In other words, leaders can ask the question: What is adequate in providing each student what he/she needs to reach standards at high levels?

Another way to analyze instructional needs is to examine how money is allocated to various parts of a campus and to reflect on which areas need resources reallocated so that student achievement is the first priority. Of course, when doing this, principals face great scrutiny from stakeholders that are negatively affected by shifts in allocations. Principals are more successful in this work when they enlist the support of a variety of stakeholders.

Finally, it is critical that principals make their practices public—to faculty, to parents, to the district, and to the community. Of course, small monetary issues are outside the interest of most stakeholders, however, the information should be available—and even discussed—as school funds are derived from taxpayers. Furthermore, when monetary decisions are public, support for decisions are much more easily acquired.

Many educators have found that outside funding, in the form of grants, allows them to provide their students with educational experiences and materials their own districts can't afford. Unfortunately, many school districts are limited in the number of state and federal grants in which they can apply for. Grant writing can take months, in some instances a year or more, before you receive any funds, depending on the costs applied for and the amount of funding,

Educators can start the process by searching online and library resources. They can also consider local government agencies, educational and civic organizations, and also private and commercial businesses as possible sources of funding. Often times the best funding sources are philanthropic organizations, education-related businesses, state department of education programs, and the U.S. Department of Education programs.

Documentation needed for the project:

- **Mission Statement**. Identify the project's potential outcome.
- **Goals and Objectives**. Make sure they are specific and measurable.
- **Planned Assessment Tools**. Be specific.
- **Framework Information.** Identify the need for your project with demographics and test results
- **Required materials, supplies, and personnel.**
- **Total Cost of project**.

Having this information in hand will make it much easier to locate appropriate funding sources -- and to complete the grant application when the time comes. Speak personally with a contact person involved with the funding who can answer your questions and provide advice and guidance. Be sure to ask how projects are reviewed, how decisions are made, and how and when funding is dispersed. Develop a relationship with your contact person and keep the lines of communication open throughout the application process.

**Procedures**

- Make sure the stated goals are measurable and realistic.
- Educators and administrators should have a clearly defined plan for their project.
- Find out in advance what kinds of projects the granter will and will not fund.
- Create and write material that will be impressive to the granter in order for your grant stand out from the many submissions.
- Statistics should be included to prove your points.

## Skill 11.3 Identify characteristics of school budgets, stages in the budgeting process, and strategies for working effectively with stakeholders to develop the school budget.

Administrators are required to understand and implement the processes of planning, developing, implementing and evaluating a district budget. The district budget is provided by the legislature and is dispensed according to the number of students in school buildings on October 1 of each school year. The budget includes a specific allocation amount for regular education students and greater amounts for special education and bilingual students. The amount for special education students is generally around 4K per student which includes additional monies for Instructional Aids and special IEP (Individual Education Plans) provisions that the student may require. The bilingual budgets are also allocated to provide additional resources to Instructional Assistants and provide additional resource materials for students.

Building a school budget based on the monies distributed to each school by a District is difficult. A proactive administrator creates an excel sheet showing budget allocations for each department over a three year span. Showing the trends and usage of monies can indicate where shifts of funding need to occur to maximize program outputs for both staff and students. Administrators bring budget decision making to the Building Leadership Team who votes to accept or reallocate funding amongst the various departments and/or programs.

Since monies are so tight for schools, budgets are huge for schools struggling to implement basic academic core programs and provide intervention programs for struggling students. Most school budgets are designed to cover the basics, so an Administrator must cover the basics with funding before any extra monies can be given to programs or additional staffing. The majority of the school's budget goes to staffing and then is used to finance additional funding proposals voted on by the Building Leadership Team.

Within the budget are additional dollars given to Special Education Programs and Bilingual Programs. This additional money will go towards providing specialized Instructional Assistants who can support student learning as interpreters or in other duties as assigned. The Administrator who can creatively use a budget to address the majority of instructional and facilitator concerns in a building is truly a transformational leader and constructive accountant.

School administrators must be knowledgeable in basic accounting principles to provide appropriate fiscal management for the economic and efficient operation of the school. Accounting is the process used by administrators to record, present, summarize, and interpret accurate records of the financial data collected by the school through its daily operation. These basic accounting principles lead practicing administrators to the recognition of revenues and expenditures for the pre-established accounts of the school.

General principles of school cost accounting require the utilization of an accrual basis for accounting rather than a cash basis. This means that the financial transactions of the school must be recorded as revenues or expenditures at the time the transaction occurs and there should never be cash exchanged for goods or services. This generally accepted principle is called the accrual basis of accounting. In this process, revenues earned at the time of the transaction become assets, and expenditures become liabilities, regardless of when the cash receipt or reimbursement occurs. In this system of accounting assets are inventory, investments, accounts receivable, building and fixed equipment, furniture, motor vehicles, etc. while liabilities are salaries, benefits, accounts payable, construction contracts, etc. Unlike private enterprises for profit where there is owners' equity, schools are owned by the taxpayers. Therefore, balances are known as fund equity, which include reserves, retained earnings, contributed capital, and other fund equity.

Schools must adhere to specific rules governing their internal funds as prescribed by State Board Rules. All school organizations must be accountable for receipts and expenditures of funds obtained from the public. Additionally, sound business practices are expected for all financial transactions of the school. For example, in an effort to raise money to benefit programs of the school, fund-raising activities should not conflict with the programs administered by the school board.

All purchases from internal funds must be authorized by the principal or designee and district's pre-approved, serially numbered receipt forms must be used to record any cash received and to record the accounting transaction. Each school must have a bank checking account and each monthly statement must be reconciled as soon as it is received. Each account should have two authorized check signers, one being the principal. The principal should be never pre-sign checks or purchase orders, under any circumstances. Monthly written financial reports must be made for the purpose of school decision-making, and annual reports must be made for the district's annual financial statement.

The sponsors of classes, clubs, or department student activities (such as athletic events, musical, and the like) are responsible for providing the financial documents and records to the principal or designee. The collection received must be deposited in the school internal fund in the respective classified account (athletics, music, art, Latin Club, and others). All disbursements by the dub or organization must be made by check from internal funds. A financial report must be filed with the principal's office at the close of each fundraising activity.

Records and documents of school financial transactions used for its internal fund and accounts must be examined periodically through the auditing process. This auditing process, whether internal or external, provides an adequate safeguard to preserve the property of the public school system. This process secures evidence of propriety of completed transactions; it determines whether all transactions have been recorded, whether these transactions have been accurately recorded in the appropriate accounts, and whether the statements have been drawn from the accounts.

Good auditing reviews are the result of excellent accounting practices. Drake and Roe (1994) define the accounting cycle as continuous and inclusive of the processes of documenting, analyzing, recording, and summarizing financial information. Documenting includes recording all financial transactions including the authority or initiator of the transaction, ensuring that the debt incurred is within the limit of allotment, that every financial transaction is identified with a unit or fund, and that each fund is restrictive and limited in use. The process of analyzing requires that each transaction is analyzed and classified into debits and credits, and that each debit and credit is referenced to a specific account under the affected fund.

The school operation must be very conscious of its fiscal control to avoid over-expenditure and maintain a positive balance in each of its accounts. Therefore, an encumbrance system must be used to charge each purchase order, contract or salary to an appropriation. Once paid, these transactions are canceled and ceased to be an encumbrance as soon as the liability is recorded.

Future resources for education are planned through student enrollment forecasts. From the appropriated funds, the district builds its budget. At this point, the budget becomes an important device for translating the educational plan into a financial plan. The budget is, in effect, the translation of prioritized educational needs into a financial plan, which is interpreted for the public in such a way that when it is formally adopted, it expresses the kind of educational program the community is willing to support financially and morally for a one-year period (Drake and Roe, 1994).

The budget must be managed through a financial system of accounting. Revenues are categorized by sources. Sources of revenues can be either federal, state or local. Expenditures on the other hand, are categorized by dimensions which include funds or account groups, objects, functions, facility, project, and reporting.

The funds or account groups are accounting entities with a self-balancing set of accounts that supports specific school activities to attain specific objectives. Therefore, funds or accounts can only be used for specified purposes.

At the school level the district allots a certain number of dollars based on a predetermined local formula to allow expenditures from the General Fund related to the day-to-day operation of the school. Additionally, the school may have an Activity account and a School Internal account. The Activity account is derived from class fees, athletic contests and events, plays, yearly photos, and other special programs. While the proceeds belong to the school, they must be used for students' learning benefits such as award ribbons, trophies, and the like. These proceeds must be identified and accounted in the same manner as any other funds of the school.

The school internal account usually originates from vending machine sales in the teacher's lounge and from related faculty activities and must be used to benefit faculty and staff. Again, these proceeds must be identified and accounted for in the same manner as any other funds or accounts of the school.

Zero-based is a form of budgeting in which all expenditures must be justified each new period, as opposed to only explaining the amounts requested in excess of the previous period's funding.

**Skill 11.4　Apply knowledge of effective procedures for managing scarce resources and creative strategies for seeking new resources to support student learning, including grant money and other nonbudgetary resources.**

There are three major sources of school funding for school districts. Approximately 50% of the financial support comes from state sources, 43% from local sources and 7% from the federal government.

The state support for education comes from the state's general revenue funds (mainly from taxes), state school trust funds, lottery, and other funds that are appropriated to meet the needs of categorical programs and specific allocations. Other state funds come from proceeds from licensing of motor vehicles and gross utility taxes which support capital outlay, racing commission funds and other minor sources such as mobile home licensing.

Local support for education originates when the school boards levy the millage required for the local tax effort, which is determined by the state statutory process. Additionally, voters may approve other tax levies such as maintenance bonds and operation user fees. Federal funds to support education are administered by the Board of Education. These funds are provided to support federal mandates such as the National School Lunch Act, the Americans with Disabilities Act, and others.

From the appropriated funds, the district builds its budget. At this point, the budget becomes an important device for translating the educational plan into a financial plan. The budget is, in effect, the translation of prioritized educational needs into a financial plan, which is interpreted for the public in such a way that when it is formally adopted, it expresses the kind of educational program the community is willing to support financially and morally for a one-year period (Drake and Roe, 1994).

The funds or account groups are accounting entities with a self-balancing set of accounts that supports specific school activities to attain specific objectives. Therefore, funds or accounts can only be used for specified purposes. There are eight major funds or account groups: General Fund, Debt Services Funds, Capital Project Funds, Special Revenues Funds, Enterprise Funds, Internal Services Funds, Trust and Agency Funds, General Fixed Assets, and General-Long-Term Debt. Of all the funds, the General Fund is perhaps the most important to schools and school districts because it deals with the day-to-day operation of the school.

At the school level the district allots a certain number of dollars based on a predetermined local formula to allow expenditures from the General Fund related to the day-to-day operation of the school. Additionally, the school may have an Activity account and a School Internal account. The Activity account is derived from class fees, athletic contests and events, plays, yearly photos, and other special programs. While the proceeds belong to the school, they must be used for students' learning benefits such as award ribbons, trophies, and the like. These proceeds must be identified and accounted in the same manner as any other funds of the school.

The school internal account usually originates from vending machine sales in the teacher's lounge and from related faculty activities and must be used to benefit faculty and staff. Again, these proceeds must be identified and accounted for in the same manner as any other funds or accounts of the school.

The management of resources at a school is a very difficult task. Principals are required to maintain budgets, but also find funds from external sources, manage staffs of usually twenty to one hundred teachers (in addition to support personnel), and keep track of material resources, such as office supplies, building materials, and instructional resources. How can a principal effectively do all this? First, every district has specific policies and procedures. The first thing a new principal should do is learn those procedures. Second, where a principal has discretion, attention should be given to the school's mission and vision. When resources are not directed at meeting the vision and mission of a school, those important elements are not cultivated or attended to. Third, a principal can get the assistance of school personnel, parents, and other interested parties. Often, when schools have site based management committees, those groups can represent various school needs that are affected by resource allocation.

After taking all those issues into account, as resources are actually allocated, various procedures should be followed to keep track how things are done. For example, as staff is hired, principals can demonstrate alignment between the desired qualifications, the actual qualifications of the hired individual, the district policies, and the school's mission and vision. Doing such things helps to prevent concerns about decisions that are made.

The management of human, material, and financial resources requires careful documentation, clear policies, and effective communication. Resources of all types carry emotional and personal weight with school community members. Principals who forget about the political elements of running a school often find themselves having to repair relationships. Proactive principals, however, consider all the political elements that might surface as decisions are made.

**Skill 11.5 Identify basic principles of financial and cost accounting, methods for financial record keeping and reporting, and effective procedures for managing activity funds.**

See Skill 11.2

**Skill 11.6 Demonstrate knowledge of current technologies and information systems designed to facilitate management, business, and scheduling practices.**

The last few decades have witnessed a number of electronic devices' debut in America's public schools. These devices were grouped under the heading of technology. Each of these devices, however, has particular capabilities and advantages, that when applied in the interactive experience of teaching and learning, makes the process stimulating, relevant, and constructive. As well, when these electronic tools are applied to administrative tasks, they yield results specific to administrative goals.

Given the assortment of technology available to schools and the range of capabilities of specific devices, a challenge facing school administrators is to identify the capabilities of technological devices and make a determination regarding the utility of that technology in the school environment and its ability to ultimately accomplish school objectives.

It is rarely useful to have technology in a school but not be able to apply it to solving school problems. Since technology is expensive to acquire and maintain, it is important that the introduction of given technological devices be related to addressing specific school goals and objectives. Very little benefit, if any at all, accrues for students, teachers, and administrators when technology is idle in the school's educational process.

There are a number of administrative tasks in schools to which technology can be applied to make a time-saving and organizational difference. Some of the task areas are scheduling, accounting, purchasing, inventory, attendance, grading, testing and library automation. The appropriate use of technology in these areas can make a difference in personal productivity, efficiency, and time expenditure. An administrator's ability to identify the capabilities of technological devices available in the marketplace and to subsequently match that technology with the needs, goals, and objectives of the school's curriculum and administrative functions is a primary skill.

A computer is an electronic device that processes information, usually numeric data, according to a body of instructions. A computer system is a collection of components that includes the computer and all the devices that people use with a computer. A computer by itself is limited in relation to what it can accomplish in a work or other productivity related environment. For a computer to actualize its potential and demonstrate its capabilities requires it to operate in relation to a number of other elements. When the computer and other hardware are combined, the result is a computer system.

A computer system consists of hardware and software. The hardware component of a computer system is defined by the physical components. The software component of a computer system consists of the program applications that tell a computer what to do. In effect, a computer system is delineated by the software which provides instructions to the computer and the hardware which executes the commands.

School administrators need to be aware of the components that make up a computer system. This is because a collection of some components will allow certain productivity operations to occur, while a collection of other components will not permit an objective to be realized. The appropriate computer system must be used to accomplish specific tasks. Understanding the components of a computer system and the capabilities of those components allows administrators to determine the kind of technological devices needed in a school environment to accomplish specified objectives. Computer technology, like other tools applied to work situations, will only accomplish that which they are designed to do.

As the information age progresses, more and more organizations are relying on computer systems to accomplish the bulk of the organizational work. Schools too, have found the utility of computer systems to automate its tasks and can even be transformed by its capabilities. Computer technology is having a profound impact on the administrative functions of schools. The popularity of computers is reinforced by their ability to get tasks completed in less time and with greater efficiency. It is the software part of the computer system that is to be recognized for accomplishing certain tasks with this efficiency.

The acquisition of software is an expensive proposition. Therefore, it is not something to engage in lightly. Mistakes can be made, and mistakes have been made, in the selection and purchase of software programs intended to accomplish certain school-related objectives. Software evaluation is a critical skill for administrators. The following are several steps to keep in mind when selecting software for administrative use. One, identify the objectives that are to be accomplished by introducing the software in the school environment. Two, determine if the features and capabilities of the software match administrative goals and objectives. Three, determine if the software actually does what it describes and if what it does is what is needed. Four, be sure to ascertain that the software is compatible to the computer system in operation at the school.

In school administration, the right application must be selected and applied to the appropriate task. Seldom can curriculum applications be applied to school administrative functions with desirable results. And likewise, seldom can administrative software be applied to the curriculum. The efficiency and effectiveness of the accounting software to handle school budget matters does not translate to the teaching and learning environment of the classroom.

Lack of knowledge about how to use technology is common in the educational world (Kearsley & Lynch, 1994). It is important for the school administrator to distinguish between software designed for accounting, scheduling, information management, and communication purposes. An administrator needs to be aware of what software programs can and cannot do. A leadership role in technology requires an ability to describe major hardware and software components and to be a role model for teachers.

The information age brings with it considerations of privacy and confidentiality of group and individual information. Who has access to certain records and who should not have access to certain records are important determinations to make. The question of security is always an issue when significant amounts of information are stored in one location. Not only are enormous amounts of information stored on computers, but that information is often of a sensitive nature, meaning not everyone needs to have access to it. Information can be used in inappropriate ways especially if that information is student data. A breach of professional ethics occurs when student data is disseminated publicly to those who do not have a need for the information. The confidentiality of school records is a paramount issue. In this time of computer hackers, the security and safeguard of school records becomes a high priority. Access to computers with school records engenders another problem also, that of computer viruses. Vigilance must be exercised regarding access to prevent the possibility of a virus and, hence, the destruction of school records.

Because information can be used for inappropriate purposes, it is important for school administrators to limit access to that information and to also safeguard school data. The ways in which this can be accomplished by a school administrator are an important part of the professional repertoire of skills the administrator needs.

# TEACHER CERTIFICATION STUDY GUIDE

## COMPETENCY 12.0 UNDERSTAND PRINCIPLES OF HUMAN RESOURCE PLANNING AND MANAGEMENT.

### Skill 12.1 Demonstrate knowledge of procedures and legal requirements (e.g., EEOC, ADA) for recruiting, screening, and selecting personnel.

The educational leader in schools must possess a number of competencies. The most time-consuming competency involves human resource management and development. Educational leaders must know and understand human relations as a primary area of emphasis since schools are labor intensive and use 80% to 90% of a school's budget. Personnel management roles for school administrators have expanded over the years. An understanding of the many aspects and importance of personnel management in achieving the vision and mission of schools is absolutely essential in creating and maintaining a successful and efficient school organization.

The role of the principal in selecting instructional and non-instructional personnel is often considered the most important aspect of the many tasks that a principal performs as leader of a school, a business enterprise of greatest importance. An understanding of the significance of this function of the principal is crucial to successful schools. It is through people that the principal leads the staff in a collegial environment to achieve the mission of the school and to provide satisfying, useful work for the instructional and non-instructional personnel. The principal must possess an attitude that people are of greatest importance in organizations, particularly in schools. The personnel in a school constitute one of the set of customers that the principal must do all within her or his power to provide with the best working conditions, because the personnel will be empowered subsequently to do what is best for the students.

In selecting instructional personnel, the principal has many appropriate responsibilities. Planning, recruitment, and selection are essential aspects of securing personnel. Planning requires the principal to look at the current staff and plan for future short-term and long-term personnel needs. The planning should occur within the context of site-based management. The principal involves the school personnel in developing and revising the personnel plan for the school. All other aspects of the school's program have to be considered in this process.

Thus, personnel are looked at in terms of the current strengths and needs of the staff, students, parents, community, school district, state laws and rules, and federal rules and regulations. Facilities, equipment and other factors must be reviewed at this time also. Planning must be comprehensive and must take place well in advance of the need. The plan must allow sufficient time for the principal to prepare papers and get approval through the district system. The principal must know the process used in the school district to select personnel, including how assignments are determined and the impact of the collective negotiation contract (if there is one in the district). The plan must also provide for emergencies such as unexpected promotions, illnesses, resignations, and terminations that may occur with personnel.

Once the plan is completed, recruitment becomes the next step in obtaining personnel. Recruitment is critical to successful human resource functions of the principal. Only persons in the applicant pool may be considered for employment. Thus, it is important to recruit sufficient numbers of qualified persons for each vacancy or anticipated vacancy. The major factor should be the quality of the applicants. Each district has its own procedure for recruiting personnel. If the district does the recruiting, the principal has to inform the district early and get approval to fill the positions. The principal who has to recruit the staff must make contacts early. College and university career offices, as well as schools of education that promise the greatest possibility of supplying the kinds of personnel needed, must be contacted. Career fairs on college and university campuses, at the state level and on the local level provide other means to secure personnel. Dialogue with colleagues and current school staff also offer other opportunities to recruit new employees. Recruitment activities must use special effort if the desire is to diversify staff members. The process of obtaining staff is best handled through a selection committee.

The selection process involves screening the paperwork, interviewing candidates and checking references. Using the job-related criteria for each position, the selection process requires that each applicant's papers are evaluated against the criteria. Those applicants whose qualifications do not meet these criteria are removed from the pool of applicants. The quality of the application is also judged for such factors as neatness, comprehensiveness, job stability, competencies, English errors, and training.

Certification in field is also a crucial factor to consider in selecting staff members. These files are confidential and should only be used by trained teachers, parents, students, and others who serve on the selection committee.

Those applicants who are selected as meeting the training and experience qualifications for the position are reviewed and a determination is made to interview. The interview takes the most amount of time in the process of selecting personnel. The selection committee determines and notifies each applicant who is being interviewed of the time and location for the interview. Prior to the interview, the committee must determine questions to be asked and criteria to judge responses to the questions. Each candidate for the same position must be asked the same questions and the same criteria must apply in judging the responses. The selection committee submits the names of the most qualified applicants, usually three to five persons, listed alphabetically, to the principal.

The principal reviews the work of the committee, interviews the potential employees and does a reference check. Persons on and not on the reference list should be contacted. Visitation to the person's place of employment is another good strategy to use. Principals often contact persons at the institutions that trained the potential employee to get professional judgments about the candidate. Fingerprint records should receive attention to ensure that known criminals are not employed. The principal recommends to the superintendent the person who should be employed.

Finally, with *No Child Left Behind* and its emphasis on "highly qualified teachers," principals will have to abide by state and federal laws regarding certification levels and degrees. For example, all secondary subject-area teachers must have a degree (or demonstrate extensive competency, usually through a very rigorous exam) in the subjects they will be teaching.

A compensation and reward system is required in any organization. A compensation program is directed at attracting and maintaining quality employees, motivating employees, creating incentives for continual growth, and maintaining budgetary control in school districts (Webb, Greer, Montello, Norton, 1996). The district must have a compensation policy. Merit pay, paid leave, child care, cost of living increase, salary schedules, extracurricular stipends, early retirement plans, tax-sheltered annuity, and medical plans are types of compensation and rewards. Social Security, retirement plans, severance pay, sick leave, annual leave, sabbatical leave, religious leave, military leave, professional leave, and transportation allowance are among the many types of compensations and rewards available to school personnel. Supply and demand often determine the extent of the package available to employees.

Newly hired employees receive assistance through the induction process. Beginning teachers need more assistance than experienced individuals. The first part of the induction process is orientation. Teachers new to a school must be oriented to the procedures, paper requirements, teaching and learning expectations, rules, and all aspects of the school culture. In some districts, the district does the orientation, with the school providing additional orientation for those factors unique to that school. The socialization process is critical since it can determine how well new personnel become or fail to become contributing members of the teaching/learning community.

Many districts are currently experimenting with pay for performance plans, where teachers who are more adept at increasing test scores are given bonuses. This has been highly controversial, though, as statistical models to determine teacher impact on student test scores is rather complicated and imprecise.

The induction process ranges from 90 days to a full school year. The best induction approach is one in which the teachers are assisted throughout the year by a mentor teacher who teaches the same grade level and subjects. The induction process should be based upon the orientation and should extend the orientation to cover every aspect of the work for the position.

### Skill 12.2  Analyze issues of equity and diversity in human resource management.

The principal is the gatekeeper of a school's resources, and resources are more than monetary. Resources include the district budget, student activity funds, Title I and other grant monies, the human resources of parents, staff and volunteers, as well as material resources of the school building.

Each financial expenditure requires the signature and approval of the administrator. Rather than making the spending decisions based on whim or favoritism, the principal should always be guided by the campus improvement plan and the school goals. For example, if funds are requested for an autism conference, but there are no school goals or student needs in this area, then this request should not be funded. However, if the school goals include literacy development, then a request for funding for additional library books or for a teacher to attend a literacy conference may be approved.

The principal also controls the human resources, or staffing of the school. School staffing models vary from district to district, but all principals have some control of how many teachers and support staff is hired. Principals may make decisions about job descriptions, duties and assigned responsibilities, as well as appraisal and development of the school staff. It is a waste of human resources to have ineffective staff members continue on the school payroll, so principals should work to document and remove employees who do not contribute to the school goals. When a need for additional support surfaces, the principal must take an overall look at how staff is being used, and reallocate the human resources to meet the need. An example of this happens when teachers are absent and there are not enough substitute teachers to cover the classes. The principal must decide who will teach the classes, by combining students or reassigning office staff or support staff to fill this need.

Resources are always limited, and conflict can occur when stakeholders are denied their requests for spending. Involving the school leadership team in these decisions and keeping the group focused on student achievement will help the principal maintain integrity and will keep the focus on the school vision.

The school principal looks at the school's needs when recruiting and hiring human resources. Preference should not be given to people of a certain race or color. They need to be selected based on the needs of the school and the qualifications and experience of the applicants. Care should also be taken to recruit teachers and paraprofessionals that will be most effective at delivering the curriculum to all students – the regular mainstream classes and the students with special needs.

Within the school setting, the principal needs to know which teachers are best suited for which classes and assignments. The assignments should not be handed out randomly nor should they be based solely on what the teachers want to do. All factors need to be carefully weighed and considered in assigning staff in the school.

**Skill 12.3** **Examine the relationship between personnel practices and quality and justice in the workplace.**

All staff need and deserve to be treated with respect, whether they are part of the teaching staff or the custodial staff. Staff members need to know that the administration is there to help in any situation and will do so in confidence if need be.

Administrators should not show favoritism to any one teacher or give more attention to one more than the other. Aspects of dealing with members of the staff include:

- Interpersonal communication
- Retention of staff
- Civility
- Reward and recognition
- Developing teams
- Establishing trust
- Managing stressful situations
- Supporting staff in times of change

When a new administrator comes into a school, he/she has to develop a sense of trust with the staff. They need to know that the administrator will support them in cases of problem students or if problems arise with parents. Staff that do an exceptional job need to be recognized and this should be done at a staff meeting. However, the administrator should look for exemplary teaching or behavior in all staff, but at the same time rewards and recognition should not be handed out frivolously.

Developing teams is something that will take time, but the administrator has to make sure that the members of the team do get along. Teams with members that cannot work together will not function effectively.

An administrator also has to be able to manage stressful situations without panicking or becoming distraught. This will let the teachers know they have a leader on whom they can depend. At the same time, the administration has to support the school district in bringing in policies and programs with which the teachers may not agree. Therefore there will be times when teachers who are used to doing something the same way all the time will be forced to change. Change is not easy, which is what the administrator has to realize. The teachers should be coached to take small steps leading to change.

## Skill 12.4 Apply knowledge of skills and procedures for supervising and evaluating school personnel.

Appraisal of personnel is a significant responsibility of the principal. Most districts use a district-wide criteria developed through a diverse committee, representative of the school community. The criteria establish objective measures that can provide the principal with reliable methods of appraising staff. The most reliable methods provide the teacher with the criteria and understanding of how the criteria are used in evaluating the staff. Gossip, unsigned notes, and other such techniques are deemed unreliable and should not be used.

The principal must know those responsibilities at the building level and those at the district level. The principal evaluates building level staff and must know the criteria and how to apply each. With the advent of performance-based appraisal in many states, principals need training to tie performance to student learning. The principal knows that the district, state, university teachers, professional organizations, and consultants afford the best opportunities to acquire information on the development and implementation of the appraisal process. Teacher mentor programs provide assistance to new and experienced teachers new to teaching. The assistance of a peer teacher and a variety of induction activities enabled the teachers to receive assistance without the implied threat of evaluation. This open system enables these teachers to seek help when or before it was needed.

Appraisal of personnel is a significant responsibility of the principal. When the evaluation process is done correctly, teachers grow professionally and students benefit from increasingly effective instruction. Most school districts use district-wide criteria to judge teacher effectiveness. These objective measures should be published and discussed early in the year. Teachers should set professional development goals based on weak areas and should receive recognition for areas of strength.

The processes for gathering the data used to rate teachers on the district criteria should also be published and discussed. Most often, there are formal, planned classroom observations, as well as, informal walk-throughs and other informal methods for viewing a teacher's work. Teacher performance ratings should be directly tied to student achievement, so student achievement data should be part of what is used in determining appraisal scores. Teaching hasn't happened unless students have learned! Teachers should be given clear feedback about whether their performance is adequately satisfying the criteria of the appraisal instrument. Delivering this feedback to the teacher in a face-to-face conference allows the appraiser to establish a dialogue with the teacher about instructional practices. Very few people change because someone talks to them. To change behavior, you must change the thinking behind the behavior by asking questions that cause teachers to reflect on their own practices.

As a principal, your goal is to improve your staff so that student achievement will be optimized. You will encounter underperforming teachers who are in need of assistance. With the underperforming teacher, agree on two or three improvement goals and concentrate on making progress in these areas before moving on to other areas of need. Document the improvement plan and progress, or lack of progress, toward the selected goals. Poorly trained teachers need to observe excellent models, so allow release time for observations in other classrooms. Conferencing with them after the observation will assist them in applying what they observed in their own classroom situation. When a teacher is working through an improvement plan, the principal should make more frequent visits to the classroom and look for signs of improvement. Document every visit and intervention. Ineffective teachers can improve with a principal's support, training and mentoring.

The appraisal process is also a way to provide recognition for outstanding teachers. When a teacher's performance is highly rated, this provides encouragement to continue instructional practices that benefit students. Appraisal systems allow for the structured feedback that teachers need to improve instruction and grow professionally.

**Skill 12.5  Apply knowledge of procedures for disciplining and dismissing staff in accordance with due process.**

The processes and procedures that Administrators use for discipline, dismissal, and nonrenewal of school employees are contractual ones that are predetermined by staff voting with their respective Unions. Procedures must be followed using the protocol set in contractual handbooks before employees can lose their jobs in school communities. Any technicalities determined by Union representatives that have not been followed concisely may result in a dismissal or discipline being overturned irrespective if staff performance warrants the intended decision-making by the Administrative team.

The final decision for staff dismissal and nonrenewal comes from the District's Human Resources Director who reviews the final paperwork submitted by the Administrator involved in the evaluation of the specific staff member. Before a staff member reaches this stage of evaluation, the Administrator must verify through written evaluations that the staff member has received unsatisfactory job performances over a period of time, usually a year of formal evaluations. The next step is working with the staff member to improve instructional practices. Improvement of instructional practices is typically coupled with professional development opportunities that an employee can use to strengthen and diversify his/her abilities to facilitate learning in the classroom. When the Administrative decides to move ahead in using procedural methods to address the removal of a staff member, a comprehensive improvement plan is created that includes all issues that have been observed to contribute to an educational climate of decline.

Administrators must work proactively with a strong teachers union before a teacher can be dismissed, discipline or nonrenewed. It is more difficult to terminate the contract of a teacher, than it is for nonrenewal of contracts. Administrators understand that first year teachers have nonrenewal contracts, so if their job performance is unsatisfactory in the two formal and one annual written evaluations during the school year, a simple check on the nonrenewal form is all that's necessary to terminate the contract. However, teachers can request a hearing before to protest nonrenewal before the termination takes place.

In order to dismiss an employee, the Administrators must demonstrate consistent use of formal and informal written observations, along with documentation that shows an active encouragement for the employee to seek professional development opportunities to restructure and improve instructional practices. Along with a series of meetings with Union representation, each employee is presented with the quantitative data to dispute or accept with recommendations for restatements of the facts or dismissal of the facts.

Once the meetings have been resolved, the employee is given a form to sign that defines his/her dismissal from the teaching position. Oftentimes, the form contains a provision that states that the employee may or may not be given a satisfactory letter of recommendation from the District or Administrator for future employment in other Districts. The definitive aspect of dismissal is that the employee will not be allowed to work in the current school District again.

Employees are disciplined all the time by Administrators. However, it is when the discipline becomes formal and written and a matter of public record in his/her file, that a grievance is filed with the Union to have any discipline paperwork removed from his/her files. Administrators must always allow due diligence and due process when admonishing employees who are demonstrating ineffectiveness in the classroom.

The evaluation process for Administrators is a contractual obligation that must be be met in a timely manner for staff. The time factor includes a formal evaluation twice a year with written feedback, along with pre and post-conferences to gather data on the observations. The evaluation criteria are predetermined and voted on by the teacher's Union and must be utilized in providing feedback to staff on progress in instructional practices. Typical evaluation for teachers includes the following:

- Professional skills
- Classroom management
- Active engagement in student learning
- Possessing effective instructional practices
- Knowledge of subject content area
- Engagement in professional development

The same criteria of typical for Administrator evaluation as well with the knowledge of subject content area encompassing knowledge of all staff subject content area and implementation. Administrators must be able to provide staff with proactive strategies or professional development for growth or redirection in instructional practices. The ability to possess administrative skills and development that can be role modeled for the school community is the strength of an effective and proactive Administrator.

Administrators must create a consistency in monitoring teacher instructional practices in the classroom by creating snapshots of observations beyond the required two formal observations. Snapshots will include an observation when school begins to ascertain which evaluation criteria should have a more timely concentration of evaluation. Timeframes for snapshots should provide Administrators with 10-15 observation periods at the beginning, middle or end of a class period, so Administrators can see how class time is utilized at the beginning of the class period and see how students are engaged halfway through the period and at the end of the learning opportunity.

In order to provide timely feedback to others on the Administrative team, weekly meetings are called by the Principal to solicit feedback and input about the impact of the school environment on each team member's daily expectations. In looking at discipline issues and staff, student or parent concerns that may redirect time consumptions and scheduled calendars is an example of feedback that is impacting on the team.

In order for Administrative feedback to be processed and implemented by staff and the Administrative team, feedback must be timely and factual. Administrators must have written records of issues and concerns that impact teacher instructional practices and Administrative evaluations of staff and the Administrative team.

When students misbehave in school or break the school rules, there is a due process that administrators must follow. The first course of action is to interview the student and try to determine the reasons for the behavior. If the behavior is of a minor nature, the principal may decide to give the student an after school detention. The parents are notified of the event.

In-school suspensions where the student is not permitted to have contact with his/her peers during the day or part of the day are also quite common in certain cases. If the misbehavior is of a major nature, the student is likely to receive a in-school suspension for the first offense. The parents and the school board should be notified in writing. Schools have their own rules for how many in-school suspensions must occur before the student is suspended from school for a period of time.

The type of punishment handed out to students also depends on the age and grade level. For middle school and high school students, suspensions of up to 15 days are possible after the second or third event. In high schools, some events may actually be illegal and the law enforcement agency has to be called in.

Any parent who does not agree with the suspension or punishment meted out has the right to grieve the situation. This is done by meeting with the administration and the teachers involved. If this meeting does not resolve the situation, then a further meeting may be required with the superintendent.

The Due Process Clause indicates that no state can deprive any person of life, liberty, or property without due process of law. Liberty and property have been broadly defined to refer to a wide range of substantive rights. For example, educators' contracts provide them with a property interest and expectation of employment for the terms of the contract. Tenure provides an expectation of future employment and so endows the individual who has tenure with a property interest. Liberty interest has been defined to encompass a wide range of personal freedoms. The courts have described liberty as fundamental rights that are "essential to the orderly pursuit of happiness by free men." The due process clause declares that no STATE can deprive a citizen of the United States of a substantive right WITHOUT according that citizen due process of the law.

This clause has major implications for educators for several reasons. It makes the earlier amendments applicable to the states. Prior to the Fourteenth Amendment, the earlier amendments applied to the federal government only. Another important factor lies in the nature of public education; it is a state governmental function. When educators are acting in their professional capacities, they are "the state". So, when administrators interact with teachers and students, they must be sure that they are functioning in a way that does not deprive an individual of his/her substantive rights. In addition to the substantive interests cited above, the freedoms identified in the earlier amendments are considered substantive. For example, if a teacher is fired from his/her position for speaking out on an issue of public interest in the middle of the school year, the teacher could bring legal action in the federal courts because the state (the school system) deprived him/her of free speech rights. The teacher would also have to be accorded procedural due process because of the property interest in the remainder the annual contract. In another example, before a student can be suspended for a significant period of time, he/she must be accorded procedural due process because the right to an education accrues to the student as a property interest through the state constitution. The sources of substantive rights are multiple and varied, but regardless of the source, the due process clause of the Fourteenth Amendment will protect them. The major elements of procedural due process are notice, a hearing, and an impartial tribunal.

**Skill 12.6    Identify requirements and effective practices in situations involving contract negotiation and management and employee grievances.**

Collective bargaining is the process of determining a contract between the management of a school district and the teachers' union, the representative unit of the teachers within a district. Collective bargaining is the term used for the negotiation between the two units. Although monetary issues comprise the majority of items in most collective bargaining sessions, other issues of working conditions (such as job duties, hours on campus, etc.) are negotiated, as well.

A principal may serve on a collective negotiation team for a district. In this case, the principal is on the management team. The negotiation process is lengthy and usually involves multi-year contracts. The process involves team determination, unit recognition, planning and preparation, agreement and implementation, and strategies to reach agreement, counterproposals, and others needed to get a contract.

While collective bargaining has typically been viewed as a divisive process in most school districts, progressive unions and sensitive districts have found that working together can be more beneficial to both sides.

# TEACHER CERTIFICATION STUDY GUIDE

## COMPETENCY 13.0 UNDERSTAND HOW TO MANAGE THE SCHOOL'S PHYSICAL PLANT AND AUXILIARY SERVICES TO ENSURE A SAFE AND EFFECTIVE LEARNING ENVIRONMENT.

### Skill 13.1 Identify the features of a safe and effective learning environment.

Schools must be safe places for students to learn and for teachers to work. When emergencies occur, clear procedures must be in place to ensure that the school community responds in an orderly fashion. Details for planning and implementing safety plans are explained in the next section. This section, however, will discuss specific strategies to ensure that safety is a priority in a school building.

First, the building must be in an operable condition. Any broken item that could pose a safety risk should be dealt with. Furniture that gets in the way of door areas must be moved. All doors should be completely operable and able to be opened quickly in an emergency. Windows should be able to be opened. Air conditioners, heaters, gas systems, plumbing, and electricity should all be able to be turned off easily and quickly if the need arises. This last point is a particular concern for many schools. Often, a specific custodian knows how to complete all those procedures. However, if that individual was not on campus at a particular time, other individuals would also need to know how to operate such equipment.

In planning for evacuation, routes should be drawn so that each hallway has the least amount of students walking through it possible, with no student having to walk too far. In other words, usually, the quickest route out of a building may clog a hallway, thereby making the route much slower. However, it would also be unwise to have a whole classroom full of students walk far around a particular hallway and still be in a potentially dangerous location. Often, fire departments or safety consultants can assist in designing solid, quality evaluation plans.

The opposite of an evacuation plan would be a lock-down plan. A lock-down plan would consist of various rules and procedures for getting or keeping all students in a secure location, such as a classroom. The problem with a lock-down is often that communication suffers. Many schools around the country are now insisting that school personnel look at their email accounts as soon as a lock-down occurs, as email is often a very efficient way to communicate to many people quickly.

In all, the best method of keeping students and staff safe is careful planning. But, as we will see in the next section, it is crucial that all school community members know those plans well.

**Skill 13.2    Examine strategies for ensuring the safety of students and school personnel and for addressing suspected problems related to safety.**

To ensure student and personnel safety, a variety of levels of planning must be implemented. First, plans must exist for ensuring safety in a variety of situations. Local natural disasters must be accounted for, as should plans for ensuring safety when, for example, the police are searching for a loose criminal in the surrounding neighborhood. Many schools may even have to consider safety plans for local terrorist attacks, particularly if the school is located near a busy or popular area.

Plans should include methods for getting students in a safe area, as well as communication among staff members and communication between administrative personnel and parents or media.

The next level of ensuring safety concerns communicating those plans to staff, parents, students, and the district. Fire drills, for example, do not command great attention from most staff and students, typically because most people have never experienced a fire in a large institution, such as a school. However, good administrators find creative ways to ensure that all staff members and students know the procedures. Clear directions, however, should be posted all over a campus for clarification when events do occur. Directions and procedures should be mailed home to parents annually, as well.

When disasters or safety concerns do occur, school leaders must behave like flight attendants: Calm, collected, but decisive and clear. People in the school community will be more likely to behave in a positive, productive manner in a disaster when the leadership gives clear instructions, is open and honest, and maintains a sense of peace among decisive action.

After events that compromise safety, school leaders must do a few things. First, they must report all factors immediately to district administrators, local police, parents, students, and sometimes media. Second, they must sit down with other staff members and discuss the performance of the school community in responding to the crisis. From that discussion, the team can then make informed modifications to the plans. New plans, of course, must then be communicated to all stakeholders

**Skill 13.3    Identify procedures for crisis planning and for responding to crises.**

See Skill 13.2

**Skill 13.4　Demonstrate knowledge of public school safety, security, and emergency procedures.**

See Skill 13.2

**Skill 13.5　Identify procedures for monitoring and evaluating the operation, use, maintenance, and efficiency of school facilities.**

School leaders are charged with providing students a safe, efficient, comfortable school building, conducive to rigorous academic learning. While school districts and funding levels do play significant parts in the aesthetics of a school building, basic safety and comfort issues are the responsibility of a school's administrative team. Various strategies can be put into place in order to promote satisfactory levels of building safety and efficiency.

First, a principal—or designee, such as an assistant principal—should be responsible on a daily basis to make rounds on a campus in order to verify a checklist of items. Such items might include visiting restrooms to ensure that everything is working properly and that students have clean, well operating facilities to use. A checklist might also include examining blacktop in the athletic areas to ensure that students would be safe running or playing on outside surfaces.

Another area a principal can be responsible for is in advocating for building comforts at the district and community level. While not all districts can afford air conditioning, principals can make needs clear to local taxpayers (with superintendent approval), as one example.

While many school districts pay for utilities, school building leaders can examine utility usage for efficiency. Problems may be noted in terms of air drafts, heating duct problems, and plumbing.

Finally, school leaders should report to the district buildings manager if certain problems exist that pose safety or privacy concerns. For example, if a bathroom stall door does not work properly, either a building level custodian must fix it, or if the building level resources are not available, a district support staff member should fix it. The same is true for issues of safety, such as a ceiling panel that is about to fall off in a classroom.

In many districts support services are being outsourced. Whether "in house" or outsourced, it is important for the principal to build relationships with the employees so that there is open dialogue concerning what is best for the children and the school. It is important that all employees, including food service, maintenance, and transportation are included in the planning and decision making for the school. It is also important to include these staff members as members of the school community, participating in activities and celebrations.

### Skill 13.6 Identify legal issues related to the operation and maintenance of school facilities (e.g., providing access for individuals with disabilities).

In 1990, Congress created an education bill of rights for children with disabilities. To meet the challenge of educating these students, school designers must provide students with disabilities the maximum possible access to general education within the classroom. However; chronic problems in the design of parking, restrooms, ramps and drinking water fountains have materialized.

The Americans with Disabilities Act (ADA) of 1990 prohibits discrimination on the basis of disability. The ADA requires school districts to provide programs and services that are readily accessible and usable by individuals with disabilities. Section 504 and IDEA contain two concepts that affect the planning and design of facilities used by students with disabilities.

1.) The first concept of appropriate education requires that schools provide all students receiving special education services with an individualized education program (IEP). The IEP specifies the levels of performance, goals, and educational services to be provided.

2.) The second concept of least restrictive environment requires students with disabilities to be positioned where they can obtain the best education at the least distance from mainstream education classes. To the greatest extent possible, these students must be educated with non-disabled students. Students with disabilities who are not initially placed in the public school district or in a general education public school should be integrated into the appropriate public school as soon as possible.

One of the most difficult school planning and design decisions is how to provide students with disabilities, particularly those at the higher severity levels, the least restrictive environment. The primary factor influencing this decision will be the IEP. Unless the IEP dictates otherwise, students should be educated in the schools they would attend if they did not have a disability.

Special education spaces should not be clustered or isolated in a single area of the building. While some special education functions clearly need to be adjacent or in proximity to one another, the balance should be dispersed throughout the school (while keeping travel distances in mind). For example, students with attention deficit disorders and emotional disabilities often require greater physical and acoustical separation between activities to reduce distractions, making single-space classrooms inadequate for their needs. A more appropriate arrangement consists of a large common classroom area, an alcove off the classroom, and a small room adjacent to the classroom that is acoustically isolated but visible from the common classroom area.

Basic guidelines to make a school handicap-accessible:

- Design wide halls and doorways throughout the facility
- Provide an accessible stall and sink in each bathroom throughout the building.
- Install elevator(s) in the most logical location to minimize travel time from first to second floor classrooms.
- Provide accessible seating in auditoriums, lecture halls, and sports facilities.

School planners and designers should always consider ways of maintaining the dignity of students with disabilities. Accommodations should avoid separating them from their peers in instructional settings, drawing unusual attention to them, or limiting their educational opportunities.

**Skill 13.7** **Demonstrate knowledge of regulations, issues, and procedures related to purchasing, food services, transportation services, information management services, and health services in the school.**

School leaders are charged with providing students a safe, efficient, comfortable school building, conducive to rigorous academic learning. While school districts and funding levels do play significant parts in the aesthetics of a school building, basic safety and comfort issues are the responsibility of a school's administrative team. Various strategies can be put into place in order to promote satisfactory levels of building safety and efficiency.

First, a principal—or designee, such as an assistant principal—should be responsible on a daily basis to make rounds on a campus in order to verify a checklist of items. Such items might include visiting restrooms to ensure that everything is working properly and that students have clean, well operating facilities to use. A checklist might also include examining blacktop in the athletic areas to ensure that students would be safe running or playing on outside surfaces.

Another area a principal can be responsible for is in advocating for building comforts at the district and community level. While not all districts can afford air conditioning, principals can make needs clear to local taxpayers (with superintendent approval), as one example.

While many school districts pay for utilities, school building leaders can examine utility usage for efficiency. Problems may be noted in terms of air drafts, heating duct problems, and plumbing.

Finally, school leaders should report to the district buildings manager if certain problems exist that pose safety or privacy concerns. For example, if a bathroom stall door does not work properly, either a building level custodian must fix it, or if the building level resources are not available, a district support staff member should fix it. The same is true for issues of safety, such as a ceiling panel that is about to fall off in a classroom.

In many districts support services are being outsourced. Whether "in house" or outsourced, it is important for the principal to build relationships with the employees so that there is open dialogue concerning what is best for the children and the school. It is important that all employees, including food service, maintenance, and transportation are included in the planning and decision making for the school. It is also important to include these staff members as members of the school community, participating in activities and celebrations.

# Sample Test

## School Vision

1. The method to use to assist participants in staff development activities to retain information and apply it in the classroom is

    A. Role-play

    B. Case study

    C. Lecture

    D. Active learning that uses all senses

2. The best way to improve a school through staff development activities is to

    A. Obtain a nationally recognized authority on the topic determined by teachers

    B. Involve teachers in initiating, planning, implementing, and evaluating the program

    C. Have a few teachers set up the program

    D. Have the principal plan and let a few teachers review the plan

3. Which of the following represents the proper sequential order in the communication process?

    A. Ideating, decoding, transmitting, receiving, encoding, acting

    B. Ideating, encoding, transmitting, receiving, decoding, acting

    C. Ideating, transmitting, encoding, receiving, decoding, acting

    D. Ideating, encoding, transmitting, receiving, acting, decoding

4. Communication in which a school principal receives feedback from the faculty/staff is

    A. Downward

    B. Lateral

    C. Upward

    D. Diagonal

5. Which of the following is *not* true of the educational grapevine?

   A. It is the least reliable source of transmitting information

   B. It is the means by which most information is passed laterally among employees

   C. Its most negative feature is the transmission of unsubstantiated rumor

   D. It can be used effectively by administrators to test employee reactions that facilitate the decision making process

6. Which of the following is an example of the communication barrier *filtering*?

   A. In an in-service planning meeting, the district director of student in instruction recommends that CPR training be deleted from the mid-year, full in-service day, citing the reason that PE teachers always fill the classes instead of registering for other educationally sound offerings

   B. Parents at an elementary school improvement committee meeting interpret the principal's reference to declining scores on the fourth grade writing assessment as a result of poor teaching. The principal fails to explain that scoring standards were increased and therefore all schools showed a slight lowering of rubric points

   C. A janitor has been asked not to clean the blackboards in a classroom shared by two social studies teachers, Mr. Anderson and Mrs. Clark. Mr. Anderson, who was never told of his colleague's request, complains to the head custodian that his room is not being cleaned properly

   D. In a middle school faculty meeting, language arts teachers become upset when the principal, having informed them that a number of language arts positions will be transferred due to population shifts within the district, cannot cite how many teachers and which schools will be affected

7. **The first step in using good group persuasive techniques is to**

   A. Plan an in-depth report of facts and statistics to support your argument

   B. Analyze the biases, emotions, and interests of the group to be addressed

   C. Make an impassioned, emotional appeal

   D. Solicit listener opinion before stating your objective

8. **Which statement best describes communication in an effective school?**

   A. Top down formal and informal communication

   B. Bottom up formal and informal communication

   C. Lateral formal and informal communication

   D. Informal communication between teachers and between teachers and administration

9. Which of the following is an example of the communication barrier *filtering*?

   A. In an in-service planning meeting, the district director of student in instruction recommends that CPR training be deleted from the mid-year, full in-service day, citing the reason that PE teachers always fill the classes instead of registering for other educationally sound offerings

   B. Parents at an elementary school improvement committee meeting interpret the principal's reference to declining scores on the fourth grade writing assessment as a result of poor teaching. The principal fails to explain that scoring standards were increased and therefore all schools showed a slight lowering of rubric points

   C. A janitor has been asked not to clean the blackboards in a classroom shared by two social studies teachers, Mr. Anderson and Mrs. Clark. Mr. Anderson, who was never told of his colleague's request, complains to the head custodian that his room is not being cleaned properly

   D. In a middle school faculty meeting, language arts teachers become upset when the principal, having informed them that a number of language arts positions will be transferred due to population shifts within the district, cannot cite how many teachers and which schools will be affected

10. An article appears in the local newspaper congratulating the winners of the district PRIDE contests. The small district has only two high schools, thus winners in the four content areas are selected from the combined senior classes. Because three of the winners attend the same school, the reporter makes a biased statement concerning the lack of qualified candidates from the second school. How should the principals of these schools react?

    A. Ignore the comment, assuming that the readers in the community will realize the fallacy of the statement

    B. Call the reporter and ask for clarification and rectification of the printed comment

    C. Collaboratively pen a letter to the editor, which explains the selections in the correct light

    D. Use the comment as a positive device to fire school rivalry

11. **The first step in using good group persuasive techniques is to**

    A. Plan an in-depth report of facts and statistics to support your argument

    B. Analyze the biases, emotions, and interests of the group to be addressed

    C. Make an impassioned, emotional appeal

    D. Solicit listener opinion before stating your objective

12. **In the acting phase of the communication process, which of the following is not a proper receiver behavior?**

    A. Storing the message for later processing

    B. Ignoring the message

    C. Reacting to the message

    D. Transmitting the message

13. **Consideration refers to a principal's behavior that is friendly, supportive, and open. Initiating structure refers to a principal's behavior that is task and achievement oriented. Select the statement that best describes initiating structure behavior.**

    A. The principal uses suggestions made by the faculty.

    B. The principal informs the faculty of administrative expectations.

    C. The principal shows concern for the welfare of faculty members.

    D. The principal regularly compliments faculty members.

14. Smithsonian School has been the site of undesirable publicity over the past years. Although the same and worse situations occur at a school attended by more affluent children, the information rarely hits the media. However, most of the bad news at Smithsonian School is headline news in the local media. As new principal of Smithsonian, what would be the LEAST appropriate measure to improve the image of Smithsonian School?

    A. Have an assembly and solicit student support for better grades and behavior.

    B. Conduct a survey of parents and faculty on measures to take.

    C. Develop a brochure and distribute it widely.

    D. Meet with the assistant principals, department chairpersons, and deans of students to discuss the problem and determine preliminary action steps.

15. The local media has written a story about the decline of school morale among students and teachers at Inman Elementary School. As principal, you were not aware of this alleged pervasive problem. Action you would take now is to

    A. Determine the nature of the alleged problem and meet with the news media

    B. Determine the status of morale and send the news media a press release

    C. Gather data on the situation, prepare a news release and meet with the press to share the news release and answer questions

    D. Gather data on the situation and meet with the press to share the data and answer questions

16. The students in Callaway Pre-kindergarten School have been exposed to a curriculum that emphasizes the latest brain research information. As they graduate to kindergarten, each of the children is demonstrating abilities not previously seen by students as they leave Callaway. As principal, you would

    A. Call your liaisons at the local television station and newspaper to inform them of the changes and to share a press release with them

    B. Fax a press release to the local television station and newspaper

    C. Send a press release to your superintendent

    D. Inform the press through a telephone call

17. Which statement best describes communication in an effective school?

    A. Top down formal and informal communication

    B. Bottom up formal and informal communication

    C. Lateral formal and informal communication

    D. Informal communication between teachers and between teachers and administration

18. Which of the following statements best illustrates the administrative model of decision-making?

    A. This strategy considers only alternatives that are similar to the existing situation, analyzes only differences between the current and proposed outcomes, and ignores outcomes beyond the decision makers narrow interests.

    B. This strategy is completely rational and is characterized by a series of sequential steps.

    C. This strategy's basic approach is satisfying, which emphasizes finding a satisfactory solution rather than the best solution.

    D. This strategy is found in organizations where ambiguity accompanies steps of the decision-making process, cause-effect relationships are impossible to determine, and there is rapid turnover of participants.

19. Which of the following best describes the process of school planning?

   A. The visionary principal who knows about the needs of the school, developing the school plan

   B. Principal, teachers, parents, business partners, and other community members developing the school plan

   C. Principals, teachers and parents developing the school plan

   D. A visionary team of teachers and administrators developing the school plan

20. Which of the following should mark the initial stages of school-based planning?

   A. Developing a plan of action

   B. Evaluating the process

   C. Clarifying and articulating the mission and goals

   D. Analyzing the plan of action

21. Recommended practice suggests that which of the following should be involved in the decision-making process concerning school improvement?

   I. Teachers
   II. Community Partners
   III. Administration
   IV. Parents and students

   A. I and III only

   B. II and III only

   C. I, III, and IV only

   D. I, II, III, and IV

22. After reviewing the reading scores of students on the state mandated reading test, the school principal has decided upon a new intervention to support the school's reading program. A memo to teachers contained the following specifications: "Beginning January 1st and continuing to the end of the year, all classroom teachers will implement the new reading program changes which will be made available immediately. All classroom teachers will incorporate the strategies and techniques outlined in the new reading program." Which of the following statements best describe the above planning process?

   A. The planning process follows the impact analysis model of planning.

   B. The planning process adheres to management by objectives criteria.

   C. This process conforms to the PDSA cycle.

   D. The nominal technique is being implemented in the above planning process.

Curriculum

1. Which of the following are best sources of curriculum?

   A. Textbooks and bibliographies

   B. Students and society

   C. Teachers and administrators

   D. Parents and community groups

2. Which choice best represents balance in the curriculum?

   A. Equal time for each of the courses offered

   B. More time for reading and math because they are difficult subjects

   C. Concepts linked to continuity and integration

   D. Opportunities provided for the development of concepts and skills applied to real life experiences

3. Which statement does not describe the curriculum of an effective school?

   A. The curriculum is planned with enough flexibility to address the changing needs of students

   B. The curriculum is planned a year at a time and encompasses basic skills that are learned in the classroom

   C. The curriculum is planned collaboratively with attention to basic skills and problem solving in the classroom and community

   D. The curriculum is planned with clear goals and objectives along with instruction activities and student assessment

4. Which statement best describes effective classroom planning?

   A. The teacher begins with the gathering of instructional materials to give meaning to the goals and objectives

   B. The teacher begins by gathering the best textbooks with sequential outlines to cover the subject matter

   C. The teacher begins by setting up the evaluation system with quizzes and tests to assess learning at the end of the chapter

   D. The teacher begins by specifying the instructional goals and objectives followed by the strategies for learning

5. The method to use to assist participants in staff development activities to retain information and apply it in the classroom is

   A. Role-play

   B. Case study

   C. Lecture

   D. Active learning that uses all senses

# TEACHER CERTIFICATION STUDY GUIDE

**Budgeting**

1. **Which of the following best describes the purpose of budgeting?**

   A. A yearly and periodic task to defined and justify expenditure

   B. Financial plan to expend funds

   C. Continuous planning to put the educational goals into a financial plan

   D. A statement of anticipated revenues operate the organization

2. **_____deals with the day-to-day operation of the school.**

   A. Internal Services Fund

   B. General Fund

   C. Debt Services Fund

   D. Special Revenue Fund

3. **The district financial officer shared information about a fund that could be used for specific types of expenditures. He made reference to_____**

   A. A group of accounts

   B. A sum of money

   C. A cash balance

   D. A ledger

4. **Which of the following is not a principle of school accounting?**

   A. Revenues and expenditures are recorded as the transaction occurs

   B. An accrual basis is used for transactions

   C. A cash basis is used for transactions

   D. Revenues earned are recorded as assets and expenditures are liabilities

5. Which of the following statements best describe zero based budgeting process?

   A. It examines each item in relation to expected revenues

   B. It begins with empty accounts to then justify the continuation of the expenditure

   C. It begins with accounts for the past three years and looks at the history of spending to justify new expenditures

   D. It integrates long-range planning with the resources provided to meet specific needs

6. Which of the following statements best describe the Incremental Budgeting process?

   A. It integrates long-range planning with the resource provided to meet specific needs

   B. It begins with empty accounts to then justify the continuation of the expenditure

   C. It begins with accounts for the past three years and looks at the history of spending to justify new expenditures

   D. It examines each item in relation to expected revenues

**Assessment**

1. **Crisis intervention methods are above all concerned with:**

   A. Safety and well-being of the staff and students.

   B. Stopping the inappropriate behavior.

   C. Preventing the behavior from occurring again.

   D. The student learning that outbursts are inappropriate.

2. Ricky, a third grade student, runs out of the classroom and onto the roof of the school. He paces around the roof, looks around to see who is watching, and laughs at the person standing on the ground. He appears to be in control of his behavior. What should the teacher do?

   A. Go back inside and leave him up there until he decides he is ready to come down

   B. Climb up to get Ricky so he does not fall off and get hurt

   C. Notify the crisis teacher and arrange to have someone monitor Ricky

   D. Call the police

3. Educators who advocate educating all children in their neighborhood classrooms and schools propose the end of labeling and segregation of special needs students in special classes, and who call for the delivery of special supports and services directly in the classroom, may be said to support the:

   A. Full service model

   B. Regular education initiative

   C. Full inclusion model

   D. Mainstream model

4. Grading should be based on all of the following EXCEPT:

   A. Clearly-defined mastery of course objectives

   B. A variety of evaluation methods

   C. Performance of the student in relation to other students

   D. Assigning points for activities and basing grades on a point total

5. Which would not be an advantage of using a criterion-referenced test?

   A. Information about an individual's ability level is too specific for the purposes of the assessment

   B. It can pinpoint exact areas of weaknesses and strengths

   C. You can design them yourself

   D. You do not get comparative information

6. Which is NOT an example of a standard score?

   A. T score

   B. Z score

   C. Standard deviation

   D. Stanine

7. The most direct method of obtaining assessment data, and perhaps the most objective, is:

   A. Testing

   B. Self-recording

   C. Observation

   D. Experimenting

8. Skills as an administrator and background in client, consulter, and consultation skills are examples of which variable in a successful consultation program?

   A. People

   B. Process

   C. Procedural implementation

   D. Academic preparation

# TEACHER CERTIFICATION STUDY GUIDE

## ANSWER KEY

**School Vision**

1. D
2. B
3. B
4. C
5. A
6. D
7. B
8. C
9. D
10. C
11. B
12. B
13. B
14. C
15. A
16. D
17. C
18. A
19. B
20. C
21. D
22. B

**Curriculum**

1. B
2. D
3. B
4. D
5. D
6. B

**Budgeting**

1. C
2. B
3. A
4. C
5. B

**Assessment**

1. A
2. C
3. C
4. C
5. D
6. C
7. A

# TEACHER CERTIFICATION STUDY GUIDE

## SAMPLE QUESTIONS WITH RATIONALE

**School Vision**

1. **The method to use to assist participants in staff development activities to retain information and apply it in the classroom is**

    A. Role-play

    B. Case study

    C. Lecture

    D. Active learning that uses all senses

**D  Skill 1.1**
The more senses that are involved in the learning process, the better the information is retained and accessed.

2. **The best way to improve a school through staff development activities is to**

    A. Obtain a nationally recognized authority on the topic determined by teachers

    B. Involve teachers in initiating, planning, implementing, and evaluating the program

    C. Have a few teachers set up the program

    D. Have the principal plan and let a few teachers review the plan

**B  Skill 1.1**
Involving more teachers in staff development planning and activities will increase accountability and feeling of ownership and promote success.

3. Which of the following represents the proper sequential order in the communication process?

   A. Ideating, decoding, transmitting, receiving, encoding, acting

   B. Ideating, encoding, transmitting, receiving, decoding, acting

   C. Ideating, transmitting, encoding, receiving, decoding, acting

   D. Ideating, encoding, transmitting, receiving, acting, decoding

**B Skill 1.1**
The six steps of communication:
Ideating: development of idea or message to be communicated
Encoding: organization of idea into conveyable symbols
Transmitting: delivery of message through a medium
Receiving: claiming of message by receiver
Decoding: translation of message by receiver
Acting: Action taken by receiver in response to message.

4. Communication in which a school principal receives feedback from the faculty/staff is

   A. Downward

   B. Lateral

   C. Upward

   D. Diagonal

**C Skill 1.1**
Upward communication is from personnel to a supervisor.

# TEACHER CERTIFICATION STUDY GUIDE

5. **Which of the following is _not_ true of the educational grapevine?**

    A. It is the least reliable source of transmitting information

    B. It is the means by which most information is passed laterally among employees

    C. Its most negative feature is the transmission of unsubstantiated rumor

    D. It can be used effectively by administrators to test employee reactions that facilitate the decision making process

**A  Skill 1.1**
The educational grapevine is an important means of disseminating information. The grapevine should not be used for sensitive or confidential information, but is an ideal system for quickly sending announcements which the entire staff must be aware of. A grapevine should be developed early in the year and fully explained so that all staff is included.

# TEACHER CERTIFICATION STUDY GUIDE

6.  **Which of the following is an example of the communication barrier *filtering*?**

    A. In an in-service planning meeting, the district director of student in instruction recommends that CPR training be deleted from the mid-year, full in-service day, citing the reason that PE teachers always fill the classes instead of registering for other educationally sound offerings

    B. Parents at an elementary school improvement committee meeting interpret the principal's reference to declining scores on the fourth grade writing assessment as a result of poor teaching. The principal fails to explain that scoring standards were increased and therefore all schools showed a slight lowering of rubric points

    C. A janitor has been asked not to clean the blackboards in a classroom shared by two social studies teachers, Mr. Anderson and Mrs. Clark. Mr. Anderson, who was never told of his colleague's request, complains to the head custodian that his room is not being cleaned properly

    D. In a middle school faculty meeting, language arts teachers become upset when the principal, having informed them that a number of language arts positions will be transferred due to population shifts within the district, cannot cite how many teachers and which schools will be affected

**D  Skill 1.1**
In this situation filtering from the central office level is preventing the principal from providing the staff with all of the details regarding the personnel decisions. This barrier in communication will create strife as the staff begins to worry without complete knowledge of the details. The principal must make a decision of whether to share the filtered information or wait until he or she has all of the details.

7. **The first step in using good group persuasive techniques is to**

    A. Plan an in-depth report of facts and statistics to support your argument

    B. Analyze the biases, emotions, and interests of the group to be addressed

    C. Make an impassioned, emotional appeal

    D. Solicit listener opinion before stating your objective

**B Skill 1.1**
Analyzing the emotions, interests and biases will allow one to prepare an argument that takes these into consideration, with stronger chances of persuasion.

8. **Which statement best describes communication in an effective school?**

    A. Top down formal and informal communication

    B. Bottom up formal and informal communication

    C. Lateral formal and informal communication

    D. Informal communication between teachers and between teachers and administration

**C Skill 1.1**
Lateral communication refers to communicating with each other on an equal footing. When teachers communicate with each other as equals or the administration communicates with the teachers in an informal way that treats them as professionals, there is increased communication in the school setting. No one wants to be talked down to or given orders. When there is a conversational tone, the ideas and directives come across more effectively.

# TEACHER CERTIFICATION STUDY GUIDE

9. Which of the following is an example of the communication barrier *filtering*?

   A. In an in-service planning meeting, the district director of student in instruction recommends that CPR training be deleted from the mid-year, full in-service day, citing the reason that PE teachers always fill the classes instead of registering for other educationally sound offerings

   B. Parents at an elementary school improvement committee meeting interpret the principal's reference to declining scores on the fourth grade writing assessment as a result of poor teaching. The principal fails to explain that scoring standards were increased and therefore all schools showed a slight lowering of rubric points

   C. A janitor has been asked not to clean the blackboards in a classroom shared by two social studies teachers, Mr. Anderson and Mrs. Clark. Mr. Anderson, who was never told of his colleague's request, complains to the head custodian that his room is not being cleaned properly

   D. In a middle school faculty meeting, language arts teachers become upset when the principal, having informed them that a number of language arts positions will be transferred due to population shifts within the district, cannot cite how many teachers and which schools will be affected

**D Skill 1.1**
In this situation filtering from the central office level is preventing the principal from providing the staff with all of the details regarding the personnel decisions. This barrier in communication will create strife as the staff begins to worry without complete knowledge of the details. The principal must make a decision of whether to share the filtered information or wait until he or she has all of the details

10. An article appears in the local newspaper congratulating the winners of the district PRIDE contests. The small district has only two high schools, thus winners in the four content areas are selected from the combined senior classes. Because three of the winners attend the same school, the reporter makes a biased statement concerning the lack of qualified candidates from the second school. How should the principals of these schools react?

    A. Ignore the comment, assuming that the readers in the community will realize the fallacy of the statement

    B. Call the reporter and ask for clarification and rectification of the printed comment

    C. Collaboratively pen a letter to the editor, which explains the selections in the correct light

    D. Use the comment as a positive device to fire school rivalry

**C Skill 1.7**
This would be the most effective and professional way to refute the information

11. The first step in using good group persuasive techniques is to

    A. Plan an in-depth report of facts and statistics to support your argument

    B. Analyze the biases, emotions, and interests of the group to be addressed

    C. Make an impassioned, emotional appeal

    D. Solicit listener opinion before stating your objective

**B Skill 1.7**
Analyzing the emotions, interests and biases will allow one to prepare an argument that takes these into consideration, with stronger chances of persuasion.

12. In the acting phase of the communication process, which of the following is not a proper receiver behavior?

    A. Storing the message for later processing

    B. Ignoring the message

    C. Reacting to the message

    D. Transmitting the message

**B Skill 1.7**
Ignoring the message is never an appropriate response, since it does not actively respond to the content.

13. Consideration refers to a principal's behavior that is friendly, supportive, and open. Initiating structure refers to a principal's behavior that is task and achievement oriented. Select the statement that best describes initiating structure behavior.

    A. The principal uses suggestions made by the faculty.

    B. The principal informs the faculty of administrative expectations.

    C. The principal shows concern for the welfare of faculty members.

    D. The principal regularly compliments faculty members.

**B Skill 1.7**
This is the only example where the principal is performing an achievement oriented behavior. Answers A, C and D show consideration rather than initiating structure behavior.

14. Smithsonian School has been the site of undesirable publicity over the past years. Although the same and worse situations occur at a school attended by more affluent children, the information rarely hits the media. However, most of the bad news at Smithsonian School is headline news in the local media. As new principal of Smithsonian, what would be the LEAST appropriate measure to improve the image of Smithsonian School?

   A. Have an assembly and solicit student support for better grades and behavior.

   B. Conduct a survey of parents and faculty on measures to take.

   C. Develop a brochure and distribute it widely.

   D. Meet with the assistant principals, department chairpersons, and deans of students to discuss the problem and determine preliminary action steps.

**C Skill 1.1**
Simply distributing counter information will not be effective alone in improving the school image, since the school already has little credibility. Answers A, B and D will likely result in more effective measures.

15. The local media has written a story about the decline of school morale among students and teachers at Inman Elementary School. As principal, you were not aware of this alleged pervasive problem. Action you would take now is to

   A. Determine the nature of the alleged problem and meet with the news media

   B. Determine the status of morale and send the news media a press release

   C. Gather data on the situation, prepare a news release and meet with the press to share the news release and answer questions

   D. Gather data on the situation and meet with the press to share the data and answer questions

**A Skill 1.7**
Meeting with the media to correct the problem is not sufficient without investigating the truth of the problem at the school.

# TEACHER CERTIFICATION STUDY GUIDE

16. The students in Callaway Pre-kindergarten School have been exposed to a curriculum that emphasizes the latest brain research information. As they graduate to kindergarten, each of the children is demonstrating abilities not previously seen by students as they leave Callaway. As principal, you would

    A. Call your liaisons at the local television station and newspaper to inform them of the changes and to share a press release with them

    B. Fax a press release to the local television station and newspaper

    C. Send a press release to your superintendent

    D. Inform the press through a telephone call

**D Skill 1.7**
Communication is most effective when it takes the shortest route and is in person.

17. Which statement best describes communication in an effective school?

    A. Top down formal and informal communication

    B. Bottom up formal and informal communication

    C. Lateral formal and informal communication

    D. Informal communication between teachers and between teachers and administration

**C Skill 1.1**
Lateral communication refers to communicating with each other on an equal footing. When teachers communicate with each other as equals or the administration communicates with the teachers in an informal way that treats them as professionals, there is increased communication in the school setting. No one wants to be talked down to or given orders. When there is a conversational tone, the ideas and directives come across more effectively.

18. Which of the following statements best illustrates the administrative model of decision-making?

   A. This strategy considers only alternatives that are similar to the existing situation, analyzes only differences between the current and proposed outcomes, and ignores outcomes beyond the decision makers narrow interests.

   B. This strategy is completely rational and is characterized by a series of sequential steps.

   C. This strategy's basic approach is satisfying, which emphasizes finding a satisfactory solution rather than the best solution.

   D. This strategy is found in organizations where ambiguity accompanies steps of the decision-making process, cause-effect relationships are impossible to determine, and there is rapid turnover of participants.

**A Skill 1.4**
Administrative decision-making is guided by the existing situation. Consideration is limited to possible outcomes of the current situation rather than analysis considering implications beyond the boundaries of the present situation. It is a limited form of decision-making, but it allows for expedient decision-making.

19. Which of the following best describes the process of school planning?

   A. The visionary principal who knows about the needs of the school, developing the school plan

   B. Principal, teachers, parents, business partners, and other community members developing the school plan

   C. Principals, teachers and parents developing the school plan

   D. A visionary team of teachers and administrators developing the school plan

**B Skill 1.4**
A school plan needs input from all stakeholders. In a democratic process, everyone that is affected by the school has to have information about the budget, the programs and the activities that are planned for the year. This ensures that all students get the best possible education. This process must also be ongoing so that it is continuously monitored and changed if need be.

# TEACHER CERTIFICATION STUDY GUIDE

20. Which of the following should mark the initial stages of school-based planning?

   A. Developing a plan of action

   B. Evaluating the process

   C. Clarifying and articulating the mission and goals

   D. Analyzing the plan of action

**C Skill 1.4**
Before any planning can take place, the stakeholders must identify their mission and goals. This sets out what they want to accomplish. The next step is to outline possible steps in accomplishing this goal.

21. Recommended practice suggests that which of the following should be involved in the decision-making process concerning school improvement?

   I. Teachers
   II. Community Partners
   III. Administration
   IV. Parents and students

   A. I and III only

   E. II and III only

   F. I, III, and IV only

   G. I, II, III, and IV

**D Skill 1.4**
Strategic planning for school improvement should include all stakeholders. All parties should have representation in the identification of improvement goals and the plan to attain them.

PRINCIPAL COMMON CORE

22. After reviewing the reading scores of students on the state mandated reading test, the school principal has decided upon a new intervention to support the school's reading program. A memo to teachers contained the following specifications: "Beginning January 1$^{st}$ and continuing to the end of the year, all classroom teachers will implement the new reading program changes which will be made available immediately. All classroom teachers will incorporate the strategies and techniques outlined in the new reading program." Which of the following statements best describe the above planning process?

   A. The planning process follows the impact analysis model of planning.

   B. The planning process adheres to management by objectives criteria.

   C. This process conforms to the PDSA cycle.

   D. The nominal technique is being implemented in the above planning process.

**B Skill 1.7**
The planning process conforms to management by objectives since the changes made were aimed to affect certain changes by a specific date.

# TEACHER CERTIFICATION STUDY GUIDE

**Curriculum**

1. Which of the following are best sources of curriculum?

   A. Textbooks and bibliographies

   B. Students and society

   C. Teachers and administrators

   D. Parents and community groups

**B  Skill 8.1**
Since the changes in society have a direct impact on what students need to learn in school, it should be any surprise that society will also be one of the best sources of the school curriculum. Since students are expected to stay in school, the curriculum should also be relevant to their needs and interests. Through discussions with students, parents, teachers and others involved with the children, curriculum needs can be determined, as well as areas that are posing problems for the students and areas that need to be more challenging.

2. Which choice best represents balance in the curriculum?

   A. Equal time for each of the courses offered

   B. More time for reading and math because they are difficult subjects

   E. Concepts linked to continuity and integration

   D. Opportunities provided for the development of concepts and skills applied to real life experiences

**D  Skill 8.2**
When planning lessons, teachers should ensure that they allow the students time to explore the concepts on their own so that they can make sense of them as they apply to their own lives. Students may understand the concepts and even do well on a test, but they will not be able to apply them to real life situations without having opportunities to do so. This can include such things as discussions in class, performing science experiments, doing projects alone and in a group.

3. Which statement <u>does not</u> describe the curriculum of an effective school?

   A. The curriculum is planned with enough flexibility to address the changing needs of students

   B. The curriculum is planned a year at a time and encompasses basic skills that are learned in the classroom

   C. The curriculum is planned collaboratively with attention to basic skills and problem solving in the classroom and community

   D. The curriculum is planned with clear goals and objectives along with instruction activities and student assessment

**B Skill 8.1**
A, C, and D all describe what an effective curriculum should be. The reasoning given for B would not be a curriculum that progresses naturally from one grade to another. It would result in a segmented curriculum in which the students would not graduate as well-rounded citizens

4. Which statement best describes effective classroom planning?

   A. The teacher begins with the gathering of instructional materials to give meaning to the goals and objectives

   B. The teacher begins by gathering the best textbooks with sequential outlines to cover the subject matter

   C. The teacher begins by setting up the evaluation system with quizzes and tests to assess learning at the end of the chapter

   D. The teacher begins by specifying the instructional goals and objectives followed by the strategies for learning

**D Skill 8.4**
All students need to know what they will learn in a unit of study and how they will be evaluated. The teacher should translate the instructional outcomes into "I can" statements and post them in the classroom. Then the students know exactly what is expected of them. When teachers use exemplars to show students what the expectations are for mastering the outcomes they are better prepared for success.

# TEACHER CERTIFICATION STUDY GUIDE

5. **The method to use to assist participants in staff development activities to retain information and apply it in the classroom is**

    A. Role-play

    B. Case study

    C. Lecture

    F. Active learning that uses all senses

**Budgeting**

1. **Which of the following best describes the purpose of budgeting?**

    A. A yearly and periodic task to defined and justify expenditure

    B. Financial plan to expend funds

    C. Continuous planning to put the educational goals into a financial plan

    D. A statement of anticipated revenues operate the organization

**C Skill 11.3**
The budget portrays the type of educational plan that the district wants to have in place for the students. The financial plans must be in place so that schools know how much funding they have for the teachers and students and what kinds of programs they can engage in for the year.

2. _____deals with the day-to-day operation of the school.

    A. Internal Services Fund

    B. General Fund

    C. Debt Services Fund

    D. Special Revenue Fund

**B Skill 11.2**
The General fund is the one of most importance to the school. It is the one that funds the programs, supplies, substitute teachers and all the supplies needed for the school. It also takes care of the staff salaries.

3. **The district financial officer shared information about a fund that could be used for specific types of expenditures. He made reference to_____**

    A. A group of accounts

    B. A sum of money

    C. A cash balance

    D. A ledger

**A  Skill 11.2**
The district budget consists of eight different types of accounts- some of which deal with the school and some deal with the district as a whole

4. **Which of the following is not a principle of school accounting?**

    A. Revenues and expenditures are recorded as the transaction occurs

    B. An accrual basis is used for transactions

    C. A cash basis is used for transactions

    D. Revenues earned are recorded as assets and expenditures are liabilities

**C  Skill 11.2**
Cash is never used as payment for anything that is paid for from the school budget. Checks leave a paper trail, which makes it easier to reconcile bank statements and to perform audits.

# TEACHER CERTIFICATION STUDY GUIDE

5. **Which of the following statements best describe zero based budgeting process?**

    A. It examines each item in relation to expected revenues

    B. It begins with empty accounts to then justify the continuation of the expenditure

    C. It begins with accounts for the past three years and looks at the history of spending to justify new expenditures

    D. It integrates long-range planning with the resources provided to meet specific needs

## B Skill 11.2
This process starts out with no money and then adds expenditures and revenues. In this manner, those involved in the budgetary process can make sure that the money is raised in a proper way and is spent as it should.

6. **Which of the following statements best describe the Incremental Budgeting process?**

    A. It integrates long-range planning with the resource provided to meet specific needs

    B. It begins with empty accounts to then justify the continuation of the expenditure

    C. It begins with accounts for the past three years and looks at the history of spending to justify new expenditures

    D. It examines each item in relation to expected revenues

## A Skill 11.2
Incremental Budgeting looks at the long term, such as two or more years based on projected enrolments in the school. This gives the stakeholders the information they need to help plan for activities that might extend over several years.

## Assessment

2. **Crisis intervention methods are above all concerned with:**

    E. Safety and well-being of the staff and students.

    F. Stopping the inappropriate behavior.

    G. Preventing the behavior from occurring again.

    H. The student learning that outbursts are inappropriate.

**A Skill 13.1**
It encompasses B, C, and D.

2. Ricky, a third grade student, runs out of the classroom and onto the roof of the school. He paces around the roof, looks around to see who is watching, and laughs at the person standing on the ground. He appears to be in control of his behavior. What should the teacher do?

   A. Go back inside and leave him up there until he decides he is ready to come down

   B. Climb up to get Ricky so he does not fall off and get hurt

   C. Notify the crisis teacher and arrange to have someone monitor Ricky

   D. Call the police

**C. Skill 13.1; 13.2**
The teacher cannot be responsible for both Ricky and his or her class. He must pass the responsibility to the appropriate person.

3. Educators who advocate educating all children in their neighborhood classrooms and schools propose the end of labeling and segregation of special needs students in special classes, and who call for the delivery of special supports and services directly in the classroom, may be said to support the:

   A. Full service model

   B. Regular education initiative

   C. Full inclusion model

   D. Mainstream model

**C. Skill 4.3**
All students must be included in the regular classroom

# TEACHER CERTIFICATION STUDY GUIDE

4. **Grading should be based on all of the following EXCEPT:**

    A. Clearly-defined mastery of course objectives

    B. A variety of evaluation methods

    C. Performance of the student in relation to other students

    D. Assigning points for activities and basing grades on a point total

**C. Skill 1.2**
Grading should never be based on the comparison of performance of other students. It should always be based on the student's mastery of course objectives, the methods of evaluation, and the grading rubric (how points are assigned).

5. **Which would not be an advantage of using a criterion-referenced test?**

    A. Information about an individual's ability level is too specific for the purposes of the assessment

    B. It can pinpoint exact areas of weaknesses and strengths

    C. You can design them yourself

    D. You do not get comparative information

**D. Skill 1.2**
Criterion-referenced tests measure mastery of content rather than performance compared to others. Test items are usually prepared from specific educational objectives and may be teacher made or commercially prepared. Scores are measured by the percentage of correct items for a skill (e.g., adding and subtracting fractions with like denominators).

6. **Which is NOT an example of a standard score?**

   A. T score

   B. Z score

   C. Standard deviation

   D. Stanine

**C. Skill 1.2.**
A, B, and D are all standardized scores. Stanines are whole number scores from 1 to 9, each representing a wide range of raw scores. Standard deviation is **not a score**. It measures how widely scores vary from the mean.

7. **The most direct method of obtaining assessment data, and perhaps the most objective, is:**

   A. Testing

   B. Self-recording

   C. Observation

   D. Experimenting

**C. Skill 1.2**
Observation is often better than testing, due to language, culture, or other factors.

8. **Skills as an administrator and background in client, consulter, and consultation skills are examples of which variable in a successful consultation program?**

   A. People

   B. Process

   C. Procedural implementation

   D. Academic preparation

**A. Skill 1.1**
Consultation programs cannot be successful without people skills.

**XAMonline, INC. 21 Orient Ave. Melrose, MA 02176**

Toll Free number 800-509-4128

*TO ORDER Fax 781-662-9268 OR www.XAMonline.com*

CERTIFICATION EXAMINATION FOR OKLAHOMA EDUCATORS - CEOE - 2007

PO#         Store/School:

Address 1:

Address 2 (Ship to other):
City, State Zip

**Credit card number**\_\_\_\_-\_\_\_\_-\_\_\_\_-\_\_\_\_        expiration\_\_\_\_
EMAIL _____
**PHONE**              **FAX**

| 13# ISBN 2007 | TITLE | Qty | Retail | Total |
|---|---|---|---|---|
| 978-1-58197-781-3 | CEOE OSAT Advanced Mathematics Field 11 | | | |
| 978-1-58197-775-2 | CEOE OSAT Art Sample Test Field 02 | | | |
| 978-1-58197-780-6 | CEOE OSAT Biological Sciences Field 10 | | | |
| 978-1-58197-776-9 | CEOE OSAT Chemistry Field 04 | | | |
| 978-1-58197-778-3 | CEOE OSAT Earth Science Field 08 | | | |
| 978-1-58197-794-3 | CEOE OSAT Elementary Education Fields 50-51 | | | |
| 978-1-58197-795-0 | CEOE OSAT Elementary Education Fields 50-51 Sample Questions | | | |
| 978-1-58197-777-6 | CEOE OSAT English Field 07 | | | |
| 978-1-58197-779-0 | CEOE OSAT Family and Consumer Sciences Field 09 | | | |
| 978-1-58197-786-8 | CEOE OSAT French Sample Test Field 20 | | | |
| 978-1-58197-798-1 | CEOE OGET Oklahoma General Education Test 074 | | | |
| 978-1-58197-792-9 | CEOE OSAT Library-Media Specialist Field 38 | | | |
| 978-1-58197-787-5 | CEOE OSAT Middle Level English Field 24 | | | |
| 978-1-58197-789-9 | CEOE OSAT Middle Level Science Field 26 | | | |
| 978-1-58197-790-5 | CEOE OSAT Middle Level Social Studies Field 27 | | | |
| 978-1-58197-788-2 | CEOE OSAT Middle Level-Intermediate Mathematics Field 25 | | | |
| 978-1-58197-791-2 | CEOE OSAT Mild Moderate Disabilities Field 29 | | | |
| 978-1-58197-782-0 | CEOE OSAT Physical Education-Health-Safety Field 12 | | | |
| 978-1-58197-783-7 | CEOE OSAT Physics Sample Test Field 14 | | | |
| 978-1-58197-793-6 | CEOE OSAT Principal Common Core Field 44 | | | |
| 978-1-58197-796-7 | CEOE OPTE Oklahoma Professional Teaching Examination Fields 75-76 | | | |
| 978-1-58197-784-4 | CEOE OSAT Reading Specialist Field 15 | | | |
| 978-1-58197-785-1 | CEOE OSAT Spanish Field 19 | | | |
| 978-1-58197-797-4 | CEOE OSAT U.S. & World History Field 17 | | | |
| | | | **SUBTOTAL** | |
| FOR PRODUCT PRICES GO TO WWW.XAMONLINE.COM | | | Ship | $8.25 |
| | | | **TOTAL** | |